D1238262

England, Upstate New York, and the Upper Middle West; Pennsylvania and the Lower Middle West; the Upper South; and the Lower South. Using photographs, maps, and geographically oriented charts, they illustrate cultural variation and similarity in housing type as well as a range of housing characteristics. Photographs of houses from Mattapoisett, Massachusetts, Grundy Center, Iowa, and Apalachicola, Florida, illustrate such diverse types as the hall and parlour cottage, salt box house, and raised ranch house, and such characteristics as height, roof form, and facade material. Geographical charts plot regional variations, revealing for example the prevalence of pre–World War I housing in the Middle West and of post–World War II ranches in the South or the near dominance of white facades, six- to eleven-room houses, front porches, and double-pile houses through every region.

Exploring on a broad scale how Americans house themselves in the 1980s, the authors provide the tools that allow scholars, students, and "house-watchers" to comprehend how houses define and differentiate the changing cultural landscape.

John A. Jakle is a professor of geography and landscape architecture at the University of Illinois, Urbana-Champaign. Among his many books are *The Visual Elements of Landscape, The Tourist: Travel in Twentieth-Century America,* and *The American Small Town: Twentieth-Century Place Images.* **Robert W. Bastian** is a professor of geography at Indiana State University. **Douglas K. Meyer,** a professor of geography at Eastern Illinois University, is the author of *Pictorial Landscape History of Charleston, Illinois.*

DISCARDED

COMMON HOUSES IN AMERICA'S SMALL TOWNS

The University of Georgia Press

Athens and London

COMMON HOUSES IN AMERICA'S SMALL TOWNS

The Atlantic Seaboard to the Mississippi Valley

John A. Jakle, Robert W. Bastian, and Douglas K. Meyer

© 1989 by the University of
Georgia Press
Athens, Georgia 30602
All rights reserved
Designed by Mary Mendell
Set in Palatino
The paper in this book meets the
guidelines for permanence and
durability of the Committee on
Production Guidelines for Book
Longevity of the Council on Library
Resources.
Printed in the United States of America
93 92 91 90 89   5 4 3 2 1
Library of Congress Cataloging in
Publication Data
Jakle, John A.
Common houses in America's small
towns, the Atlantic Seaboard to the
Mississippi valley / John A. Jakle,
Robert W. Bastian, and Douglas K.
Meyer.
p. cm.
Bibliography: p.
Includes index.
ISBN 0-8203-1006-9 (alk. paper)
ISBN 0-8203-1074-3 (pbk.: alk. paper)
1. Architecture, Domestic—United
States. 2. Vernacular architecture—
United States. I. Bastian, Robert W. II.
Meyer, Douglas K. III. Title.
NA7205.J34 1988
728.3'7'0974—dc19   87-23291
                                    CIP

British Library Cataloging in
Publication Data available

ECC/USF LEARNING RESOURCES
8099 College Parkway, S.W.
      P. O. Box 06210
Fort Myers, FL 33906-6210

For our children

and their children.

May the American

landscape never fail

to fascinate.

CONTENTS

PREFACE

Common houses are readily taken for granted in the American landscape. A traveler moving across the United States might be struck by the seemingly unique houses of a given place. But, in the main, the same types of dwellings would appear over and over again in varying combinations, a blur of familiarity. It is our purpose in this book to cut through that blur: to make more explicit the kinds of houses now common in the American scene, and to reveal how they vary regionally. We do this in order to heighten interest in common houses and, indeed, to heighten interest in the observation of landscape generally.

The study of common dwellings is not new. For well over a half-century scholars have labored to identify basic house types, to establish their origins and paths of geographical diffusion, and to determine both the functional and symbolic mean-

ings associated with them. Our objective is to fill gaps in the already substantial body of literature descriptive of American houses. Whereas much previous scholarship has been focused on folk housing we attempt to embrace all types of permanent single-family dwellings. If nineteenth-century Cape Cod cottages are important, so also are their twentieth-century revival forms as well as more numerous bungalows and ranch houses. We also endeavor to focus on urban houses, previous scholarship being weighted toward the rural. By treating small towns we emphasize places derived not only from the nation's rural past, but also molded in the image of recent metropolitan suburbs. In undertaking these tasks we have devised a lexicon for naming houses reflective of language currently in vogue among scholars. Our most important objective is to describe house types in terms of form. We make a conscious effort to

x

divorce concern for the basic elements of structure from traditional emphasis on decorative detail.

We report here the results of an inventory of single-family dwellings completed in twenty sample towns in the Eastern United States. Towns arrayed across New England, Upstate New York and the Upper Middle West; Pennsylvania and the Lower Middle West; the Upper South; and the Lower South are compared according to prevailing house forms. We present our findings in a regional frame of reference in order to pose hypotheses intended to facilitate town-to-town comparisons. Through a series of some sixty maps we lead the reader toward a comprehension of the geography of common houses in the Eastern United States as mirrored in our towns.

We have organized the book as follows. Chapter 1 introduces the study of common dwellings through a brief literature review. Chapter 2 describes our house survey, how it was organized, and what we hoped to accomplish. Our study towns are described in chapter 3. Chapter 4 focuses on constituent house elements, describing apparent regional preferences for building material, color, roof configuration, and building height among other characteristics. Chapters 5 and 6 concern the specific structure types categorized as single-pile and double-pile respectively.

Single-pile structures are square or rectangular in shape and one room in depth whereas double-pile structures are two rooms deep. Irregularly massed dwellings comprised of varying geometrics are treated in chapter 7, and bungalow and ranch dwellings in chapters 8 and 9. Chapter 10 offers synthesis outlining the commonalities between towns, suggesting how these commonalities do or do not reflect underlying cultural differences from region to region. Finally, in a glossary we offer a more formal definition and description for the sixty-seven specific dwelling types analyzed.

Our emphasis is clearly geographical. Houses may be studied from many points of view: the architectural historian focusing on stylistic ornamentation and architectural design, the folklorist on building tradition and use, the sociologist and anthropologist on values. We focus on identifying different kinds of houses according to structural form, naming these distinctive types, and establishing the outlines of their distribution as they vary geographically both individually and in combination one with another. This kind of effort we view as an important prerequisite to other kinds of analyses concerned with builder, function, and symbolism such that a comprehensive understanding of common houses, systematically based, might accrue. Ours is a "back to basics" stance built around two primary questions:

1) Which common houses predominate in the Eastern United States? and 2) How do they vary geographically within that area?

We thank the hundreds of individuals across the twenty study towns (especially the various town clerks, police chiefs, realtors, newspaper editors, librarians, and local afficionados of architecture) who aided us in our endeavor. We also would like to thank the National Endowment for the Humanities, which funded field work, and the Research Board of the University of Illinois, which funded the computer analysis. We also thank Robert Kreger, our research assistant; James Bier and Steven Johnson, our cartographers; Leona Kuhn, who oversaw all contracts; and Barbara Bonnell, who is an excellent and most indispensable typist. We extend special thanks to Keith Sculle who aided in the initial conceptualization of the project and to Wilbur Zelinsky, Peirce Lewis, Dick Pillsbury, Terry Jordan and those anonymous others who reacted to early research proposals and reviewed subsequent manuscripts.

COMMON HOUSES IN AMERICA'S SMALL TOWNS

CHAPTER I   INTRODUCTION TO THE STUDY OF COMMON HOUSES

Houses are significant in so far as they reveal the living conditions of a period and the capacity of the people who occupied them. They are a record of human society and of the peculiar genius of a given community.

HELEN REYNOLDS

What follows is a report of architectural exploration in twenty small towns in the Eastern United States. We were curious to know what kinds of houses shelter small-town Americans in the 1980s in that section of the country between the Atlantic Seaboard and the Mississippi Valley. Altogether we recorded observations on some seventeen thousand dwellings. As no universally accepted naming system existed to describe houses, we applied a categorization scheme focused on dwelling form or structure. This scheme enables us to present this treatise on house morphology quite unlike any heretofore written on a broad geographical scale. The significance of our endeavor will be obvious to all students of the American cultural landscape who value the discovery of cultural differences and similarities from place to place across wide areas. We hope this book will instill in our readers an enthusiasm for looking at common houses not only as intrinsically interesting artifacts but also as features that mirror social and cultural variations regionally distributed.

Our work attempts to add another facet to an already rich literature on house types. Scholarly focus on common houses dates back many decades involving architectural historians, cultural geographers, folklorists, social historians, and other students of what is now called material culture. Before we review our own work, it is appropriate that we examine existing literature to demonstrate from whence our inspiration derives and to point up how our work both reinforces and departs from that of others. With practitioners from many disciplines bearing down on the common house as subject matter, it is not surprising that honest differences of opinion exist as to basic concepts, their definition, and their analytical application. There is disagreement as to what constitutes significance in question posing. Some scholars emphasize origins and changes through time; others emphasize differences and similarities across geographical space. Still others see houses solely as cultural mirrors, reflections of the values and behaviors of their inhabitants. While appreciating the validity of each of these approaches we are emphasizing geographical variations.

There is disagreement as to what constitutes an appropriate house to study. One group of scholars is primarily concerned with "stylish" dwellings either designed by or influenced by architects. Another group focuses on "folk" dwellings conceived out of traditions transferred from generation to generation. Others are attracted to every type of dwelling, placing equal value on recent prefabricated ranch houses and historic handcrafted log cabins. Our concern is with the full range of dwelling types. We wanted to know how small-town residents in the Eastern United States house themselves in the 1980s.

Architectural historians initiated the serious study of house types in America. Many have devoted some attention to common houses (Kimball 1922, Kelly 1924, Hamlin 1944, Forman 1948, Morrison 1952). A few have produced detailed analyses of ordinary types of structures (Cummings 1979). However, this

group of scholars has frequently emphasized what Amos Rapoport describes as buildings of "grand design" built to impress either the populace with the power and good taste of the patron, or the peer group of designers and cognoscenti with the cleverness of the designer (Rapoport 1969, 2).

Frank Roos, bibliographer of architectural literature, recognized the following types of studies as dominant: 1) single structures (for example a specific house), 2) structures in a given geographical area (especially at the town, state, and regional scales), 3) specific architectural characteristics (for example, a specific roof form), 4) a given architect and his work, 5) source materials (especially archival), 6) restoration and preservation, and 7) the sociological implications of architecture as physical container and cultural symbol (Roos 1968, 5). Pervading the whole, however, has been a preoccupation with style. Roos writes: "We have been too much in the habit of looking at the stylistic proportions of the exteriors and interiors and not seeing . . . buildings as the builders themselves seem to have seen their handiwork—as a series of details put together to make a whole" (Roos 1968, 10).

Style has been variously defined, both broadly and narrowly. Architectural historian William Pierson's use of the term serves to illustrate (Pierson 1970, 1–14). To Pierson, style embraces the specific identifying characteristics of a building both as the building appears to the eye and as it is known to exist in design and structure. The study of style focuses on the conspicuous characteristics which relate buildings. Four aspects of form, Pierson maintains, provide the indices for stylistic analysis: 1) organization of space, 2) proportion, 3) scale, and 4) ornament. The substance of architecture is space: that is, space enclosed by structure as defined by the shape, size, and disposition of main components. Proportion is a more precise aspect of space relating length and width in generality of outline as contained within a structure or within its elements. Scale is a relationship in size between the structure and some constant unit of measure outside and beyond. In architectural study that unit of measure is usually man. Finally, ornament embraces the detail of finished surfaces as either integral to a structure's support or applied without structural function.

Many architectural historians subsume form (analyzed as space, proportion and scale) as part of style. Others focus directly and solely on ornament as the true essence and indicator of style. Thus Pierson sees ornament as "the most obvious and therefore the most immediately useful . . . indice to style." The specific ornamental devices themselves are generally developed in a manner consistent with overall shape, proportion, and scale (Pierson 1970, 7). Focus on ornamentation has encouraged emphasis on temporal change whereby design motifs are seen to have evolved and succeeded one another. Thus Pierson focuses on "Colonial" and succeeding "Neo-classical" periods. Alan Gowans, in a historical review of American domestic architecture and furniture, focuses on the products of the "Medieval mind," the "Classical mind," the successive stylistic phases rooted in literary romanticism as subsumed under the "Victorian" rubric, and the anti-Victorian "International" style. "Above all," Gowans writes, "you need to see the broad patterns in their over-all historical development" (Gowans 1964, xiv). This emphasis on change has led to the identification of style periods generally characterized by varying ornamental motifs. Popular writers have emphasized ornamentation so strongly that it is generally perceived as synonymous with style in the public mind (Whiffen 1969, Blumenson 1977).

Cultural geographers, on the other hand, have focused not on style as decoration, but on the elements of form that characterize the folk, the vernacular, and the popular in common housing. As geographer Terry Jordan notes, "the products of folk architecture are not derived from the drafting tables of professional architects, but instead from the collective memory of a people. . . . based not on blueprints but on mental images that change little from one generation to the next. . . . an architecture without architects" (Jordan 1978, 3). The clearest example of the folk building is the house built and lived in by the same individual according to time-honored customs. But cultural geographers also include within their purview the more common dwellings built by tradesmen inspired by the popular media of plan books and catalogues. Basic house form or structure (as opposed to the ornamental aspects of style) remains the primary thrust of the literature. When cultural geographers see houses they categorize them first according to form or as structural types.

Amos Rapoport divides the folk tradition into primitive and vernacular phases (Rapoport 1969, 2–6). He characterizes the primitive as producing very few building types, housing models with few individual variations

built by all. In primitive societies a diffuse knowledge of everything is shared by all. There is little specialization. Prescribed ways of doing (and not doing) result in certain forms being taken for granted with change strongly resisted. There is a close relation between house forms and the cultures in which they are embedded. Rapoport uses the term vernacular to describe house types that are neither of the primitive nor stylish varieties. He distinguishes between preindustrial and modern vernacular dwellings. In the preindustrial category diversity is greater than in folk housing but still limited. Houses are built largely by tradesmen hired by would-be homeowners. However, everyone in the society knows the building types and even how to build them, the expertise of the tradesman being only a matter of degree. The owner-occupant is still a participant in the building process. Adjustments and variations in construction affect individual structures rather than basic types, and the small number of prototypes survive as cultural ideas or imprints. Modern vernacular housing involves a greater number of types, many of which are too complex to build in a traditional fashion. Ideas are not communicated orally, but in an often sophisticated graphic form. Thus the builder possesses special skills and he and his client no longer share a single value system. Rapoport contrasts the modern vernacular with high-style modern which contains many specialized building types, each building being an original creation designed and built by specialists.

Folklorists have traditionally focused their efforts on the primitive and the preindustrial vernacular. In the ideal vernacular, according to folklorist Henry Glassie, divisions in architectural work—design, construction, and use—are brought into unity in a single individual (Glassie 1984, 10–12). This builder knows his client and together they share a common concept of how a house ought to be built. In the modern vernacular the builder and client are strangers. The client is a mere consumer of a dwelling built according to some alien plan conceived by an anonymous designer. Nevertheless, the modern vernacular, as rooted in a commercialized "popular culture," was rapidly accepted by the vast majority of Americans. As Glassie notes: "The popular object has been accepted by the innovative individual because it saves him time, is more quickly produced or bought, and is easier to use than the traditional object—and also because it is new" (Glassie 1968a, 17, 19). As convenience became more highly valued than tradition, primitive and preindustrial vernacular

dwellings were largely abandoned except by the poor or less-well-to-do. As Jordan observes, the folk house long ago became a "badge of economic failure, to be occupied with shame by those who did not succeed" (Jordan 1978, 4). Popular material artifacts, such as houses, may be based directly on folk models. On the other hand, houses also may be patterned after high-style, architect-designed models. Most common houses of the late nineteenth and twentieth centuries have represented a mixture of the two traditions. Decoration on traditional forms, even when minimal (only mimicking established styles) carries the sense of fashion symbolic of success, affluence and taste.

It is logical that architectural historians (or those writing in the tradition of architectural history) have treated common houses rooted in folk and vernacular traditions as attenuated or diluted examples of one or another high-style. Alternatively, some architectural historians have tried to define new style categories in order to classify common houses not otherwise classifiable. However, these efforts have met with little success as evidenced by recently published guides to the study of common houses.

Mary Mix Foley in *The American House* identifies "two dominant strains" in American domestic architecture: the formal period styles and a "substratum of folk building" (Foley 1980, 7). Folk building traditions, she notes, were "remarkably sturdy" while the formal styles were "fickle and changeable" representing at each new period a break with the immediate past. Nevertheless, vernacular types were often embellished with stylish decoration: the two "strains" crossing to create new popular guides. There has been created in this way "a confused, and confusing, picture." How, she asks, can one sort out such complexities? But her attempt at sorting is inconsistent in approach and raises its own confusions.

Lester Walker's *American Shelter: An Illustrated Encyclopedia of the American Home,* besides being a "handbook of American housing styles," attempts to show "how the shape and character of dwellings came about" (Walker 1981, 16). Early vignettes do focus on "structure, plan development, and shape," starting with various aboriginal building traditions. Once a form or structure type is introduced, as for example the English hall cottage, derived variations subsequent in time, such as the single-pen log cabin of frontier Kentucky, are pursued, albeit naively. Interspersed among these structural-oriented vignettes are other sections focused on stylish decorations in which some structure types are introduced clothed in ornamental garb. The author is aware that some decorative motifs were closely associated with certain forms and, conversely, that some forms were occasionally linked with particular ornamental fashions. But sorting it all out systematically eludes him.

Virginia and Lee McAlester's *A Field Guide to American Houses* is also a series of vignettes focusing alternately on stylish decoration and form or structure. They coin many new "styles," including something called "folk Victorian" (McAlester and McAlester 1984, 308–17). Following a description of selected aboriginal dwelling types, they discuss the "pre-railroad" era emphasizing the folk structures of New England, the Tidewater South, and the Middle Colonies. Next they examine the "national" era whereupon fashionable ornamentation and not form dominates discussion. In each vignette that describes style in ornamental terms they also portray vernacular forms, but decorated minimally in the style under consideration. Rather than recognizing basic forms of folk and vernacular origins, the two McAlesters persist in seeing style even where there is little or no style to see. Their work, along with that of Mary Mix Foley and Lester Walker,

suggests that house typing schemes that emphasize folk and vernacular forms have not been systematically integrated with those in which ornament is treated as the primary key to style.

A solution to this dilemma of taxonomy lies in separating form and decoration for analytical purposes. This is what most cultural geographers and folklorists have done. Quite simply, form types have been identified and studied apart from style. Concern for ornament, defined in the narrow sense as decoration or ornamentation, appears only after form has been fully understood. The separation of form and decoration is the approach adopted in our analysis of common houses reported here. It is logical that this orientation should have derived from the work of cultural geographers and folklorists who have traditionally dealt with folk and vernacular buildings totally or largely devoid of decorative implications.

Cultural geographer Fred Kniffen pioneered the description of common house forms. He

was the first to grapple systematically with house classification using structural criteria. He recognized the difficulties at hand when he compared his work with that of natural scientists. "Neither houses nor other cultural forms can be classified in a manner exactly analogous to that used by biologists. The biologist never finds the tail of a lion grafted to the body of a cow" (Kniffen 1936, 179). Houses did not obey a simple genetic code but a complicated cultural code with which individuals as decision makers regulate their building of houses among other activities. The classifier of houses, in order to comprehend the differences and similarities between houses culturally given, has to "judiciously generalize." He could never be "completely objective" like a scientist. Nevertheless, he could look for "central themes" by temporarily obscuring minor variations (Kniffen 1936, 179).

For Louisiana, Kniffen found four general dwelling types: houses with gable roofs, those with front-facing gables, those with pyramidal roofs, and those with shed roofs. Next he identified subtypes. The gable-front house, for example, was divisible on the basis of width: the shotgun house being a single room wide and the bungalow house (the southern bungalow) being two rooms wide. He disregarded variation in length and ignored appendages where the other diagnostic elements remained the same. Having driven by automobile a network of rural roads in Louisiana to categorize some fifteen thousand houses, Kniffen then mapped the house forms discovered. His purpose, reflective of the regional emphasis of academic geography at the time, was to use common houses as a key with which to divide Louisiana into cultural regions. Louisiana's landscape, he wrote, reflected the imprint of varied "cultural strains" and houses were to serve as his criteria for isolating those strains from place to place.

It should be noted that Kniffen's focus was solely on rural houses. His cultural regions were purely rural manifestations. He writes: "Urban centers were disregarded in the enumeration, not because they are not significant, but because they introduce complexities out of all proportion to the areas they occupy" (Kniffen 1936, 179). This rural bias would continue in his work and in the work of his students and other scholars attracted to his ideas. Towns, Kniffen asserted, maintained "a large measure of independence of local cultural environment, exhibiting the varied ideas of a hetero-

geneous population and aping the practices of groups far removed" (Kniffen 1936, 179). Kniffen saw two cultures: one rural and the other urban (Kniffen 1965, 552). He was uninterested in exploring the rural-urban linkages, preferring instead to absorb himself totally in the rural landscape.

In his later work, Kniffen sought to identify the most popular folk houses of the Eastern United States by focusing on their areas of origin and their subsequent geographical diffusion (Kniffen 1965). His overall objective, however, remained the demarcation of cultural regions. Ultimately, he intended that his folk housing regions be compared to those established by linguists and other scholars based on other cultural traits such as dialectic patterns or foodways. Kniffen traveled extensively in the Eastern United States interviewing architectural historians and other students of housing and viewing the cultural landscape. It should be emphasized that he did not conduct a systematic survey in producing his classic article "Folk Housing: Key to Diffusion" (Kniffen 1965). He warned his readers that he had "painted with a broad brush and generalized beyond certain ground" (Kniffen 1965, 576). Indeed, systematic surveys of house types are limited in number, and incomplete in terms of the areas covered. Most scholars, following the lead of

Kniffen's later study, have relied primarily on personal impressions when attempting to reconstruct historic paths of architectural diffusion.

Fred Kniffen's primary contributions, viewed in retrospect, appear to be threefold. First, he recognized the importance of studying house forms. He sought taxonomies reflective of basic form or structure as a first step to comprehending houses as a cultural manifestation in the landscape. "Housing even considered alone," he wrote, "is a basic fact of human geography" (Kniffen 1965, 549). Second, he recognized the need for field survey since change in the nation's housing stock was accelerating rapidly. He wrote in the mid-1960s: "There is a strong element of urgency in dealing with the older folk housing, for it is largely unchronicled and its overwhelmingly wood composition makes it highly vulnerable to destructive forces, leaving behind little record of its character" (Kniffen 1965, 550). Finally, he introduced the concept of "initial occupance" to focus the analysis of any given cultural landscape on the first post-pioneer, permanent settlement. This preliminary imprint he saw as long lasting, surviving even when new ethnic stocks succeeded original settlers. Initial occupance provided a "base of reference for all subsequent change" (Kniffen 1965, 551). Kniffen never undertook to test the relationship between prior and subsequent housing, satisfied instead merely to build the notion of initial occupance into his work as an assumption.

Kniffen's success as a teacher prompted numerous students to focus on vernacular landscape forms: houses, barns, fences, road patterns. Indeed, a "Louisiana School of Cultural Geography" can be identified in the literature. William Wyckoff summarizes the school's approach with the following sequential model for landscape study: 1) identification of a material culture form, 2) focus on significant characteristics, 3) determination of geographical distribution, 4) determination of origins and diffusions across geographical space through time, and 5) definition of culturogeographic regions (Wyckoff 1979, 6). Underlying this methodology was the concept of culture which Kniffen saw as an active force constantly remodeling the landscape. It was not individuals who built houses and otherwise altered landscapes, but rather individuals influenced by culture who so acted. Kniffen was a student of Carl Sauer, the Berkeley cultural geographer, who had written: "Human geography . . . unlike psychology and history, is a science that has nothing to do with individuals but only with human institutions, or cultures" (Sauer 1941, 7). Such a cultural deterministic view, largely discounted today, explains Kniffen's quest to designate cultural regions. It also helps explain some

of the specific objectives pursued by his most prolific student, Henry Glassie.

A folklorist, Glassie shifted the emphasis in house type studies "inward from the item to inspect the individual and his culture" (Glassie 1968a, 15). He has departed from his mentor's quest for "hypothetical origins and unusual connections," although he does admit that: "Historic-geographic worries—types and taxonomy, systems of cultural relationship—must precede functional and psychological considerations" (Glassie 1968a, 16). But, as he emphasizes in his classic *Pattern in the Material Folk Culture of the Eastern United States*: "It will be necessary to know not only what an object is and what its history and distribution are, but also what its role in the culture of the producer and user is, and what mental intricacies surround, support, and are reflected in its existence" (Glassie 1968a, 16).

In *Folk Housing in Middle Virginia: A Structural Analysis of Historic Artifacts* Glassie studied 338 houses in Virginia's Louisa and Goochland counties. His was a search for "designing rules" whereby the mental procedures used to construct folk houses could be fully exposed (Glassie 1975, 20–21). What he thought he discovered was "a set of pure

and simple geometric ideas." Competence in the building act proceeded "from this set of geometric ideas, spiraling from the abstract to the concrete, from useless ideas to liveable habitations" (Glassie 1975, 19). Glassie can support his assertions only circumstantially and even he warns that, strictly speaking, the ideas in the mind of a maker of houses can never be enumerated. The dangers of interpreting from artifact back through behavior to culture are obvious. Glassie's approach is intellectually appealing, but certainly appropriate only to the study of small numbers of houses of a restricted time period and a limited geographical area. For large numbers of houses accumulated over long periods and across extensive areas, the strategy poses insurmountable logistical problems. Nevertheless, the attempt to get inside the heads of those who built their own houses is an admirable task to undertake. In a philosophical sense, it gives, irrespective of its practicality, an ultimate purpose to the study of house forms.

Social historians, for their part, have long emphasized the vernacular house as social organizer and social symbol. In the 1920s, historian Helen Reynolds approached her study of relic Dutch houses in the Hudson Valley by noting that houses could reveal the living conditions of a period, and thus the cultural capacities of its people (Reynolds 1929, 3). She focused on houses which expressed the common people. The study of history, she noted, had traditionally emphasized the elites, the apex of the social pyramid, and, by so focusing, had emphasized social "effects" and not social "causes." "Causes," she emphasized, "lie deep at the base of the pyramid, imbedded in the common life of all the people" (Reynolds 1929, 3). Thomas Jefferson Wertenbaker's classic work, *The Founding of American Civilization: The Middle Colonies,* served as a model for social historians. It focused on the vernacular as well as the elite by emphasizing common houses and other elements of the cultural landscape as they reflected Middle Colony life (Wertenbaker 1938).

In recent years several social historians have dealt with the American house and home, beginning with David Handlin's reviewing the "ideas that have formed the basis of American houses" (Handlin 1979, xii).

More helpful are Jan Cohn's *The Palace or the Poorhouse: The American House as a Cultural Symbol* and Gwendolyn Wright's *Moralism and the Model Home: Domestic Architecture and Cultural Conflict in Chicago 1873–1913* (Cohn 1979; Wright 1980). House form is treated only in so far as general house types are considered. Emphasis is placed squarely on the professed values of those responsible for promoting various types: architects, builders, progressive reformers, educators, journalists, women's rights activists, politicians, and hucksters. As the source material is archival, houses are not required to speak for themselves. Instead, she uses three data sources: 1) architectural books and periodicals (or the professional press), 2) builders' trade journals and pattern books of house designs (or the practical press), and 3) domestic guides and home magazines for women (or the popular press) (Wright 1980, 4–5).

Jan Cohn's thesis holds that the house has been, and continues to be, the dominant symbol for American culture. "Therefore, to examine what Americans have said about houses . . . is to examine what Americans have said about their culture" (Cohn 1979, xi). Gwendolyn Wright begins by noting that architecture reveals the designer's cultural biases and those of the larger society of which he is a part. "When something is built, the process documents underlying structures of work, technology, and economics. It also serves as a metaphor, suggesting and justifying social categories, values, and relations" (Wright 1980, 1). Domestic architecture, she emphasizes, illuminates norms concerning family life, sex roles, community relations, and social equality. Wright notes that architecture "does not directly determine how people act or how they see themselves and others, yet the associations a culture establishes at any particular time between a 'model' or typical house and a notion of the model family do encourage certain roles and assumptions" (Wright 1980, 1).

Like folklorists and social historians, cultural geographers have not been remiss in studying the social implications of housing. Nor have architectural historians missed the value of such emphasis. For example, geographer Robert Bastian attempted to demonstrate the usefulness of domestic architecture as a statement of late nineteenth-century occupational class segregation, using relic houses in Terre Haute, Indiana, in a case study (Bastian 1975, 167). Richard Fusch and Larry Ford sought to relate house-type distributions to neighborhood definitions, by surveying housing in Columbus, Ohio and San Diego, California. They discussed the societal acceptance of houses, or the staying power of particular house types, in the context of spatial-temporal urban change (Fusch and Ford 1983, 324).

Architectural historian Alan Gowans, while noting that the generalizations of much social scientific scholarship "may sometimes seem too sweeping," nevertheless admits that such insights can rescue the appreciation of domestic architecture from "degenerating into an esoteric affair of cabrioles and cabochons and comparative cornice mouldings," and "bring life into art history and art history into life" (Gowans 1964,

xiii). Regarding houses as artifacts, he writes, "You have to circle round the subject, approach it from many points of view. You have to consider examples individually, as they express the taste and outlook of the particular people who made and used them. You have to consider them collectively, as revealing in their common characteristics the national origins and fundamental ways of life in diverse states and regions. Above all, you need to see the broad patterns in their overall historical development" (Gowans 1964, xiv).

The cultural geographer's call is toward the understanding of spatial or geographical patterns. As architect Doug Swaim notes, the folk house is primarily a "mental fact," the embodiment of a slowly and collectively wrought idea of "houseness." Once that idea is performed, however, it is also a geographic fact. He continues: "The dwelling that results is located for good, or at least until man or decay removes it. The folk house is thus a record of mind in place" (Swaim 1978, 28). But given the vast area over which the pattern of American folk and vernacular housing is spread (and the hundreds of thousands of miles of street and road along which the data is strung) the relatively few students of common housing have managed barely to sample the field (Swaim 1978, 29). As can be implied from geographer

Peirce Lewis's comments, the geography of common houses is at about the same stage in the later twentieth century as geology found itself in the early nineteenth: "50 percent intelligent guesswork, 40 percent mythology, and the remaining 10 percent split between alchemy and hard facts" (Lewis 1975, 22).

For cultural geographers engaged in the study of common houses the immediate challenge is to map and analyze the geographical distribution of principal house forms, although preliminary to this task is the identification of forms in a typology of structure types. Preferably, these tasks should be undertaken systematically and with reference to large areas. Various sampling strategies are called for, as, for example, the traverse method used by geographers Robert Finley and E. M. Scott and the area sampling method used by James Shortridge. In 1939, Finley and Scott mapped over 3,400 rural houses following a traverse from Wisconsin to Texas of some 1,650 miles. Unfortunately, they sought to relate their findings to physiographic differences. Since houses and physiography are only remotely related through the economic machinations of agriculture, their findings have value only as a record of houses seen: a record which, nevertheless, provides a base against which to measure change (Finley and Scott 1940, 412). More recently, Shortridge surveyed some 1,780 rural houses in twenty-six townships in counties astride the Missouri and Kansas border. His objective was to test relationships between traditional folk building methods and mass-produced designs in what he perceived to be two distinct cultural areas (Shortridge 1980, 105).

Most geographical surveys begin with a typology of house forms, the typology applied to the inventory of houses in one or more study areas. House identification is usually based only on exterior appearances when large numbers of houses are involved. Henry Glassie warns of the inutility of surveys "conducted entirely from within the armor of an automobile" (Glassie 1975, 16). He also warns of inventories "sadly mired in numerology." We recognize the inadequacies of windshield surveys which produce extensive house tabulations without yielding cultural interpretations. We are also aware of necessary priorities if cultural interpretations are to be valid. Certain preliminary steps must precede cultural interpretation. With the very rapid changes affecting modern America, it is vital that house forms which were once common, especially those residual from the late nineteenth and early twentieth centuries, be identified and mapped. Only a

relatively few vernacular house forms, such as the I house, the Cape Cod cottage, and the shotgun cottage have been carefully examined. Many forms are recognized in the literature, but confusion reigns as to basic definitions and even as to basic nomenclatures. Other structure forms have yet to be described in print, and identifying names established. To determine both the frequency of occurrence and the range of distribution of inadequately studied house types, macro scale surveys are most appropriate. The logical sequence of study is first to identify the artifact, trace its occurrence, and then interpret it as a cultural relic.

Scholars across various disciplines, working toward a variety of goals, have sketched the outlines of American domestic history. Many have focused on houses, their form and their styling. In this book we seek to synthesize what is known about house form in a comparative analysis of common dwellings in a sample of small towns of the Eastern United States. This focus, we believe, represents a logical next step toward the more complete surveying of common

houses nationwide. As previous research has emphasized the rural, we begin a systematic focus on the urban. Yet, by restricting our endeavor to small urban places, we hope to tie back into the rural record by testing hypotheses derived from the study of rural houses. Previous research has emphasized houses rooted in the past. Our study seeks to establish a base level of comprehension regarding a select set of houses observed and recorded in the 1980s. Thus we seek to link the houses of the contemporary scene with what is known of house evolution through time. Our primary concern remains geographical. How do basic house forms vary from one part of the Eastern United States to another as reflected in our study towns?

CHAPTER II   ORGANIZING A HOUSE SURVEY

Science is built up with facts,

as a house is with stones.

But a collection of facts is

no more a science than a

heap of stones is a house.

JULES POINCARE

As with most explorations, our survey of common houses evolved by stages. Certainly, we wanted to add to the scholarly literature on vernacular architecture, but by surveying houses at a scale as yet unattempted, and by asking still unanswered questions. Thus we faced the following decisions: 1) What kinds of houses would be included in the survey and how would they be described? 2) In what kinds of places should we study common houses and on what basis would these places be selected? 3) What hypotheses would we pose and what would their testing teach us about variations in common houses across a broad section of the United States? We wanted facts, but, more importantly, we wanted to erect from our facts significant structures of understanding.

Kinds of Houses Studied

We chose to study the full range of single-family dwellings found in small towns in the eastern portion of the country today. Our purpose was not to discover generalizations that would apply to every small town. The study towns were selected in order to test a set of hypotheses about regional patterns among house types as derived from previous scholarship. We picked small urban places as study sites both in response to the rural bias in the literature and in response to the fact that most Americans today are in the broadest sense urban. A concern with small-town housing permits us to pose hypotheses related to the rural-oriented literature since the housing in most small places mirrors that of rural hinterlands. At the same time, focusing on small towns also directs attention toward the big cities since most towns also reflect the fads and fashions of large places. The small town combines traits of the countryside with those of the city.

By looking at all kinds of single-family dwellings we intended to root our efforts in previous scholarship concerned variously with high-style, folk, and the vernacular. We gave equal attention to the work of architectural historians, folklorists, and cultural geographers. We sought to cast aside blinders that might restrict our focus to only certain kinds of dwellings. We wanted to gain a broad view of how small-town residents house themselves in the 1980s. Our intent was to focus on both the old and the new in order to determine what has survived from the past as well as that which is new and popular today.

We needed a universally applicable categorization scheme in order to inventory the full range of dwellings in widely scattered places. Scholars from separate disciplines, using different traits as keys to house typing, have produced diverse and often confusing descriptive labels. Our first concern, therefore, was to formulate a typology of house types emphasizing form or structure. The house categories utilized, the lexicon we created through review and synthesis of the literature, appears in the Glossary. We should emphasize that this glossary of house types results from review not only of scholarly writings, but also from reviewing literature generated by the building industry: plan and pattern books, prefabricated house catalogues, technical writings for building tradesmen, and popular writings for prospective customers. Our classification scheme, based primarily on the writings of academics, was enlarged until it proved capable of describing the spectrum of dwellings illustrated in trade materials as well.

The classification of houses is an important academic exercise. The identification of tangible artifacts through linguistic nomination creates nothing less than cultural taxonomy. One function of language is to name the things that vision demarcates, and thereby to aid in the seeing of and the interpreting of those things (Metz 1980, 59). All research starts with the naming of the phenomena studied: the rendering of things into categories of meaning. These conceptualizations influence, if not direct, the nature of subsequent analysis toward specific kinds of comprehensions. Historian Eric Wolf notes: "The ability to bestow meanings—to 'name' things, acts, and ideas—is a source of power. Control of communication allows the managers of ideology to lay down the categories through which reality is to be perceived. Conversely, this entails the ability to deny the existence of alternative categories, to assign them to the realm of disorder and chaos, to render them socially and symbolically invisible" (Wolf 1982, 388).

Our classification scheme differentiates among dwellings according to three principal dimensions of form or structure. It emphasizes 1) ground plan, 2) height, and 3) roof configuration. Focus on these dimensions of form is not new. Robert Finley and E. M. Scott so classified the houses of their north-south traverse published in 1940 (Finley and Scott 1940, 412). Henry Glassie writing in the 1960s saw height and floor plan as "primary characteristics" with roof configuration of subsidiary importance along with a dwelling's stylish trim and appendages (Glassie 1968a, 8). Virginia and Lee McAlester, writing in the 1980s, observe that house form is not endlessly varied. Instead "a few fundamental shapes, and relatively minor variations on them, tend to be used again and again through a range of changing architectural styles" (McAlester and McAlester 1984, 21). One best proceeds, they maintain, by dividing the three-dimensional house into two separate two-dimensional components: 1) the ground plan or the pattern made by the exterior walls when viewed from directly above and 2) the front elevation or the profile made by wall and roof when viewed straight-on from ground level. These characteristics, they conclude, "combine to make several fundamental families of house shapes that dominate American domestic architecture" (McAlester and McAlester 1984, 21).

Ground or floor plan refers to the general shape of a dwelling as defined by its outline, and general room arrangement. We identified five broad generic "families": 1) single-pile, 2) double-pile, 3) irregularly massed, 4) bungalow, and 5) ranch. Single-pile and double-pile dwellings are square, rectangular, or box-like in outline, the former one room deep and the latter two rooms deep (Brunskill 1971, 204, 236; Glassie 1972, 37; Smith 1975, 550). Irregularly massed structures are asymmetrical and derive from combining rooms informally to produce L, T, or other outlines (Jakle 1976, 9). Irregular massing is not to be confused with single-pile and double-pile houses with appendages or extensions. Irregular massing involves the use of different geometrical forms in a single, fully integrated structural unit. Integration usually derives from the use of a single roof and retention of a single height throughout. Bungalows, on the other hand, display open room arrangements, often with three rooms arranged one behind the other on an axis perpendicular to the street. Ranches also feature open plans, but are elongated parallel to the street. Particular house types within each generic group are identified by considering height and roof characteristics in addition to floor plan as outlined in the Glossary.

Height we defined as the number of habitable stories a dwelling contains, a half-story being livable space immediately under a roof. The reader should note our specific use of the terms "house" and "cottage" as applied to older families of dwellings: single-pile, double-pile, and irregularly massed. Our application of height in assigning older dwellings to either a cottage or house category is borrowed from Kniffen. He defined an I "house" as one that was "two full stories in height" (Kniffen 1965, 555). Discounting subsequent appendages, the way to provide maximum additional space to a dwelling with a particular floor plan, he noted, was by means of a full second story. With this in mind, we use the term "house" to designate single-pile, double-pile, and irregularly massed dwellings with two full stories. Those without a full second story we call "cottages." We followed standard definitions in treating roof configurations (gable, front gable, hip, gambrel, etc.) (See: Blumenson 1977). A gable roof, the most common roof type, is assumed for each house type described in the Glossary unless otherwise stated.

The Glossary contains verbal descriptions of each structure type along with relevant citations. It also includes generalized graphic renderings of floor plans and front and side elevations. Although we define and illustrate photographically dwelling types when first discussed in subsequent chapters, the Glossary provides formal definition as well as ready reference. Readers already conversant with the literature of folk and vernacular architecture will discover familiar nomenclature (hall and parlor cottage, I house, Cape Cod cottage, southern bungalow, split-level ranch, for example). Names popular in the literature have been retained, although arbitrary choices among competing designations were sometimes made. Where no name had yet been coined for a dwelling type, or where competing names established in the literature seemed inappropriate, new names were created or old names modified (double-pile house, two-thirds double-pile house, composite cottage with irregular massing, ranch bungalow, for example).

There is no ideal typology of dwelling types. One attempts to select those features of a house or cottage which seem most significant. Thus we looked first at floor plan, height, and roof profile, noting the most frequently occurring configurations. However, as Amos Rapoport writes: "Buildings, as all human endeavors, obey varied and often contradictory and conflicting impulses which interfere with the simple and orderly diagrams, models, and classifications we love to construct. The complexities of man and his history cannot be encompassed in neat formulas, although the desire to do so characterizes our age" (Rapoport 1969, 11). Our structural types, as variously named, are to be considered only general categories. Nevertheless, our typology adequately described 16,542, or some 96 percent of the houses we inventoried.

In addition to categorizing houses by general form, other house characteristics were recorded: the form of the principal extension, porch and garage (if any), the nature of the front facade covering (clapboard, brick, stone, etc.), the color of the facade, and the nature of the roofing material among other variables. We also noted stylized ornamentation (or "architectural style" narrowly defined). Style differentiations were based on Blumenson's *Identifying American Architecture: A Pictorial Guide to Styles and Terms, 1600–1945* (Blumenson 1977). Separating form and stylish decoration was quite deliberate in our attempt to emphasize structure. As Henry Glassie noted regarding vernacular houses: "Ornaments are modest in scale, simple in shape, weak in reference, and they are shoved to the edges where they deflect attention from themselves and emphasize the overall form of the building" (Glassie 1984, 13). Thus we have treated ornament merely as one of several secondary house characteristics in focusing on vernacular dwellings.

The Study Towns

Towns were carefully chosen to facilitate comparison of house types and selected house characteristics both within and between first-order and second-order cultural regions as identified by geographer Wilbur Zelinsky in his *Cultural Geography of the United States* (Zelinsky 1973, 118–19). We use Zelinsky's regionalization scheme because we believe it to be the best regional synthesis yet devised, as well as the one most familiar to scholars. His scheme is all-embracing, reflecting various criteria of definition: speech patterns, foodways, building traditions. Zelinsky's culture regions are areas in which initial occupance, agriculturally based, derived from common culture hearths or core areas established during the Colonial era. The Yankee core, centered in Southern New England, and the Midland Core, centered in Southeastern Pennsylvania, are the best documented hearths relative to post-colonial migrations and cultural diffusions (Chaddock 1908, Rosenberry 1909, Alexander 1946–47, Holbrook 1968, Glass 1971, Meyer 1976). Less substantial cases for culture hearth location can be made for the Upper South and Lower South (Brademan 1939, Lynch

1943, Owsley 1945, Crisler 1948, Newton 1975). Geographer Robert Mitchell has argued for the Shenandoah Valley as a secondary hearth important to the Upper South (Mitchell 1974, Mitchell 1978). Zelinsky would look to the Seaboard South, especially Chesapeake Bay, for the Lower South's origins (Zelinsky 1973, 122).

The study towns form a nearly uniform pattern of distribution across the Eastern United States as shown in (Figure 2.1). New England, Upstate New York, and the Upper Middle West comprise an area initially occupied by settlers carrying a decidedly "Yankee" culture. New Englanders came to dominate Upstate New York following the Revolutionary War. Yankees, both from New England and New York, continued the push westward in the nineteenth century across Northern Ohio, Southern Michigan, Northern Indiana, Northern Illinois, Southern Wisconsin, and Eastern Iowa. The following towns were selected to represent New England and what Wilbur Zelinsky calls "New England Extended": 1) Mattapoisett, Massachusetts; 2) Cazenovia, New York; 3) Hudson, Michigan; 4) Chilton, Wisconsin; and 5) Grundy Center, Iowa (Figure 2.1).

The Lower Delaware Valley and adjacent coastal area centered on Southeastern Pennsylvania fostered a unique cultural milieu during the colonial period. Whereas the Puritan-derived population of New England was rather homogeneous, this Midland culture was rooted in diverse ethnic origins: English Quaker, German, Scots-Irish, and Irish among other groups. Migrants in the early nineteenth century carried "Pennsylvania" culture west across Central Ohio, Central Indiana, Central Illinois, and into Northern Missouri, laying the cultural base of initial occupance. The following towns were chosen to represent this region which spreads across the Lower Middle West: 1) Millersburg, Pennsylvania; 2) Mount Gilead, Ohio; 3) Rockville, Indiana; 4) Petersburg, Illinois; and 5) Hermann, Missouri (Figure 2.1).

Pennsylvanians also moved southeasterly down the Great Valley into Virginia joining migrants from the Chesapeake Bay area and from the Carolinas in settling Kentucky, Tennessee, and Northern Alabama. Kentuckians and Tennesseans, in turn, were predominant in the initial occupance of the Ozark Plateau of Missouri and Arkansas. The following towns represent this region of the Upper South: 1) Woodstock, Virginia; 2) Stanford, Kentucky; 3) Colum-

2.1 Study Towns

Culture regions studied

I
A   New England
B   New York
C   Upper Middle West

II
D   Pennsylvania
E   Lower Middle West

III
F   Upper South

IV
G   Seaboard South
H   Lower South

Cultural region boundaries

First order   ———
Second order   – – –

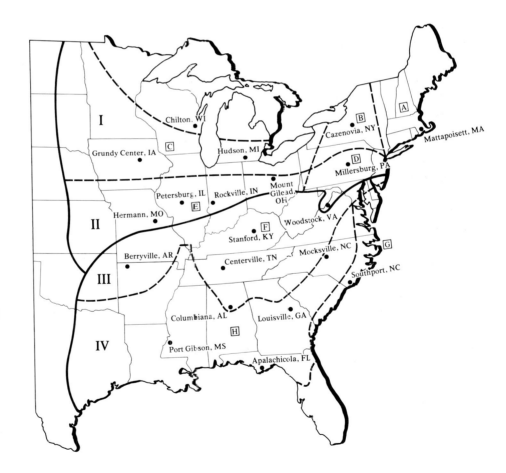

biana, Alabama; 4) Centerville, Tennessee; and 5) Berryville, Arkansas (Figure 2.1). Woodstock appropriately belongs in the Pennsylvania culture core which extends southwestward like a peninsula to encompass the northern portion of the Shenandoah Valley in Virginia. We have included Woodstock with the towns of the Upper South, however, in recognition of the Midland influence on the formation of that culture region westward. We departed from Wilbur Zelinsky's regionalization in one additional instance. According to Zelinsky, Columbiana, Alabama, is located in the Lower South. However, as we will demonstrate, our investigation suggests otherwise and thus we placed the town in the Upper South.

Compared to the Upper South, the Lower South was dominated more by plantation agriculture in its formative stage. Implicit, therefore, was a large labor force of African origin, integral to the economic functioning of the region, but kept socially separate as a distinct caste throughout the nineteenth and earlier centuries. Carolinians and Georgians migrated westward across Southern Alabama, Northern Florida, and Mississippi, to create a distinctive Lower South culture region. The following towns represent this zone: 1) Southport, North Carolina; 2) Mocksville, North Carolina; 3) Louisville, Georgia; 4) Apalachicola, Florida; and 5) Port Gibson, Mississippi (Figure 2.1).

We determined to study sample towns containing between twenty-five hundred and three thousand people (1980). We thought that towns of that size range would display, on average, between seven hundred and nine hundred single-family houses. Originally, we had intended to study larger places using a sampling technique, but a pilot study convinced us that literally every house within study communities needed to be inventoried. Being few in number, significant older houses could easily go undetected with a sampling strategy. The towns we ultimately selected vary from 2,371 people (Port Gibson) to 3,159 (Mattapoisett) (Table 2.1). A smaller population range, town to town, was impossible to obtain given other criteria of selection. Towns in this population range did contain a sufficient diversity of houses necessary for comparative study, yet were also small enough that the logistics of complete inventory in any given place were not overly burdensome. In actuality, the number of houses enumerated in the various study towns ranged from 611 (Cazenovia) to 1,089 (Mocksville). Given the time constraints for field research imposed by our funding agency, we restricted our inventory to twenty towns. The selected towns cover the width and breadth of the cultural regions identified by Wilbur Zelinsky for the Eastern United States.

We did not select our sample towns randomly. Instead, our sample is purposive and judgmental (Kish 1967, 19). We sought towns representative of their regions in terms of several criteria: 1) Our intention was to select towns that were founded during the initial occupance of their area (Mattapoisett is the only exception). 2) Each town was to have experienced growth in subsequent periods of regional economic expansion in order to contain dwellings from successive construction eras (Mattapoisett is actually a child of one of its region's later periods of growth). 3) Each town was to have had a diverse economic base throughout its history. In this regard we felt that the selection of county seats would be a good guarantee of diversity (Only Hudson, Mattapoisett, and Millersburg are not or have never been county seats). We avoided mill, resort, college, and other towns dependent on a single economic base. 4) We sought to avoid towns located in the immediate trade shadows of large cities where suburban housing of recent vintage might prevail to an abnormal degree. 5) Each town was to be located well within its culture region. Towns on or near cultural regional boundaries were avoided if possible because of our desire that they clearly reflect Zelinsky's culture regions (Columbiana, Hermann, and Mocksville are exceptions). 6) Each town was to be located on or near historically significant paths of cultural diffusion, for example, important migration and transportation routes. In this respect, towns would have been continuously accessible to the diffusion of house form innovations.

East–west arrays of towns, five in each array, were sought for four second-order culture regions. While designated according to second-order divisions each array of towns represents a principal culture region in terms of east-west migration and architectural diffusion. From north to south these include 1) Nuclear New England–New England Extended–The Upper Middle West, 2) The Pennsylvania Region–Lower Middle West, 3) The Upper (Upland) South, and 4) The Early British Colonial South–Lower (Lowland or Deep) South.

The spacing of towns in the Upper South permitted the inclusion of two third-order culture areas: the Kentucky Bluegrass and the Ozark Plateau (Zelinsky 1973, 118).

A list of potential study towns was compiled for each culture region and the towns were rank ordered. No town was accepted for study unless first-hand inspection revealed a full spectrum of housing representing all periods of growth. In several instances towns were rejected and substitutes sought. The choice of the New England town was es-

Table 2.1 Population Growth in Study Towns

Regions	Towns	1860	1870	1880	1890	1900	1910	1920	1930	1940	1950	1960	1970	1980
New England	Mattapoisett, MA	1,483	1,361	1,365	1,148	1,061	1,233	1,277	1,501	1,608	2,265	1,640	2,188	3,159
New York	Cazenovia, NY	1,632	1,718	1,918	1,987	1,819	1,861	1,683	1,788	1,689	1,946	2,584	3,031	2,599
Upper	Hudson, MI	1,489	2,459	2,254	2,178	2,403	2,178	2,464	2,361	2,426	2,773	2,546	2,618	2,545
Middle	Chilton, WI	—	363	1,132	1,424	1,460	1,530	1,833	1,945	2,203	2,367	2,578	3,030	2,965
West	Grundy Center, IA	—	—	950	1,161	1,322	1,354	1,749	1,793	2,012	2,135	2,403	2,712	2,880
Pennsylvania	Millersburg, PA	961	1,518	1,440	1,527	1,675	2,394	2,936	2,909	2,959	2,861	2,984	3,074	2,770
Lower	Mount Gilead, OH	788	1,087	1,216	1,329	1,528	1,673	1,837	1,871	2,008	2,351	2,788	2,971	2,911
Middle	Rockville, IN	728	1,187	1,684	1,689	2,045	1,943	1,968	1,832	2,208	2,467	2,756	2,820	2,785
West	Petersburg, IL	1,196	1,792	2,332	2,342	2,807	2,587	2,432	2,319	2,586	2,325	2,359	2,632	2,419
	Hermann, MO	1,103	1,335	1,314	1,410	1,575	1,592	1,701	2,063	2,308	2,523	2,536	2,658	2,695
Upper South	Woodstock, VA	998	859	1,000	1,068	1,069	1,314	1,580	1,552	1,546	1,816	2,083	2,338	2,627
	Stanford, KY	479	752	1,213	1,385	1,651	1,532	1,397	1,544	1,940	1,861	2,019	2,474	2,764
	Columbiana, AL	—	1,040	496	654	1,075	1,079	1,073	1,180	1,197	1,761	2,264	2,248	2,655
	Centerville, TN	251	175	287	498	—	1,097	882	943	1,030	1,532	1,678	2,592	2,824
	Berryville, AR	—	—	253	549	551	785	1,474	1,286	1,482	1,753	1,999	2,271	2,966
Lower South	Southport, NC	—	810	1,008	1,207	1,336	1,484	1,664	1,760	1,760	1,748	2,034	2,220	2,824
(including	Mocksville, NC	710	300	562	—	745	1,063	1,146	1,503	1,607	1,909	2,379	2,529	2,637
Atlantic	Louisville, GA	611	356	575	836	1,009	1,039	1,040	1,650	1,803	2,231	2,413	2,691	2,823
Seaboard)	Apalachicola, FL	1,904	1,129	1,336	2,727	3,077	3,065	3,066	3,150	3,268	3,222	3,099	2,102	2,565
	Port Gibson, MS	1,453	1,088	—	1,524	2,113	2,252	1,691	1,861	2,748	2,920	2,861	2,589	2,371

pecially difficult. Plainfield, Connecticut, originally ranked high for its relative isolation from large urban centers, proved to be a mill town, its older housing (mostly duplexes) constructed by a local manufacturing firm as "company housing." Clinton, Guilford, Essex, Deep River, East Hampton, and Colchester in Connecticut, Wakefield in Rhode Island, and Wareham in Massachusetts were inspected before Mattapoisett was selected. The New England choice was complicated by the difficulty of separating towns from their surrounding townships, a task easily accomplished for Mattapoisett since its center is isolated from outlying areas by marshland and an interstate highway. The choice of the Michigan town was also difficult. A preliminary reconnaissance of Hudson revealed a general paucity of post–World War II houses. However, visits to Ithaca, Chesaning, Coruna, Williamstown, and Hartford revealed similar circumstances. It was concluded that a relative lack of post–World War II construction characterized southern Michigan towns in the twenty-five hundred to three thousand population range. What at first had appeared as an anomaly for Hudson was, in fact, typical of the area's towns of its size and Hudson thus was retained.

Places with established architectural, historical, or geographical literatures were selected over alternatives equally suitable in other respects. Thus Cazenovia was selected over Skaneateles and other towns in central New York State, and Hermann was chosen over other towns in Missouri including Troy where older housing stock at the core had been razed. Where previous research had characterized a town as atypical (for example, Cazenovia's gentry orientation or Hermann's German origin) care was exercised to determine that a wide range of vernacular housing reflecting diverse social elements was present. Town aesthetics played a minor role in town selection. No town was rejected on the basis of unattractiveness and yet a quest for positive visual quality represented an underlying predisposition to accept a place that satisfied other essential criteria. It was assumed that towns with visual distinctiveness, and hence an enhanced sense of place, would provide a stronger frame of reference for the comparison of common houses, town to town.

None of the sample towns represents a perfect choice. Compromises were made. Cazenovia's location eighteen miles from Syracuse is clearly a marginal circumstance given our intent to avoid towns under strong metropolitan influence. Hermann's location near the bound-

ary of its culture region presents problems relative to its regional representativeness. However, in instances such as these, deficits were counterbalanced by other criteria. For example, Cazenovia and Hermann sit astride major migration routes with enhanced significance accordingly. The architecture of both towns has been extensively studied thus increasing our interpretative capabilities (Lamme and McDonald 1973; Gerlach 1976; Hugill 1977; Van Ravenswaay 1977). Irrespective of the pros and cons associated with any particular town, our primary objective was to create an array of towns as uniformly distributed as possible across the primary culture regions of the Eastern United States. In this endeavor we feel that we have been successful.

Hypotheses

Geographer Peirce Lewis writes: "The man-made landscape—the ordinary run-of-the-mill things that humans have created and put upon the earth—provides strong evidence of the kind of people we are, and were, and are in the process of becoming" (Lewis 1979, 15). Indeed, Lewis presents this premise as a primary axiom for interpreting ordinary landscapes. Five corollaries follow: cultural change, regional variation, convergence, diffusion, and taste. When applied to the study of common houses various assumptions emerge. In general, house types and characteristics can be expected to vary geographically in systematic fashion as mirrored in cultural variation. Thus the differences and similarities in dwellings from place to place are seen not as random occurrences, but as elements of landscape explainable in terms of culturally defined regularities.

Following Lewis's first corollary, changes through time in the popularity of different dwelling types in any given place display cultural change brought about, for example, by the disruptions of war, economic depression, or technological innovation. Lewis, in noting that landscape represents an enormous investment of money, time and emotion, writes: "People will not change . . . landscape unless they are under heavy pressure to do so" (Lewis 1979, 15). If the houses of one place look substantially different from those of another, following Lewis's second corollary, "the chances are very good that the cultures of the two places are different also" (Lewis 1979, 15). The extent to which the houses of two places have come to look increasingly alike, according to his third corollary, may reflect the increasing convergence of cultures (Lewis 1979, 16). From his fourth corollary we note that landscape is often changed by imitation. People transfer ideas as to what houses should look like from place to place. Thus the similarity of houses from place to place reveals explicit and implicit processes of cultural diffusion. Lewis's fifth corollary concerns "taste": the ephemeral fads and fashions of social status. "To understand the roots of taste," Lewis writes, "is to understand much of the culture itself" (Lewis 1979, 17). Nothing has proven more "taste-oriented" than architectural form and decoration. The study of common houses, therefore, is central to cultural landscape analysis.

Thus we sought to document regional variations in house types and house characteristics as they reflected cultural origins and diffusions and changing tastes through time and space in our sample towns. We also attempted to interpret the persistence of selected dwelling types and characteristics through time and from place to place as reflected in our regional sets of towns. Our basic conceptual hypothesis was: Dwelling types and dwelling characteristics vary systematically both within and between the principal cultural regions of the Eastern United States. These geographical variations reflect accumulations over time in the sample towns. More specifically, we hypothesized that various house types and characteristics rooted in folk traditions would be more prevalent at the eastern ends of the respective culture regions. Conversely, house types and characteristics disseminated through the media of the building industry were hypothesized to be more common to the west. These anticipations derive from Wilbur Zelinsky's notion that cultural gradients tend to be much steeper and regional boundaries more distinct in the East than westward (Zelinsky 1973, 120). Within each culture region selected folk traditions were expected to have contributed to the popularity and persistence of particular media-inspired elements in house design, a function of persisting local and regional tastes. Variations in stylish ornament were expected as reflections of differential town growth during successive building eras. It was also anticipated that the ornament imitating specific styles would vary significantly between regions. Apparent rates of adoption and periods of persistence of both dwelling forms and characteristics, such as stylish ornament, were expected to vary significantly both within and between culture regions. New houses built in towns across various cultural regions would provide, we thought, evidence of convergence: places becoming more alike or standardized in appearance given recent house construction.

Beyond the hypotheses posed, we expected to create a baseline of observation allowing future researchers to study change in our respective sample towns. Implicit is the hypothesis, untestable in the context of this research alone, that processes evident in the house data collected here will continue to produce distinctive regional and temporal configurations in the future. Certainly, a substantial proportion of America's common houses of both folk and of early builder or tradesman origin are threatened either by neglect, overt destruction, or through substantial remodeling. Fire, flood, and storm exact their toll to further the culling of housing stocks everywhere. Without systematic inventory, knowledge of the extent and persistence of this heritage would be lost.

Beyond the analyses implicit in hypothesis posing, we identified still another objective for our work. The intended description of house types and house characteristics and the analysis of their geographical distribution in the Eastern United States would stand as a kind of field guide to house study. Not only would form or structure types be illustrated in photographs, but their distributions within and between sample towns would be clearly mapped. Scholars would not only have a base line for further hypothesis testing, but lay readers would have a visual reference to house types and a clear indication as to where these forms might be found. Therefore, we present our findings in a text fully supported photographically and cartographically. Photographs and maps are central to our communicating.

The Survey

With the above objectives in mind, we launched our house inventory in Rockville, Indiana, in March 1983. During the following May and June we inventoried houses in Mount Gilead, Millersburg, Mattapoisett, and Cazenovia. In July and August we worked in Hudson, Chilton, Grundy Center, and Hermann. January 1984 found us in Port Gibson, Columbiana, and Louisville; April in Woodstock; and May and June in Centerville, Apalachicola, Southport, Mocksville, and Stanford. The last of our inventory work took us to Petersburg and Berryville in August 1984.

The streets of each town were canvassed systematically. Only habitable single-family dwellings visible from public rights-of-way were inventoried. All streets within established municipal, borough, or village boundaries were inventoried as well as streets in adjacent built-up areas. The work was divided among the three investigators as follows. All three acted as a panel to name and describe houses as viewed, appropriate information being called aloud in an established sequence. Such oral pronouncement enabled each investigator to serve as a check upon his colleague's interpretations. Differences in opinion, which were rare, were decided by majority vote. One investigator drove the automobile, a second recorded data on forms, and a third located houses on a base map. Frequent stops were made to photograph houses thought to be representative; however, no systematic photographic record was created. Occasional stops were made to question house occupants regarding dwelling age and interior layout. The details of inventory logistics (the encounters with dogs, curious residents, and the like) clearly represent the stuff of comedy and human drama, but are not relevant to this particular report.

Conducting the survey—the sequential movement through the streets of twenty towns, the viewing of every house (indeed every building), and the asking and answering of a range of questions about each dwelling— was an experience few have had. The monotony of data recording was relieved by the diurnal rhythms of each day, the observing of daily rounds conducted neighborhood by neighborhood. The viewing of different places at different seasons with the differences in social rhythm evident kept one additionally alert. But always the houses were foremost—the constant testing of the typing system and the development of new categories when established categories failed. The discovery of house forms and characteristics where expected was satisfying. The discovery of the unexpected or of the expected in numbers unanticipated

was most exciting of all. No town and no region lived up totally to anticipations as the following presentation of our results will establish. And yet our effort substantially validates past work while suggesting interesting avenues for further enhancing understanding of common houses.

Although we did not fully realize the implications of our work when we began, the data collected, once analyzed and mapped, lends itself not just to a monograph, but to a monograph approximating a "mini-atlas." As a communication device, the map is the most appropriate graphic form for presenting our findings. Some sixty maps facilitate the comparison of common houses across the study towns as grouped by region. In the next chapter we begin by describing our study towns. Then, in the following chapter, individual house characteristics are emphasized by way of further introducing readers to differences place to place. Specific structure types are treated in subsequent chapters. Having created our typology, having selected our sample towns, and having executed our

inventory, we turned eagerly to mapping distributions in order to test hypotheses. We present in the chapters which follow the more significant geographical distributions both as they stand alone as intriguing geographies and as they sum to a geographical overview of common houses.

CHAPTER III   THE STUDY TOWNS

Towns, districts, and people

all own peculiarities and

eccentricities that, by their

very deviation from ordinary

norms, lend flavor and interest

to their personalities.

PEIRCE LEWIS

Small towns in the United States share much in common. Witness, for example, the nearly ubiquitous gridirons of older neighborhoods, streets meeting at right angles to form repetitive patterns for circulation. Witness Main Streets with their near identical commerical blocks. J. B. Jackson writes: "I cannot always remember the difference between one small town and another; both will have a main street flanked by solid buildings of brick, both will contain block after block of free-standing frame houses, each with a lawn; there will be a cluster of elegant white grain elevators near the railroad tracks in both of them, and a stretch of highway bordered by drive-ins" (Jackson 1972, 155). In the newer parts of towns the grid plan changes to pockets of curvilinear subdivisions. But, more important than that, M. R. Wolfe observes, "the house-shapes become larger in plan

(one story), farther apart (wider lots), and develop new projections: carports, covered patios and decks" (Wolfe 1959–60, 12). Thus most towns have conformed to a distinctive American style of town building. Jackson calls it "classical." "A rhythmic repetition (not to say occasional monotony) is a classical trait, the consequence of a singleminded devotion to clarity and order" (Jackson 1972, 155).

Peirce Lewis reminds us that every town possesses a distinctive personality (Lewis 1972, 328). "Peculiarities" and "eccentricities" abound for no two places are alike. It is our purpose in this chapter to give some sense of local character town to town, to establish for each of our communities a clear sense of place. To interpret properly the housing patterns emphasized in subsequent chapters, the reader must have a feel for the history and geographical layout of each town. One must sense what makes each place different as a container of houses. Sorted into groups of five according to culture region, towns are described below according to settlement history and geographical configuration. The maps included with each town sketch serve not only to give a sense of urban morphology, but to define for each town the precise survey area. Only those dwellings visible from the streets outlined were included in the study.

The Towns of New England, New York, and the Upper Middle West

The dwellings and dwelling characteristics that we will describe reflect not only cultural differences expressed across regional boundaries, but temporal differences which, generally speaking, exhibit a westward progression of economic activity within regions historically. Thus population change profiles for Mattapoisett, Cazenovia, Hudson, Chilton, and Grundy Center clearly illustrate that the three eastern towns in the northernmost tier reached maturity earlier than two western towns

(Figure 3.1). Chilton and Grundy Center, although laggards early, subsequently displayed constant growth through the late nineteenth and twentieth centuries. Hudson and Mattapoisett experienced repeated cycles of sharp increase and decline reflective of shifts in industrial employment. Thus in the western towns we would expect to find accumulations of dwellings not only relatively more recent in date, but reflecting each succeeding decade more evenly. In the eastern towns, especially in Hudson, we would expect a decidedly older housing stock with certain decades contributing more.

3.1   Population Change: Towns of New England, New York, and the Upper Middle West

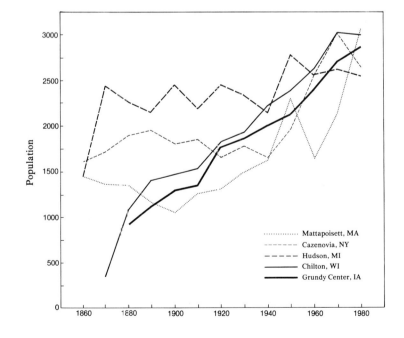

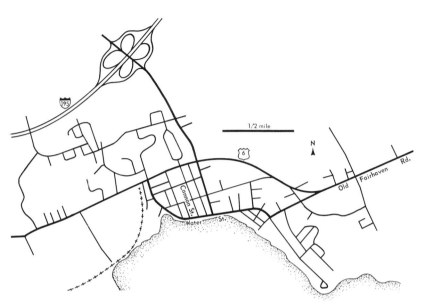

3.2   Mattapoisett, Massachusetts

3.3   Antiquity seems to pervade Mattapoisett's Pearl Street although, in fact, many houses are new and merely replicate the past.

MATTAPOISETT

The smell of salt air and the sound of gulls permeates this New England seaport at all seasons. The area was first settled in 1680, the number of farmhouses around the rock-rimmed harbor accumulating slowly. In the mid-eighteenth century shipbuilders located at the "Upper Landing" to supply sloops and small schooners to merchants at New Bedford, Nantucket, and Martha's Vineyard. By 1800 a village had formed complete with sawmills, forges, cooper shops, sail lofts, and spar yards. Between the War of 1812 and the Civil War Mattapoisett Harbor was a small but bustling whaling port to which a Boston railroad connection (now abandoned) was completed in 1854. By 1900 summer people were playing an active role in town affairs, especially through the Village Improvement Society organized in 1904 to upgrade schools and promote planting of trees along public streets. With completion of the interurban railroad over the eight-mile distance to New Bedford, Mattapoisett became a satellite of that city, a function subsequently enhanced by widespread automobile ownership.

3.4   **Tourism built around yachting anchors Mattapoisett's maritime tradition on today's Water Street.**

Commuting has contributed to the creation of an economically prosperous and amenity-rich town.

Topography, shoreline configuration, surface drainage (bogs, ponds, and streams) and an interstate highway right-of-way have contained the town geographically, and prevented undue urban sprawl (Figure 3.2). The early nineteenth-century town persists on a compact grid of narrow streets oriented to the waterfront. Pearl Street, with its slight curve, provides a quintessential maritime New England streetscape (Figure 3.3). Here classically styled folk houses are clad with wood shingles weathered gray. Water Street, a small business avenue paralleling the shore, serves the yachtsman and the tourist (Figure 3.4). Late nineteenth- and twentieth-century growth lies adjacent to the old Fairhaven Road. Here stood the village green and the Congregational Church which together formed the post–Civil War focus of the community; the area is now thoroughly obliterated by the U.S. 6 commercial strip. Oriented to this highway and the interchange of the new I-95 freeway are curvilinear streets with large lots. They form a distinctively suburban landscape with numerous ranch dwellings and modern Cape Cod revival houses. Along the harbor, streets contain a few large homes built by the early summer elite. In recent decades, additional coastal woodland has been subdivided into large lots many with ranch and colonial revival houses occupied by commuter residents. Here, as in the other suburban areas, replicas of the area's historic house forms are conspicuous in number. To the west are summer cottages built in compounds along private roads. Due to the seasonal occupancy of these dwellings, they were excluded from the house survey (*An Account of the Celebration* 1908, *Mattapoisett and Old Rochester* 1950, *Town of Mattapoisett* 1957, Bunnewith and Pursley 1976).

CAZENOVIA, NEW YORK

Cazenovia is located in the Finger Lakes area of Upstate New York, blue skies mirrored in blue waters. The town, located on the southeast shore of Lake Cazenovia, was laid out in 1794 by John Lincklaen who purchased some sixty thousand acres from the Holland Land Company, naming the place in honor of an officer of the company. Lincklaen sought settlers from New England, but by 1830 large numbers of Irish immigrants had come to the town as well. For a brief period Cazenovia was the seat of Madison County; however, construction of the Erie Canal diverted much of the area's urban growth to the north and county government was spirited away. The Buffalo-Albany turnpike, today's U.S. 20, integrated Cazenovia into the road network of west central New York. By the mid-nineteenth century some thirty mills (sawmills, gristmills, woolen mills) were located along Chittenango Creek which drains the Lake. In the early 1870s railroads (now abandoned) reached the town, but industry never thrived and Cazenovia remained primarily a farm trade center with limited resort activity added at the end of the nineteenth century. After World War II the town became a bedroom community for automobile commuters to Syracuse some twenty miles distant.

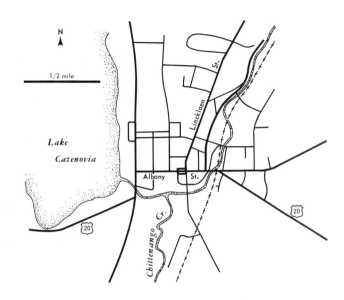

3.5   Cazenovia, New York

3.6   Cazenovia's village green, now divided by the modern U.S. 20, is suggestive of Upstate New York's New England Heritage.

3.7   Cazenovia's Lincklaen Street reflects a continuing search for gentry
status through architectural display.

3.8   Irish laborers lived near
Cazenovia's mills in the past century,
as do many of their descendants today.

Roads radiate from Albany Street's well-preserved business district (Figure 3.5). The town's irregular grid of streets is small and house density is high. The town's main focus remains the public square or green dominated by a large white frame Presbyterian Church (Figure 3.6). The radial roads of the town, and the lesser streets that fill the interstices, provide pleasant, tree-lined residential neighborhoods. Lincklaen Street is most reflective of the town's New England origins (Figure 3.7). Maple trees line the sidewalks in front of well-maintained white weather-boarded upright and wing and gable-front houses. So visually prominent is this street that it tends to blind casual visitors to the town's many ordinary streets where more modest structures crowd (Figure 3.8). Post–World War II subdivisions with modern ranch houses lie north of the town in hilly, heavily wooded terrain. A shopping center has been opened to the east (Smith 1880, Lamme and McDonald 1973, Grills 1977, Hugill 1977, Hugill 1980).

HUDSON, MICHIGAN

Yankees were attracted early to the hills of southeastern Michigan—Daniel Hudson, after whom the town was named, came from the state of New York in 1834. A complement of retail activities developed here prior to the arrival of an east-west railroad line in the 1840s, and a north-south rail connection in the 1870s. The railroads stimulated sawmilling, flour milling, and metalworking. Despite the abandonment of the railroads in the 1960s, foundries and tool and die shops continue to bind Hudson to the American manufacturing belt, especially the automobile industry centered at Toledo (forty-five miles distant) and Detroit (seventy-five miles distant). Many residents commute to nearby Adrian and Hillsdale. The population, relatively stable for over a century, has changed in composition. Today there is a larger blue collar element including recent migrants from the Upper South.

The well preserved brick storefronts of Main Street (Figure 3.9) provide the town's central focus, given the lack of a square or other ceremonial open space. The town continues to occupy three adjacent, but clearly differentiated, street grids platted in the nineteenth century (Figure 3.10). Only one very small subdivision of curvilinear streets ex-

3.9   Main Street provides a community focus for Hudson.

3.10   Hudson, Michigan

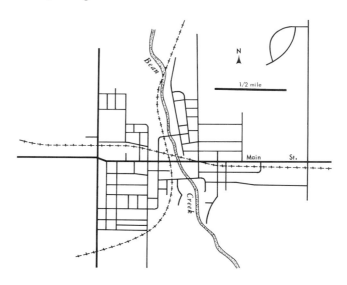

The Study Towns 29

3.11   Conversion of large houses into apartments signals social change along Hudson's gentry row west of downtown.

ists in the town's northeast periphery. There is relatively little highway-oriented commercial development, itself symbolic of the town's lack of recent growth. Residential streets are tree-lined and visually reminiscent of upstate New York and New England. The three blocks of Main Street west of the commercial district contain many large nineteenth-century gentry houses (Figure 3.11), the center piece the large brick Methodist Church. Motorists approaching the town

from the west ascend a steep grade directly into the heart of this gentry row: a juxtaposition of rural countryside and townscape of striking visual effect (Hogaboam 1876, Bonner 1909, Yager 1983).

CHILTON, WISCONSIN

Chilton stands east of Lake Winnebago in rolling dairy country. The site was first settled in 1845 by Moses Stanton, a mixed-blood Narragansett Indian from Rhode Island, who built a sawmill and later a gristmill. Chilton's early population was dominated by New Yorkers and New Englanders with Germans and Irish coming later. A village was platted in 1852, and in the next year made seat of Calumet County. The arrival of the railroad in 1871 (now the Milwaukee Road) encouraged establishment of a creamery, brewery, malt house, canning plant, and several mill work factories. The large brick malt house remains a prominent town landmark.

Chilton's radial road pattern has associated with it several separate street grids, creating distinct residential and commercial sections (Figure 3.12). Main

3.12   Chilton, Wisconsin

Street, running east-west, contains the principal commercial district, originally oriented to the now vacant millsites on the Manitowoc River (Figure 3.13). A series of dams and scenic ponds are reminders of the early mill era. Main Street also serves a railroad-oriented business district to the east now largely abandoned to retail trade. Although Chilton is the county seat, the courthouse is not the town's centerpiece—it sits at the very western edge of the community, keeping a low profile. Central landmarks of Chilton are the St. Augustine (Irish) and St. Mary (German) Roman Catholic churches whose towers may be seen from some distance. New subdivisions, extensions of the various grids, have been built during the last quarter century around the town's peripheries, especially north and south (Figure 3.14). Extensive commercial strip development is also located there. Chilton has become a retirement community for dairy farmers whose preference for new ranch houses is clearly evident. Much captured farm land lies within the city limits and supplements the already extensive open space provided by parks and playgrounds along the river (Smith 1977).

GRUNDY CENTER, IOWA

Grundy Center epitomizes the small town that many people use to stereotype the Middle West.

3.13 St. Mary's Church deflects the view up Main Street, toward the business district beyond.

3.14 Cow pastures converted to subdivisions sprout new houses around Chilton's edges.

Icons of place include the spacious uniform grid of streets, a wide business street anchored by a courthouse at one end, and grain elevators astride a railroad (abandoned in the 1970s) that touched the grid on the town's northside (Figure 3.15). Settled in

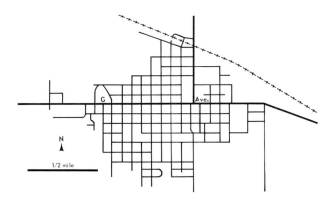

3.15   Grundy Center, Iowa

1856, Grundy Center grew very slowly until completion of the railroad in the late 1870s. Early settlers came from New York, New England, Pennsylvania, and Ohio. Traditionally, businesses have been agriculture-related (canning, grain storage, farm chemical and equipment supply). Today Grundy Center also serves as a bedroom community for workers commuting to Waterloo/Cedar Falls some twenty-five miles distant.

The checkerboard Middle Western image of Grundy Center is reinforced by the town's street names. The street-naming system designates east-west streets by letters and north-south streets by numbers. The main street is G Avenue (Figure 3.16). The town's single grid of streets has been extended in recent decades both north and south, the most affluent area being in the southwest adjacent to country club and golf course. Houses in the older parts of town are noticeably plain, having been exposed painfully to view through the recent loss of trees to Dutch elm disease (Figure 3.17). Commercial strip development, both east and west

3.16   The courthouse anchors this view westward along Grundy Center's G Avenue.

3.17   Here is Iowa at its utilitarian best, plain houses outlining Grundy Center's strict grid of streets.

on G Avenue, is anchored by farm implement and automobile dealers. Grundy Center's location on its high prairie ridge produces a visual landscape with a western feel. Perhaps appropriate to this setting are a small number of Prairie-style dwellings, a variety found in none of our other study towns. In the summer, large fields of corn and soybeans stretch off into the distance, the silos of farmsteads widely spaced. Courthouse and grain elevators punctuate the town's skyline (*Grundy Center 1977*, *Grundy Center Remembers 1977*).

Clearly, the feeling of New England drops off rapidly west of Hudson and is hardly evident in Grundy Center. That Hudson reflects its Yankee past so vividly in its white houses and tree-lined streets is undoubtedly a function of its economic and population stability over recent decades (Figure 3.1). Cazenovia also has suffered recent population reversal. But, as in Mattapoisett, old neighborhoods appear prosperous and well maintained because the residents are affluent, primarily commuter-sustained, families. In Mattapoisett recent growth is clearly revealed in new subdivisions dominated by

revival-style dwellings that mirror those at the town's traditional core. Architecture and social status are clearly linked there. In Chilton and Grundy Center there is no pretense at replicating the past in new subdivisions. Modern ranch dwellings dominate the new subdivisions. In these western towns old streets echo not so much folk traditions from the east as the commercial builder's catalogue of forms ubiquitous everywhere in the Eastern United States from the mid-nineteenth century on.

3.18 Population Change: Towns of Pennsylvania and the Lower Middle West

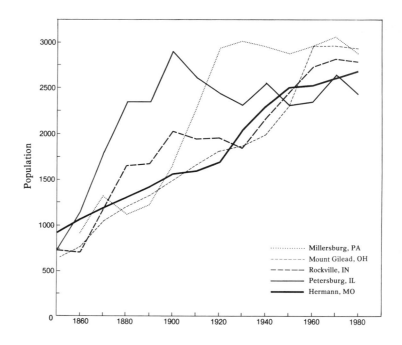

The Towns of Pennsylvania and the Lower Middle West

Although of similar size both in 1860 and 1980, the towns of Pennsylvania and the Lower Middle West experienced very different patterns of growth in the intervening years (Figure 3.18). Whereas Mount Gilead and Hermann enjoyed consistent population increase across all decades, Rockville and Petersburg reached peaks early in the twentieth century followed by sharp declines. Although recovery came after World War II, Petersburg's population still remains well below its early peak. The town's stability is related not only to declining agriculture, but to its inability to attract industry. Whereas Millersburg's economy remains substantially dependent on small scale manufacturing, its employment base has been shrinking in recent decades for manufacturing is no guarantee of sustained growth. We would expect unusually higher numbers of older dwellings in Petersburg, Rockville, and Millersburg. Immediate post–World War II houses would be more evident at Mount Gilead given its very rapid growth between 1940 and 1960. By contrast, Hermann's even growth should be reflected in a diversity of dwellings obtained from all major building eras.

MILLERSBURG, PENNSYLVANIA

Millersburg nestles beside the Susquehanna, a picturesque river town flanked by mountains. Daniel Miller of Lancaster County, Pennsylvania, laid out the town in 1808, migrating later to Ohio. Mahantango Mountain to the north and Berry Mountain to the south originally blocked land transport and thus the town's trade hinterland developed eastward. In 1856 a rail line (now Conrail) connected Millersburg with Harrisburg, the state capital and county seat of Dauphin County, twenty-four miles to the South. Shoe manufacture and a tool and die industry, the two major components of the town's present industrial base, evolved in the late nineteenth century, the skilled labor primarily of Pennsylvania German descent.

The town's simple grid of small uniform blocks has as its central focus a public square which now serves as a traffic rotary for several highways (Figure 3.19). Streets are narrow except the principal business thoroughfare which extends northward from the square (Figure 3.20). Placement of houses along the older streets is typical of Southeastern Pennsylvania: little

3.19 Millersburg, Pennsylvania

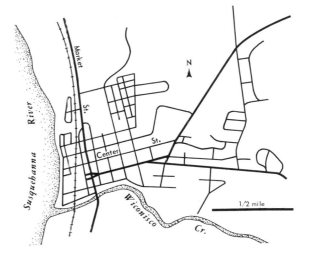

or no front yard and houses with either touching side walls or minimum separation (Zelinsky 1977, 131–38). Shade trees are planted in the brick sidewalks. North Street appears especially typical of the region with predominantly brick buildings serving a mix of commercial and residential functions (Figure 3.21). The new section of Millersburg, located east on heights above the town, contains large modern ranch dwellings on spacious lots. Here curving streets exemplify modern American suburbia (Figure 3.22). Millersburg also has a lower town between the railroad and the river where poorly maintained, older dwellings predominate (Egle 1883, Woodside 1979).

3.20 The mix of commercial and residential functions along Millersburg's Market Street typifies towns in Southeast Pennsylvania.

3.21 Houses of the 1870s, flush to the sidewalk at the left, and houses of the 1910s, behind very shallow front yards to the right, demonstrate changing fashions along Millersburg's North Street.

3.22 Millersburg's new subdivisions sprawl across the eastern heights, making postage-stamp yards a thing of the past.

MOUNT GILEAD, OHIO

Mount Gilead is what a novelist might like to typify as Ohio: a certain mixture of old and new. Settlement began in the early 1820s, but a village, at first called Whetstone and then Youngstown, did not thrive until the 1830s. Renamed to honor a Virginia town, population increased rapidly after Mount Gilead became the seat of newly created Morrow County in 1848. Most of the early settlers migrated from Pennsylvania, New York, Virginia. Some came from Germany. Being a county seat and farm trade center only partially offset the loss of two mainline railroads which bypassed Mount Gilead two miles to the west and six miles to the southwest, respectively. Only a spur line (now abandoned) served Mount Gilead and the town's growth was stunted until the automobile era. Today, the community manufactures hydraulic presses in a small plant, but most residents commute to work in cities, especially Galion and Marion.

The tight grid of streets at the center contains older houses (Figures 3.23 and 3.24). On the looser grid to the northwest, ranch dwellings prevail, owned not only by commuters but by farmers retired in town. No dominating commercial strip has evolved and thus the central business district has been left viable and structurally intact. Mount Gilead is an arterial street town with routes converging on the town square from the four

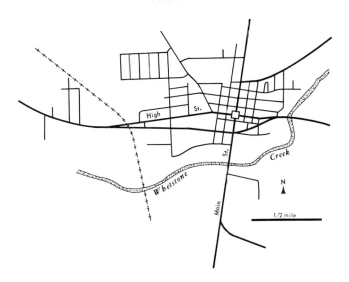

3.23   Mount Gilead, Ohio

3.24   Mount Gilead's older tree-lined streets suggest Sherwood Anderson's fictional Winesburg, Ohio.

3.25 Commerce tightly rings Mount Gilead's town square, the obelisk a strong visual anchor for the town.

ROCKVILLE, INDIANA

Rockville dates from 1824 when the courthouse of Parke County was established at what was an isolated frontier settlement some twenty-five miles north of Terre Haute. Most of the early settlers were migrants from either Ohio and Pennsylvania or Kentucky and Tennessee. The town grew slowly as a farm trade center, its economy bolstered by small mills. Bypassed by a mainline railroad (a branch railroad is now abandoned) and never successful as a seat of industry, the town has remained primarily a trade center. In recent decades Rockville has also begun to function as a bedroom community with

cardinal directions. Traffic converges in a diamond-form square enclosed on three sides by business buildings, and punctuated at its center by a tall obelisk (Figure 3.25). Although located one block distant, the courthouse visually anchors this public space. Like that of Millersburg in Pennsylvania, the diamond-form square is slightly elongated. Away from the square, Main and High streets once served as residential show streets (*History of Morrow County* 1880, Baughman and Bartlett 1911).

3.26 Rockville, Indiana

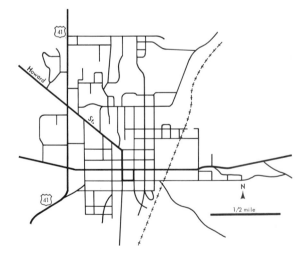

commuters oriented to Terre Haute and suburban Indianapolis. The largest local employer is a small manufacturer of electrical components.

The town is clearly divided between an older section, predominantly blue collar, and a newer, basically middle class, suburb (Figure 3.26). The former comprises a grid of streets centered on the courthouse square, the massive French Second Empire courthouse providing the centerpiece for a well preserved late-nineteenth-century commercial district (Figures 3.27 and 3.28). Howard Street angles across the top of the grid toward the northwest. This was once Rockville's most prestigious residential avenue with many of the houses on the north side of the street surrounded by very large, irregularly shaped lots. A rural aspect once penetrated to within three blocks of the courthouse here. Beginning in the 1920s, new streets were opened north from Howard Street in wooded, rough terrain (Figure 3.29). Not

3.27 Rockville's courthouse fully dominates its large square; business facades are seemingly repelled to comfortable distances.

3.28 The courthouse bell is still heard across Rockville's older grid of streets, symbolizing a sense of community cohesion.

3.29 Many of Rockville's newer streets lack a clear sense of place, and seem unconnected with the rest of the town.

until after 1960, however, did this new section mature with the curvilinear streets of the various subdivisions coalescing to form a distinctively suburban landscape. In the 1970s a commercial strip evolved north along peripheral highway U.S. 41. Since the 1950s Rockville has been the site of the annual Parke County Covered Bridge Festival, one of the largest folk festivals in the United States. The town stands at the heart of a declining farm community where land is rapidly diverting to recreational use and where tourists seasonally seek the relics of rural life rapidly passing (Beadle 1869, Strouse 1916, Davis and Davis 1978).

PETERSBURG, ILLINOIS

Petersburg lies in Illinois's Lincoln country. Lincoln matured into adulthood at nearby New Salem (now a state historical park) and played a role in surveying Petersburg in 1836. Emigrant guidebooks of the early nineteenth century portrayed the region as edenic, attracting migrants from Kentucky and the Upper South, but also from New England and the Middle States, especially Pennsylvania. A river town on the Sangamon, Petersburg was made the seat of Menard County in 1843. It grew as a farm trade center, a thriving business district established around the courthouse square. The first railroad arrived in the early 1870s (now the Chicago

and Illinois Midland) to connect Peoria and Springfield. A second line, connecting Bloomington and Jacksonville, is now abandoned.

The town is located on both the floodplain of the Sangamon, and on terraced bluffs. A grid of streets was platted in both areas, although many streets have been closed down the steepest slopes (Figure 3.30). The old commercial district is no longer thriving and many business buildings stand empty (Figure 3.31). The main highway has become a commercial strip, not only at the town's peripheries but toward its center as well. Older housing is concen-

3.30 Petersburg, Illinois

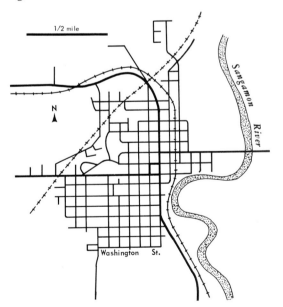

3.31 Behind Petersburg's courthouse empty storefronts mourn merchants lost to the highway. The town of Edgar Lee Masters's childhood is unravelling at its center.

3.32 Bungalows line several of Petersburg's streets up the bluff west of the square.

trated near the square (Figure 3.32) with some larger houses crowning the bluffs. Modest dwellings have been removed from the most flood-prone land along the river. One house, a small white frame cottage preserved as a museum, was a boyhood home of the poet Edgar Lee Masters. After World War II, streets were extended west of town on flat upland. A declining farm town, Petersburg has not attracted industry making it a retirement center for farmers and a commuter base oriented to Springfield twenty miles to the South (*History of Menard and Mason Counties* 1879, Plews 1974).

HERMANN, MISSOURI

Hermann was created by the German Settlement Society of Philadelphia which bought some eleven thousand acres of land on the south bank of the Missouri River along Frene Creek. There the river bluffs were carved into hills and valleys very reminiscent of the Rhineland. By the spring of 1838 some 250 colonists had built fifty houses: residents coming from Germany, Switzerland, Alsace-Lorraine, and Pennsylvania. Settlers of the surrounding area were primarily from the Upper South. The town was designated the seat of Gasconade County in 1842 and in 1854 the railroad (now the Missouri Pacific) completed its line from St. Louis encouraging town growth. Serving primarily as a farm trade center, Hermann also has light industry: several food processing plants (including wineries) and a shoe factory. The completion of a highway bridge over the Missouri River in 1929 expanded the town's trade hinterland to the north, as well as its labor shed.

A uniform street grid was imposed on the heavily dissected terrain (Figure 3.33). The oldest section of Hermann, located on a river terrace, bears the grid best. German and Pennsylvanian heritage is evident on only a few streets where houses, built of brick, stand close to the sidewalks (Figure 3.34). Two commercial districts evolved early. That near the river and the rail-

road is oriented both to retail trade and wholesaling whereas the Market and Fourth Street area, a short distance south, is oriented to retail trade only (Figure 3.35). Land use in the intervening space remains both residential and commerical as might typify the older section of a Pennsylvania town. The courthouse, St. Paul's Church (United Church of Christ), and St. George's Church (Roman Catholic) show to advantage from individual hilltops giving the town a verx distinctive skyline. Viewed from a hilltop, the town easily composes as scenery (Figure 3.36). Grid irregularity

characterizes those parts of Hermann developed after 1900 on steeply sloping higher ground. Several subdivisions of the 1960s and 1970s have curvilinear grids, but are disfigured by difficult terrain (*History of Franklin* 1888, Bek 1907, Schmidt and Schmidt 1954, Van Ravenswaay 1977, *Gasconade County History* 1979, Hesse 1981).

The Lower Middle West does not reflect its eastern origins faithfully. Something of Pennsylvania survives at Mount Gilead's square and yet, as we will demonstrate, the town's housing carries less of the Pennsylvania

3.33 Hermann, Missouri

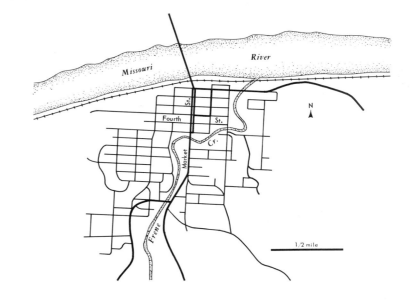

stamp than expected. Central
Ohio was originally a shatter
zone of settlement with people
coming from the Upper South
and from New York as well as
from Pennsylvania. The look of
Rockville and Petersburg owes
even less to Pennsylvania, for
the stamp of the Upper South is
prevalent. Not only are the
squares at Rockville and Petersburg configured in the southern manner, but, as we will
show, more houses are southern
descended than expected. One
questions whether a "Pennsylvania Extended" exists much beyond Eastern Ohio. Only in
Hermann, with its clear but unusual tie with Pennsylvania Ger-

**3.35   Hermann is a town of views.
Here the tower of the old German
School rises above Fourth Street as if
to define a European place.**

**3.34   German culture of the nine-
teenth century is reflected in brick and
stone carefully preserved at Hermann's
center.**

**3.36   Thrift and orderliness mark Her-
mann's newer neighborhoods as well
as its old.**

mans, is the Middle West's bond with Pennsylvania landscape re-established. Hermann's character, however, may be as much a function of its place in time as in space. The town's early start as a river port on the vital Missouri River coincides historically with the rise of Millersburg on the Susquehanna.

The Towns of the Upper South

Of the Upper South towns, Berryville displays the most consistent growth pattern, a very straight curve indeed (Figure 3.37). The other places, while showing long term increases, also show important periods of decline. Stanford's growth was interrupted at the century's turn and Centerville's growth a decade later. Woodstock declined precipitously during the economic depression of the 1930s. Tied to changes in local agriculture, these setbacks were offset in several communities by the establishment of light industry. Manufacturing based on inexpensive labor supply is especially important at Centerville, Columbiana, and Berryville. Stanford serves as a dormitory town for other more vigorous centers in the Kentucky Bluegrass and Woodstock in the scenic Shenandoah Valley has become an afflu-

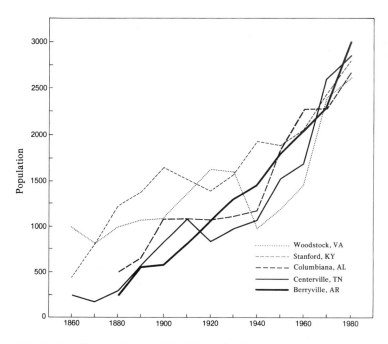

3.37 **Population Change: Towns of the Upper South**

ent retirement center. Therefore, one would expect more older dwellings at Stanford and Woodstock. Of course, one would expect new housing to predominate nearly everywhere as the bulk of town growth in the region has come in the past forty years. Relative to the northern two tiers of towns, we will show that the housing stock of the Upper South is, indeed, very recent. Older housing persists at town centers, but these traditional cores are being overwhelmed by newer housing on peripheral streets and in new subdivisions.

WOODSTOCK, VIRGINIA

Surrounded by apple blossoms in springtime, Woodstock is located in orchard country. Jacob Miller, a farmer from Pennsylvania, settled here in 1752. In 1761 the town of Woodstock was established, to be made the seat of newly formed Dunmore County (renamed Shenandoah County) in 1772. Through ensuing decades the Great Valley pike that bisected Woodstock was utilized by emigrants traveling to the Carolina Piedmont and across the Appalachians into the Ohio Valley. The town prospered as a rural crossroads market and political center, many small factories thriving during the early years of development. The railroad (now the Norfolk Southern) was completed to Woodstock in 1856. During the Civil War major battles were fought in the vicinity but without damage to the town. The automobile highway of the twentieth century (U.S. 11) brought population increase. Today, a new interstate highway places the Virginia suburbs of Washington, D.C., an hour's drive to the east. Woodstock functions as a bedroom community for commuters and as a retirement center for city folk attracted to rural, small town lifestyles.

The north fork of the Shenandoah River meanders one mile to the east with Massanutten Mountain, part of the Blue Ridge, dominating the horizon. Woodstock, built on a series of old stream terraces, occupies very hilly terrain offering spectacular views. At the center, houses built close to the street mirror southeastern Pennsylvania. Main Street remains a viable retail district with a half-dozen new banking offices and the county courthouse (Figure 3.38). A large shopping plaza is located on North Main Street and a "franchise America" retail area is developing at the I-81 interchange to the southwest along with a second shopping center.

3.38 Woodstock's Main Street, once partly residential, is now lined by stores and offices, many located in former dwellings. Shopping centers anchor both ends of the street.

44

3.39 Woodstock, Virginia

The eighteenth- and early nineteenth-century town includes the old compact, linear grid (Figure 3.39). South Church Street is strongly reminiscent of Pennsylvania with classic white, clapboarded hall and parlor houses among other folk forms (Figure 3.40). Neighborhoods chiefly of late nineteenth- and early twentieth-century origin lie in the interstices between roads which radiate to neighboring urban centers. Post–World War II housing is built on the higher levels of the town (Wayland [1927] 1976, Cartmell 1963).

STANFORD, KENTUCKY

Follow the route of the old Wilderness Road northward from Cumberland Gap and you come to Stanford, located just inside the Kentucky Bluegrass country. One of the state's oldest towns, it functioned as a place of defense against Indian raids during the Revolutionary War. Stanford grew slowly as a farm market town and seat of Lincoln County with population increasing more rapidly after 1866 with the arrival of the railroad (today's Louisville and Nashville). Population is predominantly of southern stock with roots in Virginia and the Carolinas. The town serves as a retirement community for local farmers and as a bedroom community for commuters to nearby Danville and distant Lexington.

The older portion of Stanford is comprised of a small, uniform grid of streets laid out north of Main Street (Figure 3.41). St. Asaph Creek flows just south of the business district aborting the grid in heavily dissected terrain. The Lincoln County Courthouse is situated on a block facing Main Street, but does not occupy a central square. It fits into Main Street more as an integral element rather than as a visual focus, the well-maintained business street stretching several blocks to the west (Figure 3.42). Main Street turns abruptly to the north at the western edge of

3.40   The past seems to have evaded progress on Woodstock's South Church Street.

town to form the Danville Road, traditionally the town's elite residential section. Older housing is oriented to the grid and to major arterial roads. Early twentieth-century houses are built, as in many southern towns, on streets platted in the interstices between these radial roads. Many of the town's blacks occupy older cottages on streets bordering the railroad (Figure 3.43). The largest post–World War II subdivisions are located off the U.S. 150 bypass to the north. Small ranches, little attention to landscaping, low maintenance on houses, and highly visible boats, trucks, and old cars suggest the working class status of most subdivision

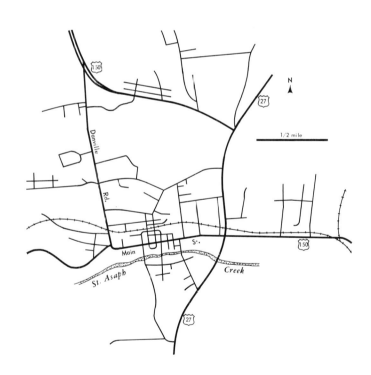

3.41   Stanford, Kentucky

3.42 Downtown Stanford retains most of its Main Street commerce, the highway held in abeyance.

3.43 Freight trains still rumble close by the alleys and short streets long home to Stanford's blacks.

families. New strip development is concentrated where U.S. 27 joins the bypass on the east. Large amounts of farm land are entrapped within the corporate limits and images of the Bluegrass state are mirrored in the surrounding agricultural landscape: dark brown tobacco barns, stone and wood fences, estate houses of gentry farmers (Dunn n.d., *Lincoln County Bicentennial* 1975).

COLUMBIANA, ALABAMA

Columbiana is found at the southernmost extent of Appalachia. Shelby County was first settled in the second decade of the nineteenth century by settlers coming from Virginia, the Carolinas, Tennessee, and Georgia. The county was organized in 1818 and the county seat moved to its present location in 1826 where the town of Columbiana evolved. Local farmers pursued a cotton, corn, and hog-based economy in this marginal agricultural area. Slaveholding was never widespread. An economic boom as a foundry center supplying the Confederate Civil War effort ended abruptly when Union forces burned the town. Although Columbiana is primarily a political seat and farm trade center for cotton and cattle, lumbering is also an important activity. Many residents commute to suburban Birmingham thirty miles to the north.

Originally, the town plan was a uniform grid of streets focused on a courthouse square (Figure 3.44). However, a portion of the grid lay on low, poorly drained land, deflecting business away from the square which, indeed, no longer exists. Two courthouse buildings dominate the Main Street, that of 1854 to the south and that of 1908 to the north (Figure 3.45). Much open space exists close to the center, especially near the former right-of-way of the north-south railroad line, which is now abandoned. Here recently erected public buildings (a new city hall, a large fortress-like county jail, and a county library) and several new shopping plazas substantially reinforce a sense of community focus. A large industrial park on the west edge of town is oriented to the east-west railroad (now the Norfolk Southern). Small factories manufacture threaded rod, wire, and alloy casts. The new and the old blend everywhere in Columbiana. Old white frame houses predominate near the revitalized town center, and suburban ranch houses along the arterial roads (Figure 3.46). Several new subdivisions for affluent white families are located on surrounding hills with commanding views. Several small black neighborhoods, noticeably poverty-stricken, cling to the town's margins, particularly in low lying areas. Dense stands of pine in this area provide visual barriers between these two types of neighborhoods (Glazner 1938, Galloway n.d., Alabama Historical Commission 1975).

3.45 The 1908 courthouse distinguishes Columbiana's Main Street. Many storefronts sport sunshades reminiscent of the South before air conditioning.

3.46 Suburbia in Columbiana means curvilinear streets dominated by ranch dwellings—a modern metropolitan image.

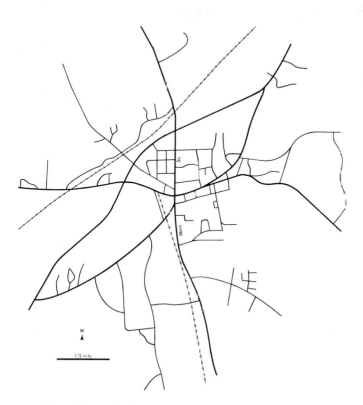

3.44 Columbiana, Alabama

CENTERVILLE, TENNESSEE

Hills of Tennessee red clay, covered once again by a forest canopy, surround Centerville. Farm settlement in the vicinity began in 1818, many of the original settlers coming from the Carolinas. The town was chosen as the seat of Hickman County in 1823 and grew very slowly as a market center for a marginal agricultural area. The thin soils of the hilly countryside support little agriculture today. Although no battle was fought at Centerville, the effects of the Civil War were great; a major loss in population followed the burning of the courthouse and adjacent businesses. Recovery was slow, real growth coming only after the arrival of the railroad (now the South Central Tennessee) in 1879. The collapse of the peanut crop prior to the Great Depression spurred a second population decline. An industrial park, developed in the 1960s, has attracted several large clothing and shoe plants, and a large factory for the manufacture of fiberglass advertising signs. The town also serves as a bedroom community for commuters to Nashville forty-five miles to the northeast. Several prominent members of the Grand Old Opry commute from Centerville. Minnie Pearl remains the town's most celebrated native.

Centerville is very clearly divided between an old town, confined to the original grid of streets and several radial roads,

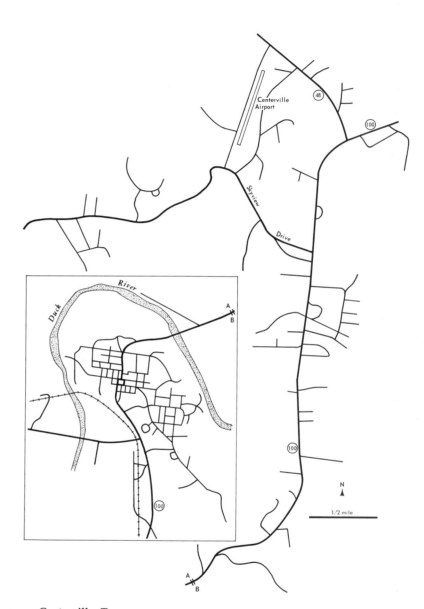

3.47 Centerville, Tennessee

and a new town, sprawled out some five miles toward the north along the Nashville highway (Figure 3.47). A major gap between the two sections, the lowlands of the meandering Duck River, clearly divides Centerville, giving the town a split personality. Old and new hardly seem connected. Old Centerville is exceptional for its plainness. Stylishness generally is not evident in its old houses, nor is it evident in the business facades surrounding the courthouse square (Figures 3.48 and 3.49). A small black population occupies the northeastern portion of the old grid. Here, along street extensions, older dilapidated cottages give way to modest ranch dwellings (Figure 3.50). Here also are found black business establishments and churches, and the abandoned shell of the former "separate but equal" school.

3.48   Newer dwellings have filtered into Centerville's older neighborhoods. There is no clear sense of the past here.

3.49   Centerville's courthouse sits astride its square with business pressing in around. But time seems only temporarily suspended here. Business seems destined to follow residential development northward several miles up the highway.

3.50   To be black in Centerville is to live in the town's southeast quadrant in cottages, bungalows, and ranches strung out along a bypassed highway.

3.51 Around Centerville's airport a kind of exurbia has evolved. Ranches on large lots have the appearance not of town, but of country things.

By contrast, the new town mirrors sophisticated big-city planning, especially along Skyview Drive which serves the airport, an industrial park, a country club, and an extensive new suburban residential development. Out along Skyview Drive a modern, exurban life-style is evident with large open lots occupied by expensive ranch houses in a country atmosphere (Figure 3.51). There is a much fragmented commercial strip along the highway (Spence 1900, *Hickman County Sesquicentennial* 1957, Ferguson 1975, Broemel and Cooper 1981).

BERRYVILLE, ARKANSAS

Berryville is situated in the Ozarks of northwest Arkansas, a region rapidly developing as a resort and retirement area. Originally, two migration routes brought settlers to the region to farm. The White River funneled emigrants from Kentucky, Tennessee, and Mississippi, while settlers from Missouri came overland. The small village which evolved around Henderson Berry's store in the 1850s was almost totally destroyed in the Civil War. But in 1876 the site was chosen as the seat of Carroll County and town building re-

3.52 Berryville, Arkansas

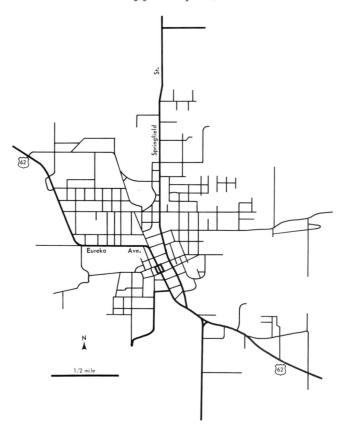

tourist attraction fourteen miles to the west.

The town's older section comprises a small street grid oriented to the east-west Eureka Springs road and to the north-south Springfield, Missouri, road (Figure 3.52). The grid centers on the courthouse square, a large open space surrounded by business buildings with the old courthouse (now housing the historical society) on the west (Figure 3.53). Behind the old courthouse looms a large water tower, a town landmark, and beyond it, easily overlooked, is the newer county building. Recent population growth has precipitated both expansion of the business district and enlargement of the old grid, especially along the arterial roads. Older dwellings have been removed from lots adjacent to the commercial core. Bungalows and other early twentieth-century houses are preserved along older arterial avenues, but on the new streets the ubiquitous ranch houses dominate. This community does not possess a high status residential street. Indeed, the entire town presents a highly utilitarian aspect. Some streets are unpaved; most are without curbs and sidewalks. Ranch houses are small and unpretentious and yards display little landscaping (Figure 3.54). Commercial strip

3.53 The old county building at Berryville faces an open square, a monument to government set into an otherwise commercial necklace of buildings.

3.54 Ranches thrive like hothouse plants in Berryville's new subdivisions.

newed. The railroad (now abandoned) did not arrive until 1901, and did little to change Berryville from a sleepy farm trade center. In recent decades several industries have been established in Berryville; the largest is a packing plant. Escaped chickens wander nearby streets, yards, and alleys on the town's north side. In addition, Berryville receives an overflow of tourists from Eureka Springs, a popular

development is fragmented, but westward toward Eureka Springs franchise restaurants, motels, and other businesses add substantially to the utilitarian theme. Throughout the town an outdoor style of life is visually evident: horses graze, trucks and four-wheel-drive vehicles sport gun racks, camping trailers and boats line driveways (Braswell 1889, Lair 1983).

From Berryville eastward the towns of the Upper South are very similar save Woodstock. Woodstock stands alone, clearly the child of Pennsylvania with its older houses built tight to the streets in a core still visually dominant. As we will show, many of its houses clearly mirror this Pennsylvania tie. The other towns of the region exhibit diversity of form in their older sections. In some the street gridirons are clearly defined. In others radiating thoroughfares are dominant and the street grids seem more like afterthoughts. But all towns share in the prodigious number of post–World War II ranch houses both on the radials and in the peripheral subdivisions. These neighborhoods easily capture attention. Whereas newness tends to be hidden away in northern towns, or held apart in a single peripheral sector, here newness surrounds, in-

filtrates and dominates. Indeed, a new kind of sprawling town is being shaped at Centerville. Centerville is becoming a "rurban" district. Here is a new kind of South if not a new kind of America.

The Towns of the Lower South

In the Lower South, Southport, Mocksville, and Louisville have grown consistently across the decades following sharp declines in the 1870s (Figure 3.55). Little or no antebellum architecture

survives in these places as a result of the Civil War. Apalachicola and Port Gibson also declined precipitously in the 1870s, although these places survived the Civil War physically intact and some very old houses may be seen. Apalachicola's fortunes as a river town waned with the decline of cotton culture in its upriver hinterland after 1900, but until recent decades it held its own, oriented to commercial and sport fishing in the Gulf of Mexico. Port Gibson's fortunes suffered in the 1960s and 1970s as a result of racial confrontation given the black community's drive for civil rights.

3.55 Population Change: Towns of the Lower South

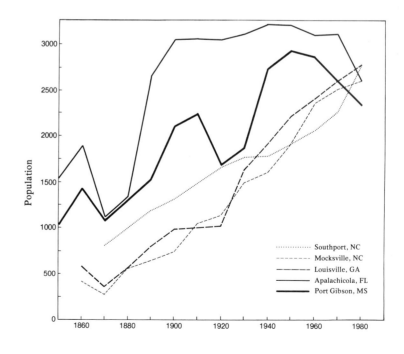

Thus we would expect more older housing in the latter place, and relatively little recent housing. As we will show, the towns of North Carolina and Georgia are more like those of the Upper South where newness predominates. Apalachicola and Port Gibson share much in common with northern towns such as Hudson, Rockville, and Petersburg. Not every place across the Sunbelt has shared vigorously in post–World War II prosperity.

SOUTHPORT, NORTH CAROLINA

The approach to Southport from the north is a half-hour ferry ride across a broad estuary. English colonists established a small fort to protect the mouth of the Cape Fear River. Smithville, now Southport, was established at the site in 1792 and in 1807 the seat of Brunswick County was transferred to the place. Rice and naval stores dominated the antebellum agricultural economy, but always under the shadow of larger Wilmington (some thirty miles upriver). Smithville remained a sleepy coastal village, home primarily to the river pilots, while boarding houses catered to summer vacationers from Wilmington. The Civil War had little effect on the town. In the 1880s a population boom was anticipated with the proposed

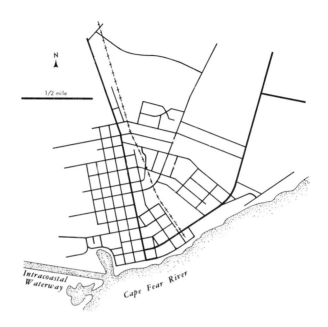

3.56 Southport, North Carolina

development of a seaport. This boosterism spawned a change in name but little else, for the town failed to develop a hinterland even after the arrival of a railroad (now abandoned) in 1911. In the mid-1970s the county seat was moved inland from the coast, although this loss was offset by construction of a chemical works and large power station. In addition, nearby Oak Island, accessible by bridge, has been developed as a resort and retirement area. Commercial strip development north and west of Southport serves the beaches.

Southport's original town plat includes Fort Johnson, now a Signal Corps communications center, located on the river (Figure 3.56). Here, older, irregular streets are lined by giant live oaks which shade modest white frame cottages and bungalows (Figure 3.57). The business district has spread along several streets and is anchored by new bank buildings which symbolize

the current economic boom
(Figure 3.58). Numerous ranch
houses have been built on streets
newly attached to the grid, as re-
placements for old dwellings previously torn down, and as infill
on lots not previously developed. The town contains a large
and relatively prosperous black
community, its economic power
symbolized by the large long-
shoremen's union hall. The
newer sections of Southport
sprawl out along the various radiating highways: suburban subdivisions with large lots and
curvilinear streets cut out of the
coastal pine forest (Figure 3.59).
A large marina for pleasure craft
dominates the riverfront
(Lounsbury 1979; Lee 1980).

3.57 Giant live oaks line several of
Southport's older streets, offering a
sense of timelessness in an otherwise
rapidly changing place.

3.58 Southport's business district appears very new, the result of recent
growth as well as renewal wrought by
fire and hurricane.

3.59 New ranch dwellings sprawl out
along Southport's arterials, many half
hidden in the coastal pine forest.

MOCKSVILLE, NORTH CAROLINA

The piedmont of North Carolina was settled prior to the Revolutionary War. Large numbers of Scots-Irish and Germans came from Pennsylvania to mix with settlers from the coastal Carolinas. Near Mocksville the parents of Daniel Boone lay buried. The original settlement site in Rowan County was known as Mock's Old Field. A post office, located there in 1810, precipitated village growth. In 1836 the northern portion of Rowan County became Davie County and Mocksville was established as court seat. The Civil War brought a depressed economy relieved only by the railroad's arrival (today's Norfolk Southern) in 1891, although Mocksville remained only a farm market center with some lumber milling. The automobile and improved highways brought the town into the commuter shed of Winston-Salem, a city twenty-five miles to the northeast. However, Mocksville's growth in recent decades is based more on local industrial development. Several furniture and clothing manufacturers, and a producer of portable air compressors, occupy large buildings. Mocksville clearly reflects "New South" prosperity.

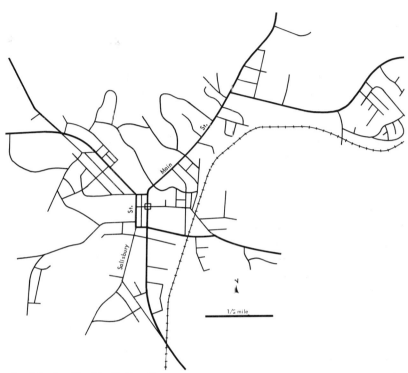

3.60 Mocksville, North Carolina

Initially, Mocksville was a linear village strung out along present-day Salisbury Street on a long ridge with views toward the east and west (Figure 3.60). Retail trade focused on the courthouse square, a diamond-form space now given over entirely to automobile traffic, the present-day courthouse sitting off to the southeast (Figure 3.61). The well-preserved business district on Main Street is surrounded by much vacant space.

The town center has numerous gasoline stations as several highways converge there. A small retail district is appended to the east and oriented to the railroad. It contains a grain elevator, farm

3.61 The courthouse anchors Mocksville's business district on the south.

Both the old and the new houses in this area tend to occupy large, extensively landscaped lots and the many boxwood hedges give this part of town a truly elegant look. To the northeast large working-class subdivisions (including one predominantly occupied by blacks) are located in close proximity to several new factories (Figure 3.62). New industrial plants have been interspersed with residential, park, and institutional land uses rather than located in one large industrial park (Wall 1969, Frank 1979).

3.62 Separate black and white subdivisions cater to blue-collar workers on Mocksville's northeast side.

supply businesses, and several black merchants oriented to the traditional black neighborhood. The rolling topography made it difficult to plat a uniform grid of regular blocks and thus the interstices between the major radial roads are filled with secondary streets graded to ridge contours. Post–World War II subdivisions have developed along the major arterial roads. Most prestigious are the curvilinear and cul-de-sac streets platted on the west side of North Main Street toward Winston-Salem.

LOUISVILLE, GEORGIA

Scots-Irish settled in the flat coastal plain of eastern Georgia in the last decades of the eighteenth century; most came from Virginia and the Carolinas. The movement of the state capital to Louisville, some 150 miles to the northwest of Savannah, had the desired effect of attracting some of these people to the interior. Louisville was surveyed in 1794 on high ground near the Ogeechee River, and the town served as the capital from 1795 to 1805. Louisville was also selected as the seat of Jefferson County, a function the town still retains. After 1800 a cotton economy based on slave labor dominated agriculture in the town's hinterland. Sherman's march to the sea produced great destruction as businesses were burned and the courthouse defaced. During the 1860s and 1870s the town's population declined sharply, but the coming of the railroad in the 1880s (now abandoned) stimulated growth. Louisville's accessibility to other places improved markedly during the automobile era with the designation of U.S. 1 through the town. Today the agricultural economy is diversified with cotton, corn, soybeans, peanuts, livestock, pecans, and peaches. Several light industries are located in Louisville in a new industrial park.

The numerous roads which converge on Louisville are intercepted by a regular grid of streets focused on Broad Street, once a wide market area but now developed as a landscaped commons (Figures 3.63 and 3.64). An old market house (or slave market) dates from the founding of Louisville and provides the town with a logo as well as a strong visual anchor for its business district. One block to the east sits the courthouse at the old state capital site. Behind Main Street along lower ground once traversed by the railroad, a large cotton gin stands idle. After World War II new subdivisions were created along the several arterial roads and, during the

3.63   Louisville, Georgia

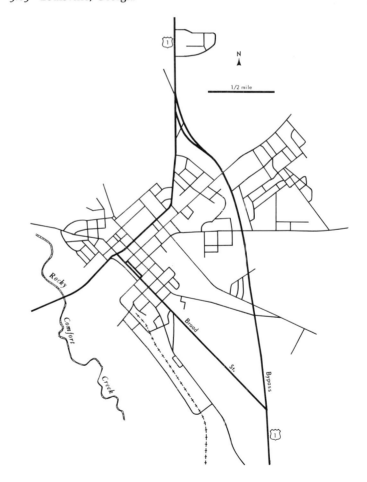

3.64 Louisville's Broad Street has been landscaped to resemble a big city suburban shopping center.
3.65 Black rental houses line unimproved streets gerrymandered beyond Louisville's eastern town limit.

past two decades, to the east off the U.S. 1 bypass highway. Commercial strip development has occurred along the old highway north of the town and in recent years along the bypass itself. Black housing in Louisville is located on the town's fringes, in most instances gerrymandered beyond the corporate limits (Figure 3.65). Much of it is rental property and substandard. The largest black residential area, Wren Quarters, is contiguous to Louisville on the east and is included in the study area. This residential district is a throwback to the Old South. It is served by red clay streets, dusty when dry and muddy when wet. Whereas many dwellings are of post–World War II vintage, they are of modest size and repetitious form (Durden 1983).

APALACHICOLA, FLORIDA

The Apalachicola River flows across the Gulf Coastal Plain, its estuary and bay protected by the sandy barrier of St. George Island. Summers are hot and humid, although tempered by sea breezes. Both the barrier island and the community are vulnerable to hurricanes. The Apalachicola Land Company acquired over a million acres of land from the Seminoles, originally part of a Spanish land grant, and settlement along the river's west bank began in 1821. The town of West Point was incorporated in 1827, to be re-named Apalachicola when the seat of Franklin County located there the next year. Steamboats initiated service to upriver cotton plantations in Alabama and Georgia, and cotton warehouses quickly came to line Apalachicola's Water Street. During the cotton boom, from 1830 to 1855, the town was eclipsed only by New Orleans and Mobile as cotton shipping points on the Gulf of Mexico. In the late 1850s railroads shifted cotton trade eastward to Atlantic ports and in the 1870s cotton production shifted westward, leaving Apalachicola to a constantly dwindling lumber trade and to fishing, oystering, and shrimping. Apalachicola's railroad (the Apalachicola and Northern) never grew beyond a short line and, indeed, the railroad no longer terminates in Apalachicola, but serves Port St. Joe twenty miles to the west. Recent completion of a causeway to St. George Island has prompted a building boom in shore houses and condominiums there. This development, along with completion of I-10 (which has diverted tourists away from coastal highway U.S. 98 running through the town) has brought recent decline. Preserved in Apalachicola, however, is a pre-1960s tourist landscape with the charm and beauty of "Old Florida" still intact.

The Apalachicola Land Company laid out a uniform grid of streets with small residential blocks (ten lots per block) interrupted by a number of squares reminiscent of those at Savannah, Georgia (Figure 3.66). Today the town divides into three sections. The first contains the business district and adjacent riverfront (Figure 3.67). Here a lone cotton warehouse among vacant lots survives as a reminder of the community's early economic base. Fishing boats lining the nearby riverfront reflect today's economy. The Franklin County courthouse sits at the south end of Market Street, a once lively business thorough-

fare, and at the foot of the Gorrie Bridge over the estuary. The second section of town, the bayside portion of the old grid, includes a designated historic district. Here streets are paved and lined by palm trees (Figure 3.68). Large houses, built during the lumber and early tourist periods, face Apalachicola Bay with smaller cottages and houses inland. The central focus of the historic district is Gorrie Square with its water tower, Gorrie State

3.66 Apalachicola, Florida

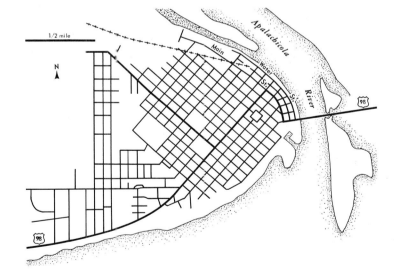

Museum (John Gorrie developed the first ice machine), and Trinity Episcopal Church. The other squares have lost their identity through conversion to hospital use, school grounds and other developments. The black community, which occupies the northern part of the old grid, possesses its own visual identity. Black-owned businesses and churches are spread throughout. Abandoned structures, dilapidated homes, and vacant lots are more common here where many streets remain of soft sand and oyster shell. The town's third section is comprised of street extensions to the west made during World War II when an Army Air Force training base (now closed) was in operation adjacent to the community. Commercial strip development with some regional flavor lines U.S. 98 west of town: seafood restaurants, wholesale and retail fish markets, and boat repair businesses. An informal, outdoor, water-oriented life-style is evident everywhere. Residents affectionately call the town "Apalach" (Lovett 1960, Owens 1966, Marshall 1975).

3.67 Apalachicola's wide Main Street recalls a time when the town was much larger.

3.68 Palmettos grace Apalachicola's older residential streets. Many neighborhoods, both affluent and poor, appear caught in an early twentieth-century time warp.

PORT GIBSON, MISSISSIPPI

U. S. Grant called Port Gibson "the town too beautiful to burn." And the fact that Union troops spared the place makes it one of the South's most attractive towns today. Samuel Gibson was granted a tract of land by the Spanish in 1788 on Little Bayou Pierre and a settlement evolved around his plantation. In 1802, under American jurisdiction, Claiborne County was created and a county seat, initially called Gibson's Landing, established the next year. Located on the Natchez Trace, and accessible by water to the Mississippi River some ten miles to the west, the site attracted settlers from Tennessee, Georgia, and the Carolinas. As an early way station for travelers returning north from New Orleans and Natchez, Gibson's Landing had numerous inns and taverns. By 1830, when Vicksburg was founded thirty miles to the north, Port Gibson was already a thriving community of some one thousand people. The town's economy has long depended upon cotton (originally produced by slave labor), lumbering, county seat functions, and farm trade activities. Over time the population of Port Gibson has fluctuated widely owing to the effects of the Civil War, the boll weevil and out-migration of blacks to the North. A large cotton gin and a railroad pulpwood loading facility are still active. The Grand Gulf Nuclear Power Station, located immediately north of town, provides employment.

The initial grid of streets ran perpendicular to Little Bayou Pierre with a courthouse square at its center (Figure 3.69). With increased population growth during the nineteenth century this original grid was expanded to the south and east along high,

3.69   Port Gibson, Mississippi

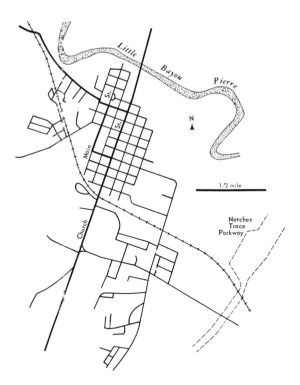

3.70 **William Faulkner's mythical Mississippi town of Jefferson could have been Port Gibson. The view here is north on Main Street past the now empty dry goods stores toward the courthouse square.**

flat ground as new residential areas were required. Main Street served as the principal commercial street anchored by the courthouse (Figure 3.70). Church Street, two blocks to the east, became the residential show street and the location of some eight churches, including a synagogue for the families of Jewish merchants. Black residential areas were dispersed throughout the town, but especially on lower ground (Figure 3.71). Blacks now outnumber whites three to one in the county and black residents now live throughout Port Gibson in every neighborhood. A black boycott of white dominated business in the 1970s substantially damaged the local retail sector resulting in a substantial downgrading of the business district. Today, commercial buildings stand empty and many have been removed (Douglas 1974, Smith 1979).

Among the towns of the Lower South, Apalachicola and Port Gibson stand apart as clear reminders of an Old South linked closely to agriculture. In these places, as in most of the northern towns, traditional town centers not only anchor but dominate the sense of visual landscape and shape the sense of place. For Southport, Mocksville, and Louisville, traditional cores are viable, but the new subdivisions and highway commercial strips dominate functionally and visually. Here is the New South reoriented to industrial jobs rather than farm labor. Instead of narrow streets of white frame houses sporting elaborate front porches enclosed with wisteria, one thinks of ranch houses set off by wide-sweeping lawns in curvilinear subdivisions.

In very general terms, the picture we paint is one of two broad classes of towns: those which have experienced the bulk of their growth in recent decades and those which have been stable being developed physically generations back. With the exceptions of Apalachicola and Port Gibson, the growth towns are largely southern. Across the South small traditional centers have had grafted on to them extensive new areas comprised not only of residential subdivisions, but of industrial parks as well.

3.71 Port Gibson's blacks continue to live in the older houses of once-segregated neighborhoods.

Commercial strips along highways offer spatial integration. In the North, recent town growth is linked to commuting to large urban centers nearby. The most prosperous communities, like Mattapoisett and Cazenovia, are those which have attracted an affluent middle-class commuter. Across the North the traditional small town, firmly rooted in the nineteenth century, abides modest modernization.

We have provided a preliminary framework for comprehending common dwellings observable in our sample towns. Cultural differences rooted in initial occupance suggest that our study towns be sorted into four regional categories. This sorting helps comprehend the older housing rooted in folk traditions. Within and between regions focus belongs on differing growth experiences, or the differences in historical development just discussed. This sorting helps in comprehending the builder traditions: builders operating in fully commercialized economies variously divorced from folk ways. We begin in the next chapter the report of our house survey by dealing with the specific characteristics of dwellings as they vary from place to place.

CHAPTER IV   HOUSE CHARACTERISTICS— GEOGRAPHICAL DISTRIBUTION

He never painted the house,

nor sought to adorn it,

but the passage of years

has given it softness and beauty,

and now we hear persons

admire its functionalism.

J. B. JACKSON

Common houses may be noticed for various attributes: decoration, color, size, construction material. What excites one viewer may be totally ignored by another. It is important in house study, therefore, to have consistent criteria that force broad awareness of the similarities and differences to be found house to house, place to place. In evaluating each of our houses we looked first to see if it was a habitable single-family dwelling. Unoccupied dwellings were eliminated from consideration if structural and utility deficiencies precluded immediate occupance. Multiple-family structures, although noted, were not further inventoried. We then categorized each house by general floor plan, assigning it to a structure group. Concern with roof form, overall height, height of basement or crawl space, size, facade covering, color, roofing material, and

stylish decoration followed. We also noted the apparent age and the extent of apparent structural change over time as well as documenting porches, garages, and carports. Only then did we identify each dwelling as a distinctive structure type. In this chapter we report on individual dwelling characteristics as they vary geographically. It is our intent to instill in readers a sense for our criteria and to lay a foundation for considering structure types, the principal thrust of our work.

In this and in subsequent chapters, we use maps to communicate our findings. Although drawn to a similar base designed to facilitate comparison town to town and region to region, information is presented in slightly different ways map to map. We ask the reader to consider carefully the key to each map. In essence, a graph is presented for each town showing the percentage occurrence for either one, two, three, or four variables.

Each graph is constructed to facilitate the eye's approximating the values given. The actual percentage figures are indicated at the top of each graph, making each map a table as well. Although they will require some effort initially, we feel that the maps will enable readers to both obtain a general, overall impression of differences and similarities town to town and region to region, and readily ascertain the specifics of the geographical variations discussed. It may help the reader to consider this work a "mini-atlas." Thus one may want to browse the maps across the various chapters before continuing with the text.

Dwelling Age

In a land as youthful as the United States there are pronounced differences in the relative age of small towns. Differences in the age and demographic history of communities determines what proportion of their housing stock displays traits of particular building eras, periods of pronounced regional differences and periods of widespread uniformity. As we have seen in chapter 3, there is a general tendency for towns to the east to be older than those to the west, but more important than geographical position relative to a generalized westward sweep of agriculture was a town's rhythm of commercial orientation. Thus Mattapoisett's rise as a shipbuild-

ing center coincides with Hermann's rise as a river port, and Cazenovia's growth as a milling center with Apalachicola's emergence as a cotton port. House survival rates, as we will subsequently discuss, vary from place to place. The Civil War brought destruction to several southern towns. Houses endure not only as a function of violence avoided, but as well of modernization evaded. Economic hard times breed impoverishment. Fewer new houses are built necessitating the continued use of old houses. How does all of this actually translate into dwelling age one study town to another?

We estimated the date of construction of every house in each study town according to the oldest visible architectural evidence following an evaluation system adapted from the geographer John Rickert for the northeastern United States (Rickert 1967, 216–19). Each dwelling was then assigned to one of the following general construction eras: 1) pre-1865, 2) 1865–1919, 3) 1920–1945, and 4) post-1945. Our choice of general eras was based on the primary role played by major wars in interrupting home building in America. The Civil War, World War I, and World War II totally consumed our nation's energies and brought house construction to a halt in 1861, 1918, and 1942 (Isard 1942a, Isard 1942b, Alberts

1962, Campbell 1963, Abramovitz 1964, Gottlieb 1976). Material shortages and economic recessions followed each conflict. These conditions further retarded dwelling construction to the point that clear temporal breaks are evident in the changed appearance of the housing stock associated with each resumption of construction. Although the volume of home building was also severely constrained during interwar depressions, especially between 1929 and 1936, it is our judgement that wartime interludes were followed by more substantial changes in the character of dwellings. War economies brought forth new fashions in design, altered structural forms, stimulated the use of novel building materials, and changed construction techniques. All of these changes were in keeping with new lifestyles stemming from the dislocations of war.

The two primary building eras in our study towns, in terms of numbers of surviving dwellings, are the 1865–1919 and post-1945 periods (Figure 4.1). The 1865–1919 period ranks first or second in eighteen study towns. Only in Mocksville, Centerville, and Apalachicola are dwellings built between 1920–1945 more numerous. Indeed, housing from the interwar years predominates in Apalachicola. Older towns in the Middle West are places where dwellings built between the Civil War and World War I survive in exceptional numbers. In Rockville they comprise a majority, and in both Petersburg and Hudson approximately two-thirds of all dwellings. The most recent construction period ranks either first or second in every town. It is responsible for a majority of the structures in seven of the ten southern towns: Stanford, Columbiana, Centerville, and Berryville in the Upper South and Southport, Mocksville, and Louisville in the Lower South. Recent construction predominates through much of the South and is clearly reflected in prevailing dwelling traits in that section of the country as we will demonstrate.

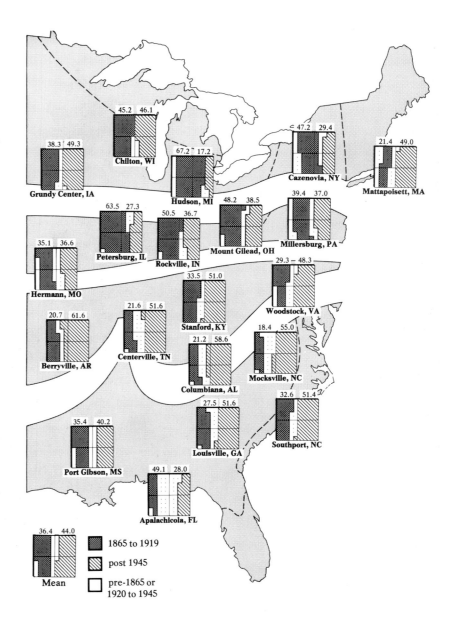

4.1   **Estimated Age of Dwellings by Period of Construction (percent)**

Structure Group Defined by General Shape

We have categorized every single-family dwelling by general shape. Although we identify each dwelling according to specific structure type, we think it valuable to also consider the common denominators of form: the elementary geometry of ground floor perimeters (disregarding appendages) and the general character of associated floor plans. Houses belonging to our "single-pile" group usually have a simple rectangular perimeter. They may be one or more rooms wide, but are invariably no more than one room deep (Figure 4.2). The different kinds of dwellings included in our "double-pile" group are also usually box-like in outline and most often two rooms wide (Figure 4.3). What distinguishes them from single-pile dwellings is their two-room depth. For convenience we placed the various shotgun dwellings in this group even though they are but one room wide and often more than two rooms deep. Here we have also placed one-third double-pile cottages and houses. These, too, are but one room in width. Dwellings comprising the "irregularly massed" group are characterized by a complex geometry and an accompanying offset arrangement of rooms (Figure 4.4).

4.2   Single-pile dwellings, like this one in Rockville, are but one room in depth.
4.3   Double-pile dwellings, like this one in Mattapoisett, are two rooms deep, ignoring all rear appendages.
4.4   Irregularly massed dwellings, like this one in Hudson, combine various geometries to achieve apparent informality of floor plan.

Dwellings of the "bungalow" group are typically rectangular in outline. Asymmetrical sets of rooms are usually arrayed from front to back, rooms often opening one to another without large hallways (Figure 4.5). Houses belonging to the "ranch" group may have either rectangular or irregular perimeters (Figure 4.6). Their long, low profiles usually spread parallel to the street in contrast to compact appearing bungalows. In ranch dwellings rooms also open one to another except the bedrooms which are usually linked by hallway. We have reserved our "other" category for rare and peculiar varieties that defy classification by our typology.

4.5 Although bungalows come in various shapes and sizes (shown here is a southern bungalow in Port Gibson) they are consistent in their internal organization (two rows of three rooms arrayed behind one another usually without benefit of large hallways) and their exterior look (use of extended eaves with brackets for example). Bungalows keep low profile and appear to hug the ground.

4.6 Ranches also come in varied shapes and sizes. Unlike bungalows, rooms are organized parallel rather than perpendicular to the street. Broad picture windows, exaggerated eaves, and other devices serve to emphasize the horizontal. Roofs offer low profile as on this Berryville ranch.

We mapped the frequencies of the three most common structure groups in each community. The most frequently encountered types of dwellings belong to the double-pile and ranch groups. Various types of double-pile houses comprise at least 45 percent of all dwellings in Mattapoisett, Cazenovia, Hudson, Millersburg, Hermann, and Apalachicola (Figure 4.7). High frequencies of double-pile dwellings are associated primarily with older towns in the Northeast where a strong residual of pre-1865 housing remains. Ranch-type dwellings are most numerous in southern towns which witnessed considerable home construction since 1945. This structure group accounts for more than 40 percent of the housing stock in each of our southern towns except Apalachicola and Port Gibson. Ranch dwellings occur at a similar level of frequency in Grundy Center, the study town of the Upper Middle West with the most youthful housing.

Irregularly massed dwellings are less widespread than either the double-pile or ranch varieties. Nevertheless, they represent the third most common structure group. Houses of complex geometry constitute more than 20 percent of the dwellings in four Middle West towns: Hudson, Chilton, Mount Gilead, and Petersburg (Figure 4.7). They are most common in Hudson where one in three houses has

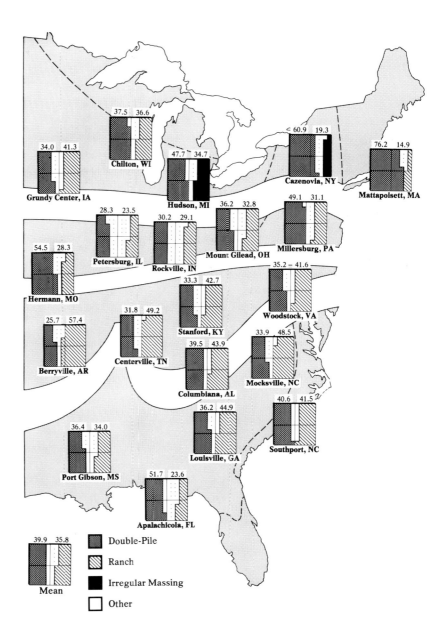

4.7   Two Most Common Structure Groups by Town (percent)

an irregular perimeter. Houses with irregular massing were commonly built during the late nineteenth century and are most closely associated with Middle West towns where vintage housing is abundant.

Roof Forms

What kinds of roof characterize houses in our study towns? In response to this question we repeated the mapping procedure employed for structure groups. We found that the three most common roof forms in the twenty towns were selected from only four varieties. They include: 1) a gable form with symmetrical front and back slopes and a ridge line running from one side of the house to the other (Figure 4.8), 2) a front gable form with matching side slopes and a ridge line running from the house front to the back (Figure 4.9), 3) a multiple-gable form with two pairs of symmetrical slopes and ridge lines that intersect at right angles (Figure 4.10), and 4) a hip form composed of long and short pairs of slopes with only the longer pair meeting at the ridge line (Figure 4.11).

The gable roof is the most common type in every town except Hudson. It defines a normative circumstance. In some towns, Woodstock, Mattapoisett, Millersburg, Stanford, Centerville, and Mocksville, it clearly

4.8   Gable roofs, as with this Woodstock house, have ridgelines parallel to the road with symmetrical front and back slopes. Gables form at both ends.

4.9   On this gable-front house in Cazenovia, one gable end faces the street, giving an appearance not unlike a classical Greek temple.

4.10   Multiple-gable roofs, as with this Louisville house, combine gable and front-gable ideas to render L and T shapes when viewed from above.

4.11   On this hip-roofed cottage in Apalachicola, pairs of long and short slopes meet, the longer pair defining the ridgeline.

dominates (Figure 4.12). Upper South towns, as they are characterized more by new ranch dwellings, display the gable roof most consistently. Only Berryville, deviates from this pattern. Multiple-gable roofs are more reflective of northern towns. They cap at least one-fifth of the dwellings in Cazenovia, Hudson, Chilton, Mount Gilead, Rockville, and Petersburg. They recur with similar frequency in only two southern towns, Berryville and Mocksville. Most often, multiple-gable roofs accompany irregularly massed dwellings. As noted above, irregularly massed dwellings are most numerous in the North.

Front gable roofs rank third in frequency of occurrence. They top more than 20 percent of the dwellings in five towns (Cazenovia, Hudson, Hermann, Apalachicola, and Port Gibson): places with large stocks of older housing (Figure 4.13). In Cazenovia and Hudson this roof form was probably inspired by the fashionable Greek Revival style of the early nineteenth century. At Hermann it reflects a German immigrant building tradition. In Apalachicola and Port Gibson front gable roofs cap shotgun cottages, southern bun-

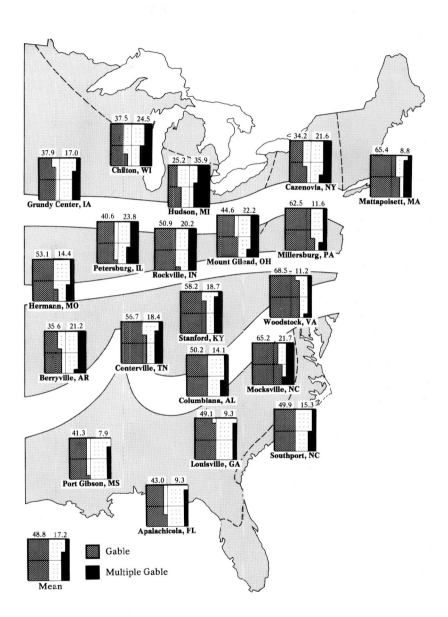

4.12   Gable and Multiple-Gable Roofs (percent)

72

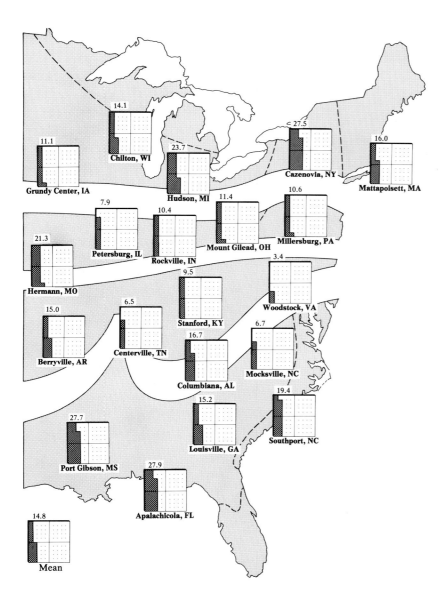

4.13 **Front Gable Roofs (percent)**

galows and similar gable-front double-pile cottages. The only other common roof form, the hip variety, displays no particular regional affinity although one-fifth of Louisville's houses display it (Figure 4.14).

A pair of infrequently occurring roof forms are worthy of mention only because of their unexpected distribution among our study towns. These are the steeply pitched pyramidal roof, that ascends to a peak rather than a ridge line, and the more complex hip with gable variety (Figures 4.15 and 4.16). Elaborate versions of the latter form may include a polygonal or conical turret. In scholarly literature both forms are attributed to southern building traditions (Glassie 1968a, 112; Lewis 1975, 20). Pyramidal roofs and hip with gable roofs are more common in our Middle West towns than among those of the South (Figures 4.14 and 4.17). In the Middle West pyramidal roofs commonly cap box-like double-pile dwellings that we call cube houses. Within the same section of the country hip with gable roofs sometimes top irregularly massed dwellings in place of more common multiple-gable roofs.

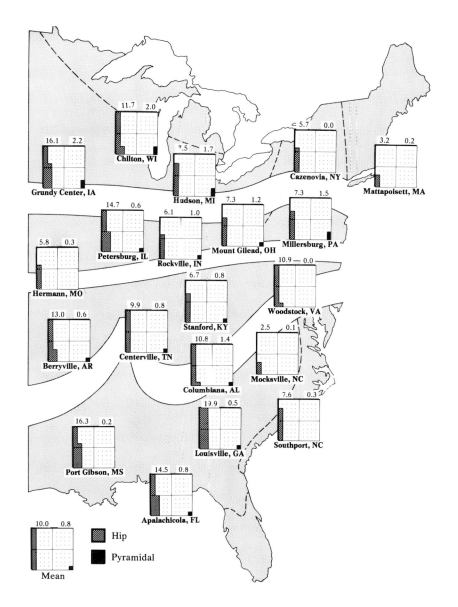

4.15 The pyramidal roof is a kind of hip roof where equal slopes meet either at a real or an implied peak. A house from Hudson illustrates.

4.16 More exotic roofs combine gable and hip roof types in various ways. One of the most popular is the hip roof with multiple gables, an example pictured from Grundy Center.

4.14 Hip and Pyramidal Roofs (percent)

74

**4.17 Gable and Hip and Multiple-
Gable and Hip Roofs (percent)**

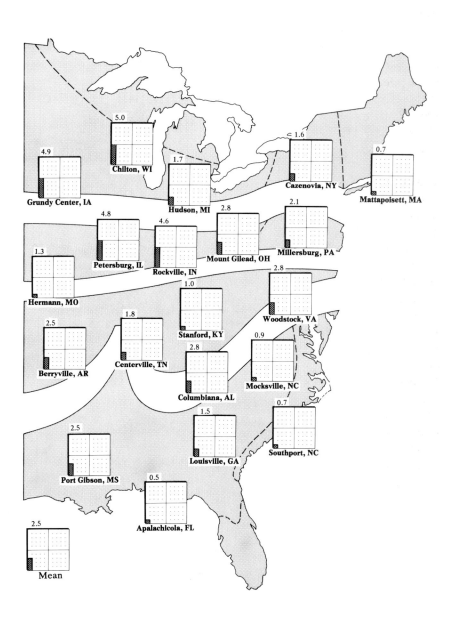

Height

Older dwellings with at least two full stories account for more than one-fifth of the housing in Cazenovia, Millersburg, Woodstock, Mount Gilead, and each of our Upper Middle West study towns (Figure 4.18). Tall houses are unusually rare in Columbiana, Centerville, Berryville, and Louisville, comprising less than 3 percent of all dwellings. The association of tall houses with northern towns and those of modest height with southern communities (other than Woodstock) is most pronounced among pre-1920 dwellings. Two-story houses account for more than 40 percent of all dwellings built before 1920 in Cazenovia, Hudson, Chilton, Grundy Center, Mount Gilead, Millersburg, and Woodstock (Figure 4.19). In Millersburg and Woodstock pre-1920 two-story houses comprise approximately three-fourths of the total which suggests that Woodstock, indeed, enjoys a close tie to Pennsylvania (Zelinsky 1973, 118–19).

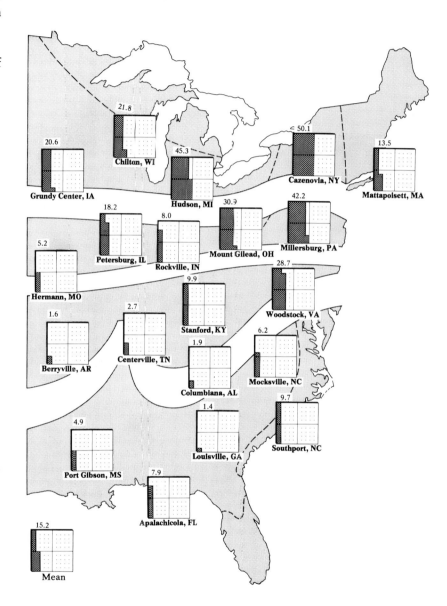

4.18   Two- and Two-and-one-half-Story Dwellings (percent)

4.19 Pre-1920 Two- and Two-and-one-half-Story Dwellings (percent)

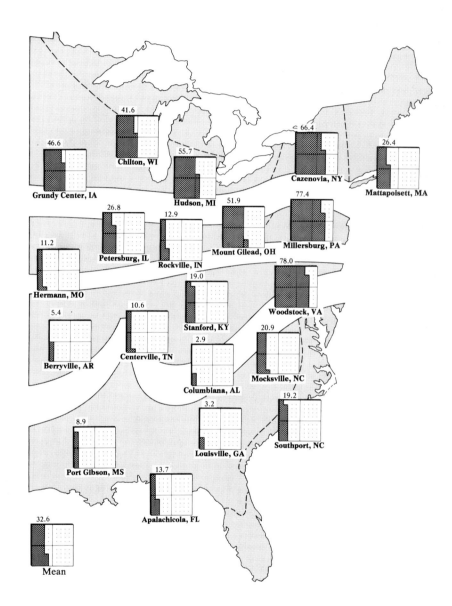

Raised Dwellings

Does an elevated first floor characterize dwellings in southern towns? We hypothesized this possibility since older houses in seaports and river towns of the Lower South are often visibly raised by means of posts or high basements. Raised first floors facilitate air circulation in hot climates. We defined raised dwellings as having first floors reached by four or more outside steps of normal height, not including steps used to ascend sloping front yards. As expected, high frequencies of raised dwellings (more than one in five) were inventoried in the southern river ports of Southport, Apalachicola, and Port Gibson. However, raised dwellings were not exclusive to the southern towns. Equally large numbers occur in such widely scattered places as Cazenovia, Chilton, Petersburg, Woodstock, Stanford, Columbiana, and Berryville (Figure 4.20). High pedestal-like basements are also commonly associated with older houses in northern towns such as Cazenovia and Chilton.

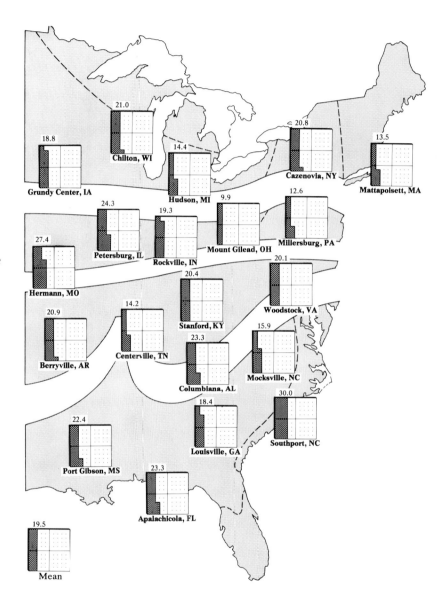

4.20   **Dwellings with Raised First Stories (percent)**

Size

We estimated the number of rooms (excluding bathrooms, hallways, and attic spaces) for each dwelling. Size was cued by the general bulk of each structure, the number of windows and doors and what we knew of floor plans typical of various structure types. Moderate-sized structures have an estimated six to eleven rooms, small dwellings five or less and large dwellings twelve or more. Moderate-sized dwellings were expected to be especially numerous in the Northeast and Upper Middle West where two-story houses are common. As expected they comprise more than 60 percent of the total in the northern tier of towns from Mattapoisett to Grundy Center and also in Millersburg and Woodstock. What we did not anticipate was a similar frequency of these dwellings in the Lower South town of Mocksville (Figure 4.21). In the North, except at Mattapoisett, the frequent occurrence of tall roomy houses reflects an earlier era of affluence and social pretentiousness. In Mattapoisett, Woodstock, and Mocksville large numbers of spacious double-pile cottages and ranch dwellings reflect recent prosperity. Large houses with more than eleven rooms are numerous only in Mattapoisett and Cazenovia as reflects exurban orientations to nearby cities as well as development as affluent summer retreats.

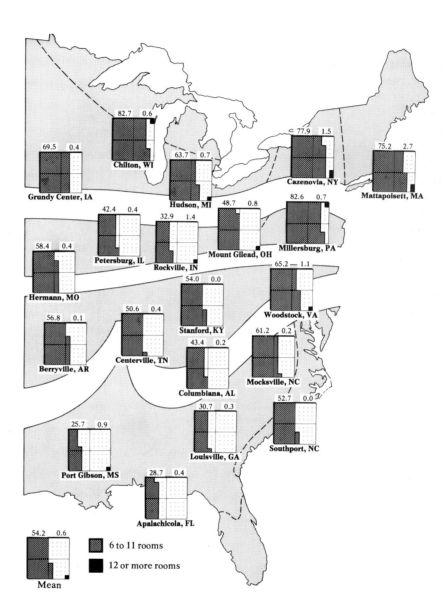

4.21 Size of Dwelling (percent)

Front Porches

How frequently are front porches
a feature of single-family dwellings and which are the most common varieties? Front porches are
associated with a majority of the
dwellings in each of our study
towns except Mattapoisett
(Figure 4.22). In most southern
towns, as well as Millersburg,
Rockville, and Hudson, more
than three-fourths of all dwellings have a porch. The scarcity in
Mattapoisett reflects the historical
and current popularity there of
forms derived from porchless
medieval English prototypes
(Brunskill 1971, Brunskill 1981).
Colonial and early federal era
houses tended not to have
porches in New England.

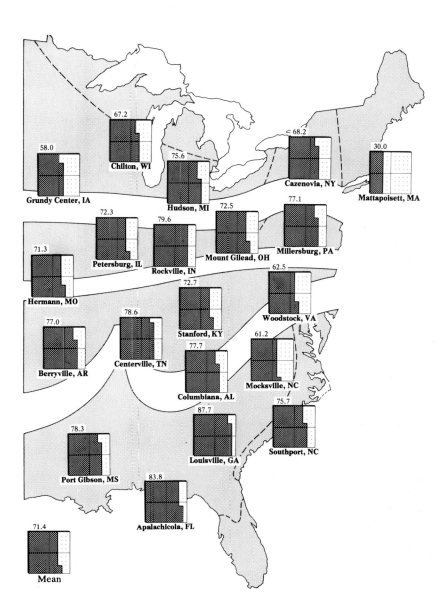

4.22   Dwellings with Front Porches (percent)

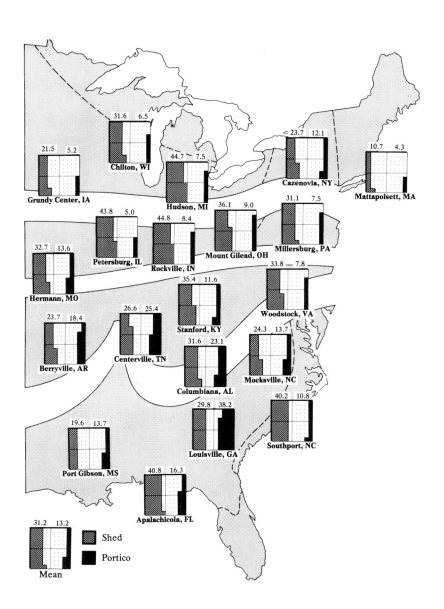

21.5 5.2
Grundy Center, IA

31.6 6.5
Chilton, WI

44.7 7.5
Hudson, MI

< 23.7 12.1
Cazenovia, NY

10.7 4.3
Mattapoisett, MA

43.8 5.0
Petersburg, IL

44.8 8.4
Rockville, IN

36.1 9.0
Mount Gilead, OH

31.1 7.5
Millersburg, PA

32.7 13.6
Hermann, MO

33.8 — 7.8
Woodstock, VA

23.7 18.4
Berryville, AR

26.6 25.4
Centerville, TN

35.4 11.6
Stanford, KY

24.3 13.7
Mocksville, NC

31.6 23.1
Columbiana, AL

40.2 10.8
Southport, NC

19.6 13.7
Port Gibson, MS

29.8 38.2
Louisville, GA

40.8 16.3
Apalachicola, FL

31.2 13.2
Shed
Portico
Mean

4.23 Shed and Portico Porches (percent)

Mapped are the two most popular varieties of porch. The shed type, that which slants away from the wall and is supported by posts on the outer side, is most common everywhere except in Louisville (Figure 4.23 and 4.24). This kind of porch is attached to more than 35 percent of all dwellings in Hudson, Mount Gilead, Rockville, and Petersburg in the Middle West and in Stanford, Southport, and Apalachicola in the South. In the Middle Western towns it tends to reflect a large number of surviving nineteenth-century dwellings. This is also true in Apalachicola and to a lesser degree in Southport. In these coastal communities of the Lower South the shed porch is a persistent reminder of an English colonial adaptation to subtropical climate.

The portico, with a front gable roof set perpendicular to the house and supported by pillars, has the strongest association with the South (Figure 4.25). Porticos are attached to almost 40 percent of the dwellings in Louisville. They are also a feature of more than one dwelling in six in Columbiana, Centerville, Berryville, and Apalachicola (Figure 4.23). In these communities a portico is often attached to ranch dwellings as an

element of Early American ornamentation, a style motif which
emerged in the 1930s. Its popularity supports stereotyped images of a genteel antebellum
South (Smith 1941).

The incised porch is another
variety primarily associated with
the South (Figure 4.26). This
kind of porch is not attached to
the house, but recessed beneath
the front slope of a gable roof. It
occurs most frequently in Port
Gibson where it is a feature of
more than one dwelling in four
(Figure 4.27). In Port Gibson,
where it is most common, it reflects a high frequency of Creole
cottages, a form rooted in French
and Spanish colonial Louisiana.

4.24   These shed porches pictured in
Stanford merely slant away from
dwelling facades, taking part of their
support from the facades.

4.25   This portico porch in Centerville
echoes the gable-front roof by also
mimicking the style of a Greek
temple.
4.26   This incised porch in Port Gibson is recessed under the main roof of
the cottage and thus is not merely attached to but is integral with the main
structure.

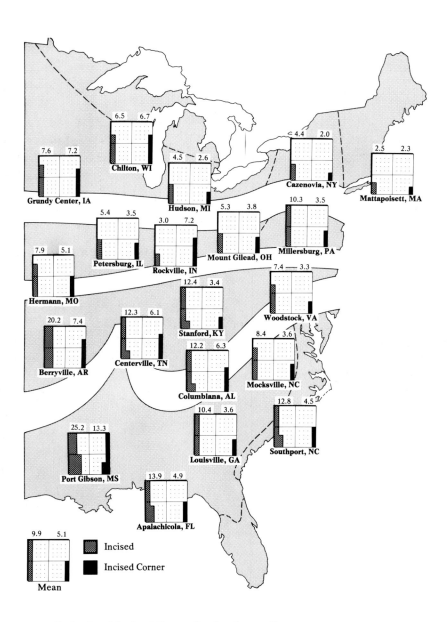

Incised

Incised Corner

Mean

4.27 Incised and Incised-Corner Porches (percent)

The town's site near the east bank of the Mississippi River suggests architectural borrowing from the Louisiana French (Kniffen 1936, 183–84, 188–89). Incised porches characterize over 10 percent of the houses in every other southern town except Woodstock, and Mocksville. In the North they are found with equal frequency only in Millersburg. There the incised porch is primarily associated with ranch dwellings, but tends to be a feature of older houses also. Incised corner porches (incised at only one corner of a dwelling) increase in frequency westward from north to south (Figure 4.27). They are most frequently associated with ranch dwellings.

The flat roof and covered stoop porch types lack clear geographical patterning. The covered stoop is interesting because of the minimal protection it offers (Figure 4.28). It consists of a very small projecting roof that is either cantilevered or supported by struts instead of pillars. Most often it is attached to dwellings of the 1920–1945 era and is somewhat common only in scattered northern communities: Chilton, Grundy Center, Millersburg, and Mount Gilead (Figure 4.29). Doorways are dressed with minimum attention, a mere genuflection to the elaborate porches of the late nineteenth-century middle class.

Facade Materials

What are the predominant materials covering houses in the small towns of the Eastern United States? The three most popular types of wall cladding are mapped. Brick is the most common facade material used. However, brick is truly notable in only a half dozen communities where it covers more than one-

4.28 These examples in Mount Gilead, although very elaborate and carrying classical ornamental implications, do illustrate the covered stoop, a porch covering without the support of posts or pillars.

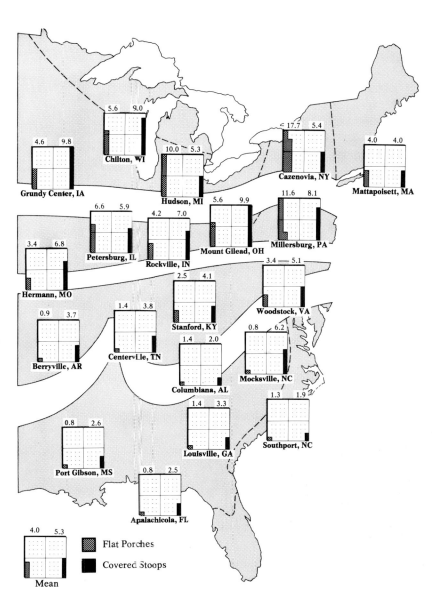

4.29 Flat Porches and Covered Stoops (percent)

third of the houses. Most of
these towns are located in the
Upper South and include Woodstock, Stanford, Centerville,
Berryville, Mocksville, and
Hermann (Figure 4.30). We refer
to brick facades rather than brick
walls since this material is used
primarily as a veneer on recently
built dwellings in the South.
Among our southern towns, at
least 80 percent of the dwellings
with brick facades were built
after World War II. In Germanic
Hermann, on the other hand,
two-thirds of the brick structures
were built before 1945 and solid
brick walls are a common feature
of older dwellings. We also expected a high frequency of older
brick structures in Millersburg.
Contrary to what was anticipated, only 28 percent of the
single-family dwellings in this
community have brick facades.
Furthermore, as in towns of the
Upper South, a large majority of
the brick dwellings (three out of
four) were built after 1945. Most
are ranches of one or another
form.

Use of cement block has a
close association with the South.
Dwellings with cement block
walls characterize more than 1
percent of all dwellings in eight
of ten southern towns (Figure
4.30). Nowhere in the North is
this material as widely used.
Block construction appears to be
strongly regionalized within
the Lower South in Louisville,
Apalachicola, and Port Gibson.
Dwellings with block walls tend

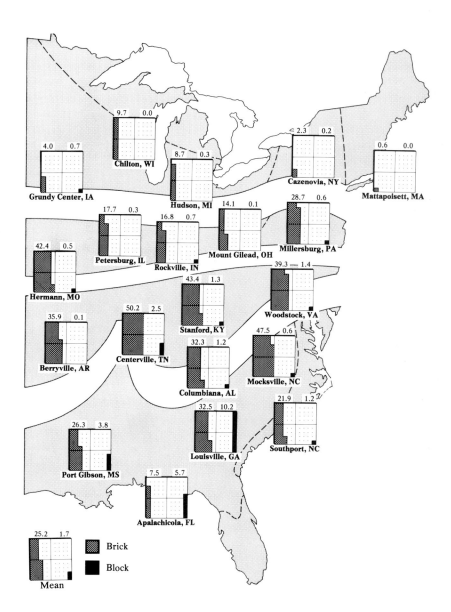

4.30 Brick and Block (percent)

to be found in neighborhoods inhabited by poor blacks. Their relative scarcity in Southport and Mocksville reflects the greater prosperity of the black communities there.

Aluminum siding and look-alike vinyl siding, were grouped together. They form the second most popular wall-facing material used in our study towns. These materials have a strong regional affinity to the Middle West. They cover more than one quarter of the houses in Hudson, Chilton, Grundy Center, Mount Gilead, and Petersburg (Figure 4.31). The only other place where they are equally popular is Millersburg. In Chilton alone the majority of the aluminum and vinyl sided dwellings postdate 1945. Because these materials were not readily available until after World War II, they were primarily used as surfacing materials on older houses, being applied in horizontal strips in a manner imitative of clapboard. Thus it is safe to assume that horizontal aluminum or vinyl siding generally covers an original clapboard surface on dwellings built before 1945.

Clapboard proves most common in the two older towns of the Lower South, Apalachicola and Port Gibson (Figure 4.31). In Apalachicola its persistent popularity can be explained in two ways. The town is both a former lumber shipping port and a community that has been in economic decline in recent decades.

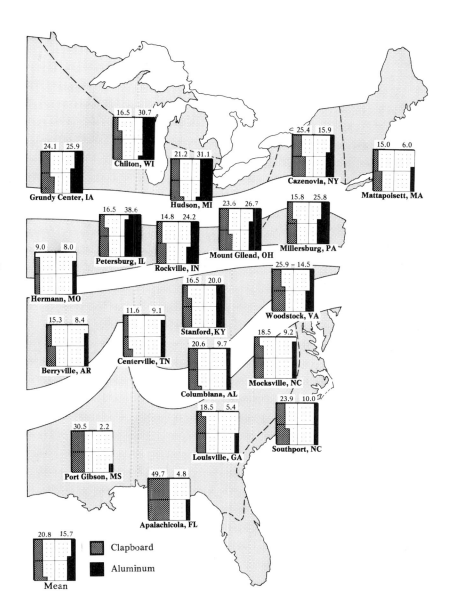

4.31 **Clapboard and Aluminum (percent)**

Wood siding was readily available during an earlier era of prosperity and recent conditions have not encouraged the residing of older dwellings with aluminum or other materials. Port Gibson too has suffered decline during the aluminum residing era. Clapboard, aluminum and vinyl siding together cover more than 40 percent of the houses in each Middle West town (except Rockville), and also in Cazenovia, Millersburg, and Woodstock. Overlapping horizontal siding is a persisting tradition nearly everywhere in the eastern third of the country. What could be more common in rural America than the white clapboarded farm house?

Our New England and upstate New York towns are the only places where wood shingles prevail as a wall cover. In Mattapoisett wood shingles cover more than two-thirds of the dwellings, and at Cazenovia more than one dwelling in three (Figure 4.32). The unusual popularity of wood shingling in Mattapoisett relates to its widespread recent application to new dwellings, such as Cape Cod cottages, which imitate, as revivals, popular early forms. The rustic appearance of wood carries a clear historical association and social status connotation. It is an affluent middle class manifestation. Elsewhere, artificial shingles are more popular than the wood variety. In several towns they rank second or third in pop-

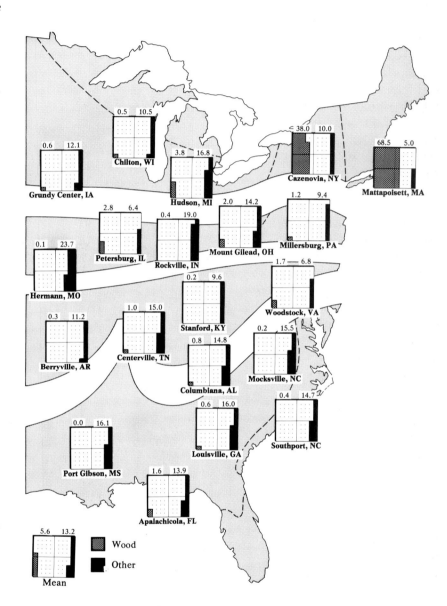

4.32 Wood Shingle and Other Shingle (percent)

ularity among the different kinds of siding, but nowhere do they represent the most common type of cladding. Nor do artificial shingles display any strong regional affinity. They were marketed primarily between 1920 and 1945 and were used both as original siding and for facade remodeling. Thus they played a role similar to aluminum and vinyl siding, but during an earlier period of relatively short duration.

Vertical board and board and batten siding, including modern artificial imitations, are not widely used. Occasional dwellings in southern towns, especially in declining black neighborhoods, display unpainted cypress board. However, in Southport vertical siding does comprise one of the three most common types of house facades. There the black community appears to be relatively stable, and, through its stability, clings to traditional building forms and cladding materials.

Color of Facade

J. B. Jackson, a keen observer of the American scene, suggests that white is the most important "color" in small towns as throughout rural America (Jackson 1967, 2) (Figure 4.33). Cultural geographer Wilbur Zelinsky notes that white is not universal. Red, for example, is the dominant hue in towns of the Penn-

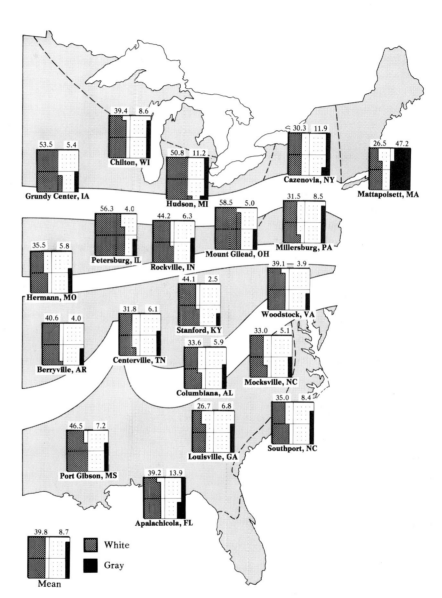

4.33 **White and Gray Facades (percent)**

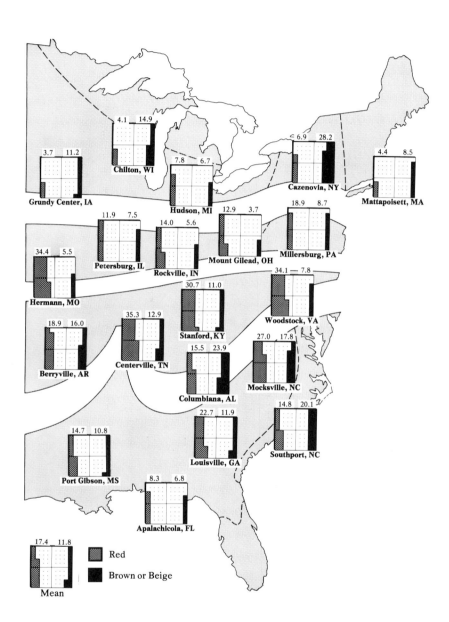

Red
Brown or Beige

Mean

4.34 Red and Brown or Beige Facades (percent)

sylvania culture area (Zelinsky 1977, 133). In order to test such assertions the frequencies of the most common house colors are mapped. White is the most common shade in every town except Mattapoisett and Centerville (Figure 4.33). Within four Middle West towns (Hudson, Grundy Center, Mount Gilead, and Petersburg) more than one-half of the houses are white. Whereas the use of white is nearly universal, Middle Westerners express the strongest preference. Unexpectedly, red is not the leading color in our Pennsylvania town (Figure 4.34). Instead, Centerville in Tennessee shows the greatest preference as related to the recent widespread use of brick on ranch dwellings there. Of the 328 red houses, 315 are brick. Generally speaking, red is most popular across the South, a function, as in Centerville, of the popularity of brick-veneered ranches.

Whether a certain color is largely the result of new construction, maintenance of traditional materials, resurfacing as an economy measure, or neglect, it relates closely to other traits. These include prevailing age, size, and facade material. Gray is the leading house color in Mattapoisett (Figure 4.33). It appears on dwellings painted this shade, unpainted but weathered to this shade, or resurfaced with artificial siding of this shade. In Mattapoisett, unstained naturally weathered wood shingles cover more than two-thirds of the houses. Gray is also an important color across New England Extended, especially at Cazenovia and Hudson, and in Apalachicola, a result not from choice so much as from long-term neglect associated with poverty mixed with salt air.

Brown and beige tones are important in the South. At Columbiana, Berryville, Southport, and Mocksville, at least 15 percent of the dwellings are so colored (Figure 4.34). Most brown and beige structures are large, brick ranch dwellings. Only at Cazenovia are these tones used significantly on other types of wall surfaces. The color yellow has a regional affinity with the Middle West (Figure 4.35). It is the third ranking color in Chilton, Grundy Center, Mount Gilead, Petersburg, and Hermann. Beyond the Middle West it occurs with similar frequency only in Apalachicola. Yellow is common with aluminum and vinyl siding that simulates traditional weatherboarding on new houses. Green has a weaker association with the Middle West as the third most popular wall color in Hudson and Rockville. Together these colors characterize 15 to 24 percent of the dwellings in half the towns. Green is strongly associated with older houses recovered with vinyl shingles.

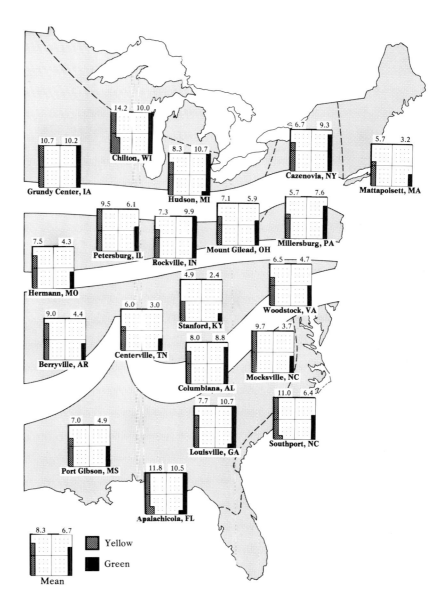

4.35 **Yellow and Green Facades (percent)**

Roofing Materials

From the house facade we now turn to the roof. Compositional shingles are the dominant roofing material throughout the Eastern United States. They cover the roofs of more than 60 percent of the dwellings in each of our study towns. Their frequency is highest in the northernmost towns from Mattapoisett through Grundy Center, in the Lower Middle West communities of Rockville and Petersburg, and in Berryville in the Arkansas Ozarks. In these communities, compositional shingles cover the roofs of more than nine of ten single-family dwellings. Because of its universal popularity we do not include a map of this type of roofing. Do minor varieties of roof covering display any regional affinities? So far as metal, slate, and tar paper are concerned the answer to this question is an emphatic yes. Metal and slate are historic roofing materials that are rarely applied to houses today. Tar paper, on the other hand, is still readily available even though it is sold primarily for use as an under layer rather than an outer surface. It is usually applied as outer roofing by those who cannot afford something more substantial.

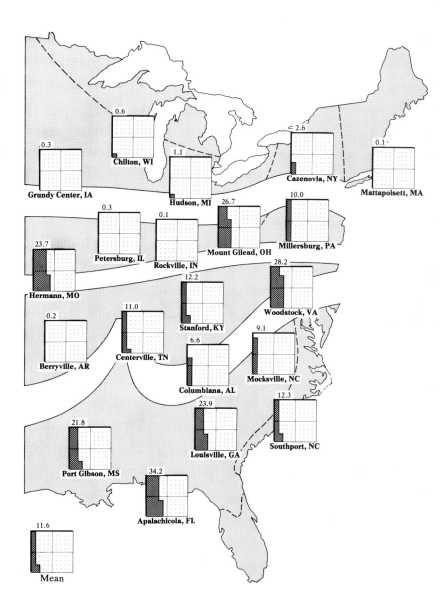

4.36   Metal Roofs (percent)

Metal roofs are conspicuously present in Louisville, Apalachicola, and Port Gibson in the Lower South, Woodstock in the Upper South, and Mount Gilead and Hermann in the Lower Middle West (Figure 4.36). In each of these towns, except Port Gibson, metal roofs are found on over one-half the houses built before 1920 (Figure 4.37). This vintage material is most widely preserved in Apalachicola where older dwellings still stand in large numbers. Here, one in three houses has a metal roof. Slate, as with metal, is a vestigial roofing material, although not as frequent in appearance. Where it remains, this type of roofing has the closest association with the Pennsylvania culture area and its nearby extensions. In the Susquehanna Valley town of Millersburg, more than 2 percent of the single-family dwellings have slate roofs whereas at Woodstock in the Shenandoah Valley almost 3 percent of the houses are so covered. But it is westward in Ohio where this roofing material is encountered most frequently: close to 9 percent of the dwellings at

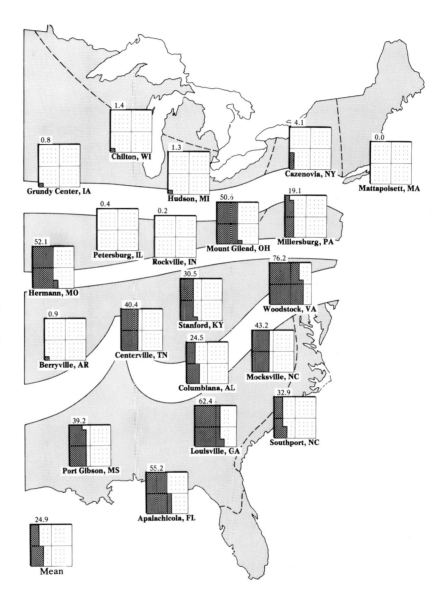

4.37   Pre-1920 Dwellings with Metal Roofs (percent)

Mount Gilead for example (Figure 4.38). In the remaining study towns slate is found on fewer than 1 percent of the houses. The association of slate roofing with towns having ties to the Pennsylvania culture area may reflect a German preference for roofs relatively maintenance free. Use of tar paper as a roofing material has a pattern of geographical distribution resembling that of cement block walling, although in lower frequencies (Figures 4.30 and 4.38). Tar paper roofs are most common in Port Gibson, Apalachicola, and Columbiana. Tar paper is associated in our Southern towns with poor black neighborhoods and represents a building material of last resort.

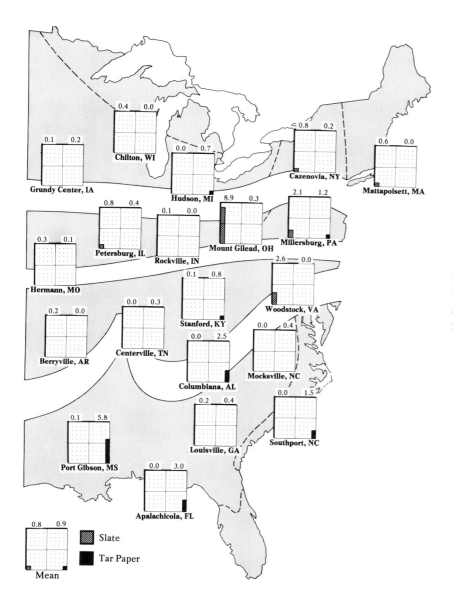

4.38 Slate and Tar Paper Roofs (percent)

Stylish Ornamentation

From concerns with form and building material, let us turn to architectural styling to see how a sense of ornamentation has affected the design of common dwellings. We define architectural style narrowly, restricting ourselves largely to matters of ornamentation. Ornament characterized nearly half of the dwellings in Mattapoisett, and as little as 2.5 percent in Berryville (Figure 4.39). Dwellings with stylish ornament are most numerous in our New England, Upstate New York, and Kentucky Bluegrass towns. Mattapoisett leads the field, a clear reflection of its affluent status. Stylish decoration continues important westward at Cazenovia (more than one-fourth of the dwellings) another affluent place. The rather recent attention given to stylish decoration in Stanford may reflect a growing appreciation of the town's aesthetic surroundings in gentleman farm country (Raitz 1980, 18–23). Mapped are the relative frequencies of the most popular varieties of stylish decoration as a percentage of total dwellings (Figure 4.40).

Early American ornament is the most common type among all dwellings in nineteen of the twenty towns. The exception is Hudson where the largest

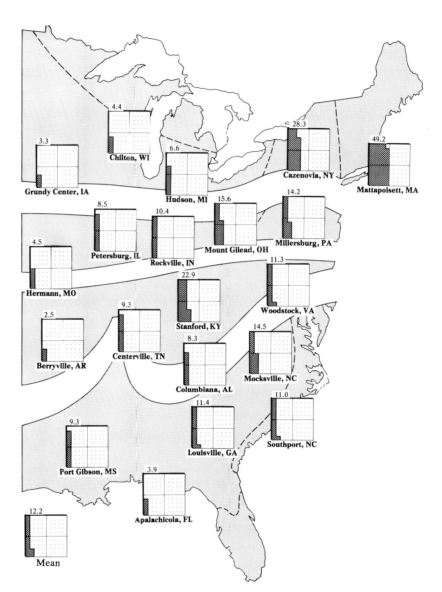

4.39   Dwellings with Stylish Ornamentation (percent)

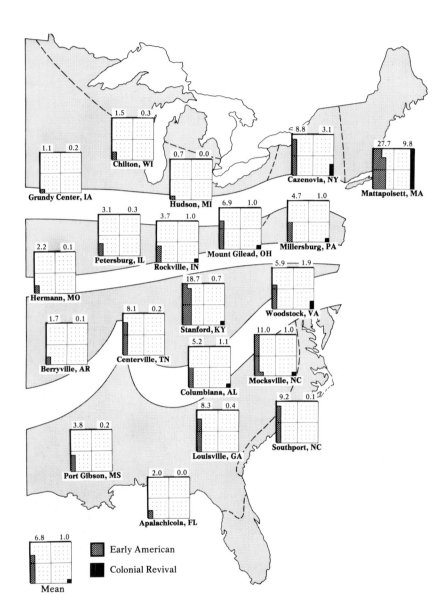

number of decorated dwellings display Italianate ornament, an indicator not of recent prosperity, but of historical persistence rooted in economic stability and decline. Early American decoration includes small paned windows (both real and simulated), decorative exterior shutters, paneled front doors with pseudo-classical frames, and porches with reproduction columns among other characteristics (Figure 4.41). Early American decoration has become popular since 1945, especially on ranch dwellings. It is applied more widely and with less regard for authenticity than was the ornament associated with earlier architectural styles. It is most popular in Mattapoisett, Stanford, Mocksville, and Cazenovia. Authentic or not, this variety of ornament is especially popular in towns which possess a sense of history as reflected in old buildings (including residences), but which also have experienced vigorous growth in recent decades.

What are the most common styles of ornament displayed on houses built before 1920? The decorative details of only three nineteenth-century designs, Greek Revival, Italianate, and Queen Anne, need concern us.

4.40　Early American and Colonial Revival Ornamentation (percent)

4.41   This Mattapoisett cottage is ornamented in the Early American Style.
The use of small-paned windows,
shutters, and end boards alludes superficially to historical precedent,
while demonstrating modern
simplicity.

Greek Revival ornament was
fashionable in America between
1820 and 1860. Among its key
features are a low pitched front-
gable roof, wide entablature
boards beneath the eaves, small
paned windows, a door surround containing a rectangular
transom and narrow side lights,
and a portico or recessed porch
supported by Doric, Ionic, or
Corinthian columns (Blumenson
1977, 26–27; Figure 4.42). Greek
Revival survives most visibly in
the Northeast and the Lower
Mississippi Valley where it deco-
rates almost 7 percent of the

4.42   This elegant dwelling on
Cazenovia's Lincklaen Street uses a
gable-front roof with abbreviated eave
returns and entablature boards to simulate the pediment of a Greek temple.
The effect is much enhanced by the
porch pillars, the whole making a
fashionable Greek Revival statement.

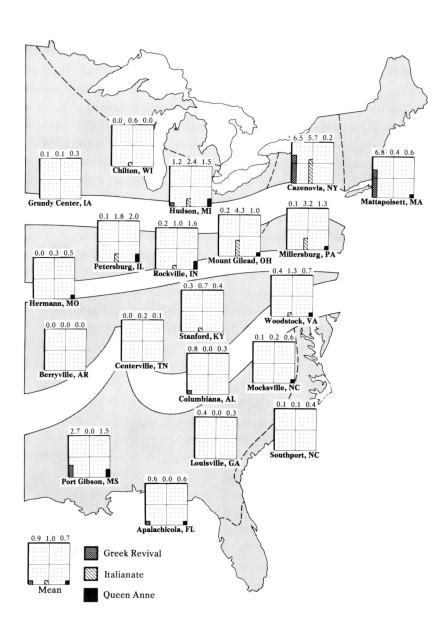

The following values appear on the map:

0.0 0.6 0.0 — Chilton, WI

0.1 0.1 0.3 — Grundy Center, IA

1.2 2.4 1.5 — Hudson, MI

6.5 5.7 0.2 — Cazenovia, NY

6.8 0.4 0.6 — Mattapoisett, MA

0.1 1.8 2.0 — Petersburg, IL

0.2 1.0 1.6 — Rockville, IN

0.2 4.3 1.0 — Mount Gilead, OH

0.1 3.2 1.3 — Millersburg, PA

0.0 0.3 0.5 — Hermann, MO

0.3 0.7 0.4 — Stanford, KY

0.4 1.3 0.7 — Woodstock, VA

0.0 0.2 0.1 — Centerville, TN

0.0 0.0 0.0 — Berryville, AR

0.8 0.0 0.3 — Columbiana, AL

0.1 0.2 0.6 — Mocksville, NC

2.7 0.0 1.5 — Port Gibson, MS

0.4 0.0 0.3 — Louisville, GA

0.1 0.1 0.4 — Southport, NC

0.6 0.0 0.6 — Apalachicola, FL

0.9 1.0 0.7 — Mean

Greek Revival
Italianate
Queen Anne

4.43   Greek Revival, Italianate, and Queen Anne Ornamentation (percent)

dwellings in Mattapoisett, over 6 percent in Cazenovia, and nearly 3 percent in Port Gibson (Figure 4.43).

Italianate design was in vogue between 1840 and 1880. Its distinguishing features include: a low pitched roof of the hip, multiple-hip, or multiple-gable variety; prominent decorative brackets beneath the eaves; tall narrow windows that are frequently arched; and a flat roofed porch (Blumenson 1977, 36–37; Figure 4.44). The decorative details of this design are most evident in New England Extended, the Pennsylvania culture area, and the older portion of the Middle West. More than 2 percent of all dwellings exhibit Italianate ornament in Cazenovia, Millersburg, Mount Gilead, and Hudson (Figure 4.43).

Queen Anne design did not become popular until late in the nineteenth century. Being flamboyant and eclectic in character it is likely to attract attention wherever it occurs. Its basic decorative elements include: steeply pitched multi-planed roofs, round towers with conical roofs or polygonal turrets with tent roofs, projecting dormers with fish-scale shingles beneath the gables, and large delicate porches (Blumenson 1977, 62–63; Figure 4.45). Dwellings with Queen Anne ornament are common in older towns of the Middle West, in Millersburg and in Port Gibson (Figure 4.43). Between 1 and 2 percent of all dwellings display the Queen Anne decoration in Mount Gilead, Rockville, Petersburg, Hudson, Millersburg, and Port Gibson.

The decorative details of only one early twentieth-century architectural style, the Colonial Revival, is common in our study towns. This design is characterized by a symmetrical facade, windows with multi-panes restricted to the upper sash often decorated with shutters, a door with oversize side lights, and large attic dormers (Blumenson 1977, 24–25; Figure 4.46). Dwellings decorated in a Colonial Revival mode are most common in study towns located in the Northeast and the Shenandoah Valley. In Mattapoisett almost 10

4.45 Queen Anne decoration resides in an exaggerated eclecticism, an earlier, much freer, and more extensive borrowing of historical precedents than the Early American. Important on this Hudson house is the varied use of facade coverings including fish scale shingles, the turret with conical roof, the many porches with their spindled posts, the finials atop the roof.

4.44 The Italianate decoration of this house on Rockville's Howard Street includes the flat roof with extended eaves supported by brackets. Windows are tall and variously hooded. Whereas the Greek Revival accentuates the horizontal, the Italianate accentuates the vertical.

4.46 The Colonial Revival decoration of this Cazenovia house lies mainly in the symmetry of its facade openings, the use of small-paned windows, and the use of the portico porch and sidelights to elaborate the front door. The basic house form is appropriate to Georgian houses of the late colonial era which this house, despite its gross liberties, manages to replicate.

percent of all dwellings display the ornament of this style with more than 3 percent in Cazenovia and almost 2 percent in Woodstock (Figure 4.40).

The vast majority (87.8 percent) of the dwellings in our study towns are not ornamented. This lack may be the most important lesson we can draw from examining ornamentation. Clearly, many decades in the early twentieth century favored clean, utilitarian designs devoid of the detail which cluttered many middle class dwellings in the nineteenth century. The new century was greeted with simplified houses which in themselves spoke as a kind of styling through lack of deliberate ornament. Nonetheless, the vernacular impulse must be considered also. Most Americans have always been satisfied with basic structures devoid of ornament both in the new houses they built or commissioned and in their failure to maintain ornamentation on old houses. The vernacular aesthetic would seem to be an impulse which embraces basic form while declining eccentric decoration.

Structural Change

Few houses remain unaltered for long. Alteration, such as stripping trim off of a house, is a characteristic of housing that varies geographically. Change includes: resurfacing walls with material different from the original, replacing windows with those decidedly at variance in size and character with the windows they replace, removing or enclosing front porches, enclosing garages or carports, and adding extra rooms. Dwellings were classified according to no change evident as well as minor, moderate, and extensive visible alteration. Minor alteration involves no more than surficial change as, for example, when aluminum or vinyl siding is used on a clapboarded house. Moderate alteration involves changes which combine to modify the structure but do not obscure its original identity as a structure type. For example, a bungalow might have its porch enclosed and dormers added. Extensive alteration involves a sufficient combination of changes as to render the original design very difficult to decipher. Only minor details remain to suggest a dwelling's initial character. Of course, we are assessing apparent changes as evidenced in a dwelling's oldest visible materials and elements.

Looking only at pre-1946 dwellings (the older structures that would be expected to show the most change) we find strong regional variation in the impulse to alter (Figure 4.47). Towns where at least 25 percent of the pre-1946 dwellings display moderate and extensive alteration are confined to Upstate New York and the Middle West. These communities include Cazenovia, Chilton, Grundy Center, Mount Gilead, Rockville, and Petersburg. In Hudson, however, well over half of the houses are conspicuously remodeled. Hudson possesses the smallest stock of new dwellings of any town.

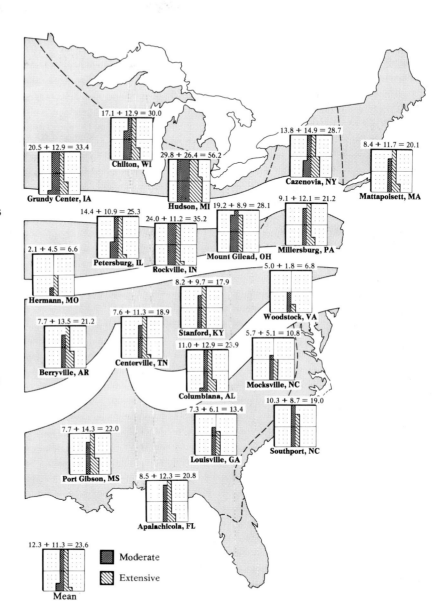

4.47   **Structural Change Among pre-1946 Dwellings (percent)**

Clearly, one factor operating in the change equation is a less prosperous town's need to recycle its traditional dwellings through structural alteration. Among the three Upper Middle West towns, a peculiar kind of alteration prevails. In Hudson, Chilton, and Grundy Center more than 10 percent of the porches are enclosed to form new rooms (Figure 4.48). Clearly, this is a response to the harsh winters of the Upper Middle West as well as a convenient and inexpensive way to capture additional interior space no longer needed for summer cooling in an age of air-conditioning. Porches are already roofed and require only walling to be winterized as interior space.

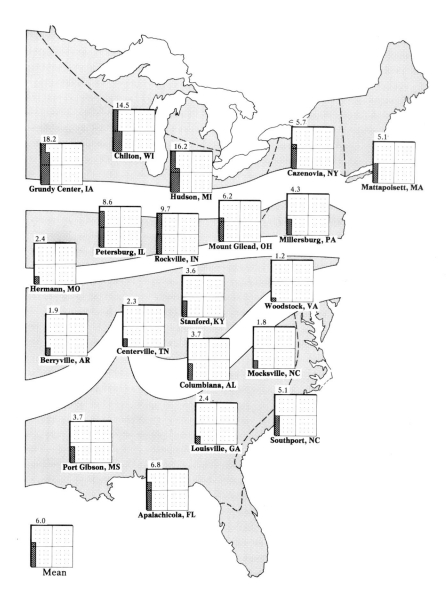

4.48 Enclosed Porches (percent)

Garages and Carports

In automobile oriented America a garage or carport is a common adjunct to the single-family dwelling. Garages are subsidiary structures fully enclosed and equipped with doors whereas carports are open sided or only partially walled and lack doors. Either may stand as separate structures or be attached to or integrated within dwellings.

Garages diminish in importance southward, although across all regions they tend to be slightly more numerous in the west than in the east. They are associated with at least 50 percent or more of the single-family residences in our New England and Middle Western towns (Figure 4.49). In the Lower South, especially in Louisville and Apalachicola, fewer than 35 percent of the houses have garages. As expected, the relative frequency of garages reflects the severity of the winter season.

Basement garages are unusually common in Hermann which is laid out on hilly terrain, many houses being built into hillsides (Figure 4.50). Carports exhibit a more or less inverse frequency to garages. At least 20 percent of all dwellings in six of our ten southern towns have them. They occur with some frequency in both Millersburg and Hermann but in the other Lower

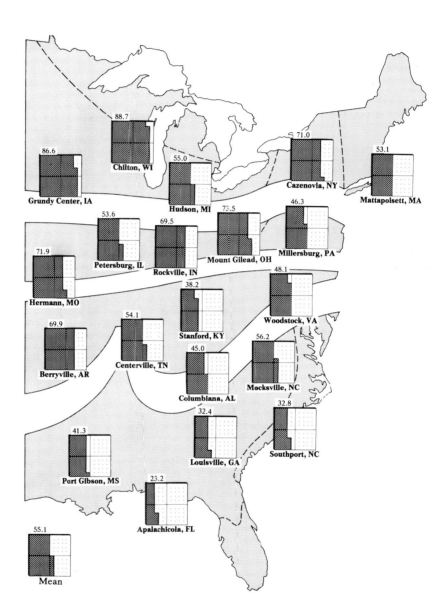

4.49   Dwellings with Garages (percent)

Middle Western communities are less common. From Mattapoisett westward to Grundy Center they are positively rare. As with garages, carports tend to mirror climatic conditions although in Apalachicola predominance of older dwellings and a lack of recent growth may be responsible for the low number of carports in this southern town of mild winters.

Mobile Homes and Duplexes

Although the focus of our study is the single-family dwelling, in many of the towns mobile homes and duplexes represent important housing alternatives. Manufactured housing is most popular in the South, accounting for 16 percent of the total dwellings (mobile homes and single-family dwellings combined) at Columbiana and Louisville and for 19 percent at Apalachicola (Figure 4.51). Mobile homes are rare across the northern tier of towns, and less important generally in the East as opposed to the West. Paradoxically, the mobile home is numerous in both the rapid growth towns of recent decades, and in slow growth places. It appears to be an appropriate dwelling with which to house people attracted by post-1960 industrial growth, but

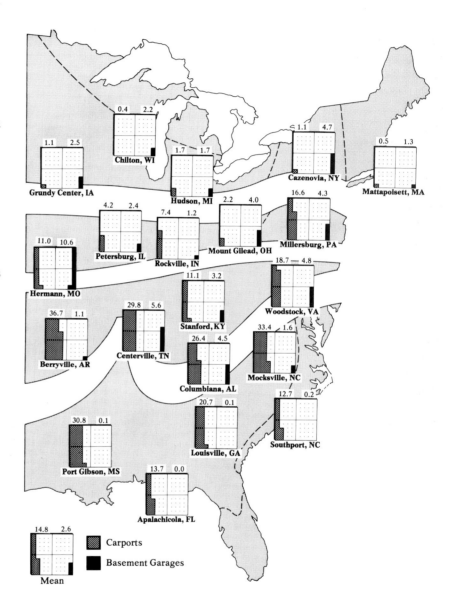

4.50 Carports and Basement Garages (percent)

also serves to fill a void where a traditional building industry is dormant. In addition, the mobile home serves as a starter home for lower class and lower middle-class families with limited financial resources.

Duplexes, dwellings built specifically to house two families (as opposed to single-family residences subsequently divided), are especially important in Millersburg (Figure 4.51). There the row or terrace house usually combines twin two-thirds double-pile houses in a single structure. Built flush with the sidewalks or with small "postage stamp" front yards, little differentiates these dwellings from detached town houses except the shared common walls. Comprising over one-fifth of the housing stock of the place, duplexes add substantially to the special visual character of streetscapes that clearly mark Millersburg as a Pennsylvania town. Duplexes are not generally popular in small towns.

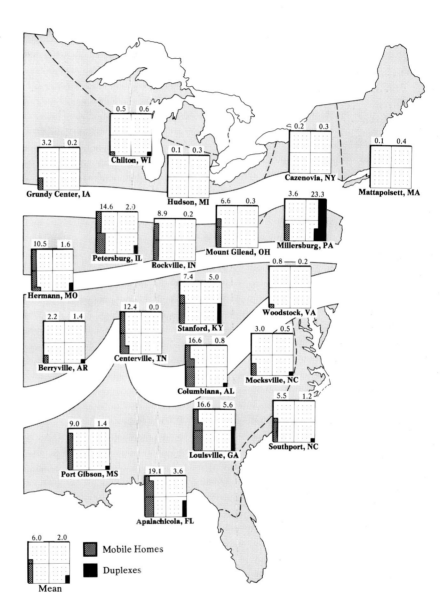

4.51 Mobile Homes and Duplexes (percent)

104

We have sought first to focus the reader's attention on major characteristics by which common houses may be described. Clear regional patterns are discernible in many instances. But how do towns share these characteristics when traits are considered in combination? Mapped is the strength of town-to-town similarity based upon the most widely shared dwelling characteristics: age (1865–1920, post-1945), form (double-pile and ranch), roof (gable, multiple ga-

ble and front gable), height (two-story), size (six to eleven rooms), porches (all types, shed, portico and incised), facades (brick and aluminum), color (red and brown-beige), roofing (composition and metal), structural change (moderate to great, porch enclosure), garages and carports, and stylish decoration (all and Early American) (Figure 4.52). Lines pairing towns symbolize the number of numerically significant characteristics held in common by respective town

pairs: i.e., five or six, seven or eight, or nine shared characteristics. Five shared traits were chosen arbitrarily as a cutoff in order to emphasize only the most intensive sharing of characteristics between towns. The map shows which towns are most alike. Lines with two arrows connect towns which are most like each other according to the number of shared characteristics indicated. Lines with arrows indicate which towns are most like each other.

4.52 Most Similar Towns: Shared Characteristics

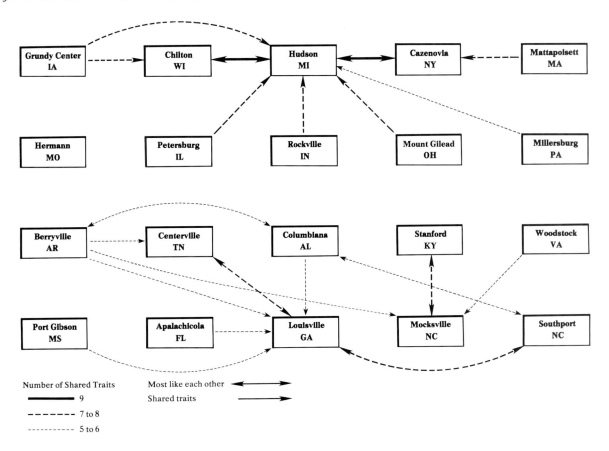

Without reiterating the specific characteristics involved, the study towns group into two distinct sets, north and south. Towns in the New England–Upper Middle West tier are most similar to one another but, except for Hermann, those in the Pennsylvania–Lower Middle West resemble Hudson. Thus Hudson epitomizes our northern towns as a kind of normative case. Hermann, on the other hand, is unique in its dissimilarity to any other study town, a reflection of its substantial German heritage. Although residents of Hermann have not built European dwelling types for well over a century, they continue as a group to choose different forms, colors, and materials for the modern houses they do build. In the Upper South, Berryville is like Centerville and Columbiana, but all three share traits with Louisville in the Lower South. Woodstock and Stanford on the other hand, are most like Mocksville. Berryville also resembles Mocksville. Among Lower South towns

Southport, Apalachicola and Port Gibson are most similar to Louisville. Thus with respect to dwelling traits, Louisville is the most typically southern place. Irrespective of how various towns relate, it is clear that there are two distinct groupings: one in the North and the other in the South. These groupings reflect substantially the geographical distribution of the specific dwelling types, the description to which our research is dedicated. We return to fuller consideration of North-South regional dichotomy in our concluding chapter, but for now we focus on specific dwelling types beginning in the next chapter with single-pile structures. Looking at houses critically requires an eye for differences that distinguish one dwelling from another. But important also is the ability to assess the whole, to note how different elements add up to define a distinctive dwelling type.

CHAPTER V   SINGLE-PILE DWELLINGS

I expected to be able

to read these houses . . .

as combinations of squares

and halves and quarters

of squares.

HENRY GLASSIE

Single-pile or one-room deep dwellings in the United States are rooted in folk tradition. This category includes single-room cabins or hall cottages built to provide minimal living space, the single room representing a primary module to be subsequently expanded through room appendage. The basic two-room planform of hall and parlor was in Britain, according to R. W. Brunskill, "the starting point for developments which eventually led to the diminution and then the extinction of vernacular characteristics in domestic architecture" (Brunskill 1981, 43). So also in the United States were rooms combined in various configurations to define new structure forms, many of which remained popular among commercial builders well into the twentieth century (Glassie 1968a, Lewis 1975, McAlester and McAlester 1984). In this chapter we focus on the principal single-pile dwellings identified in the literature on vernacular architecture by describing their geographical distribution across our twenty study towns in the Eastern United States.

The one-room deep dwelling is a traditional housing idea transferred across the Atlantic from Great Britain and Europe to the colonial culture hearths of what would later be the United States: Southern New England, the Delaware Valley of the Middle Colonies, and the Tidewater South. The single-room unit or hall cottage served as the architectural building block from which various linear plan folk dwellings originated. During the American colonial era and the later western frontier period, one-room deep dwellings were built out of various materials: logs, sawn lumber, bricks, and stone. One-room log cabins, either squared (often sixteen by sixteen feet) or slightly rectangular (often sixteen by eighteen feet), came to symbolize pioneer settlement in the forested areas of eastern America south of New England and native-settled parts of the Upper Middle West (Glassie 1968b, 351; Figure 5.1). Soon, usually within a decade, many single-pen cabins or cottages were enlarged as time, resources, and growing families permitted (Marshall 1981, 44). Thus single-room dwellings were extended sideways, rearwards, frontwards and upwards. These transformations, nonetheless, resulted in relatively few popular, standardized single-pile structure types.

By the nineteenth century these forms were being constructed not in stages but all at once. Larger dwellings of one-and-a-half or two stories exhibited specialization in living space. Ground floors were usually comprised of hall and parlor rooms with most socializing and domestic activity focused in the hall or kitchen. Sleeping, formal entertaining, or both took place in the smaller parlor with sleeping arrangements in the upstairs chambers as well (Swaim 1978, 33–34). Medieval architectural planforms were altered through assimilation of Renaissance notions. Linear planforms became more rigorously symmetrical, and facades more balanced with symmetrically arranged windows and doors. Central hallways were added producing a layout reflective of high style Georgian plans. As John Stilgoe notes:

"Common knowledge is neither folk nor literate but a complex mixture of both the 'little tradition' transmitted by generations of half-literate peasants and the 'great tradition' of the literate, innovative minority of scholars, rulers, and merchants" (Stilgoe 1982, 5).

Standardization of form and other design characteristics became the rule. In new places, as on the frontier, simplicity and stylistic constraint were often "an expression of many settlers' belief that they would soon be moving to a better house" (Wright 1981, 88). Housing

5.1   A basic hall cottage or single-pen cabin languishes at the edge of Louisville.

viewed as temporary could not deviate unduly from common taste lest equity be lost in an inability to sell when the time came to move. In a patently democratic society, social status, as symbolized by fashion, remained an exceptional impulse. The principle of difference in sameness ruled. Town lumberyards furnished standardized

plans, precut lumber, standardized components (doors, windows, etc.), fixtures and
decorative trim (McAlester and
McAlester 1984, 89). Certain
single-pile structure types became national house types with
standardized planforms widely
publicized in plan books. Even in
the early twentieth century a few
one-room deep house types were
replicated almost everywhere as
part of local builder repertoires,
particularly in working class
neighborhoods.

Geographical Distribution

By the latter eighteenth century
each culture region (New England, Midland and Tidewater)
had adopted and adapted a
number of distinctive regional
structure types. We hypothesized that the distinctive single-
pile dwellings of each culture
hearth would be more prevalent
in the eastern portions of the
principal culture regions derived.
Conversely, we anticipated substantial mixing of regional structure types in the west, as well as
a general numerical diminishing
of folk forms in favor of builder
forms westward. We expected
sharp cultural gradients from
north to south between culture
regions to be confined to the
east. Let us first describe the
general geographical distribution
of single-pile dwellings before
turning to the patterns of distribution of specific structure
types as they might test these

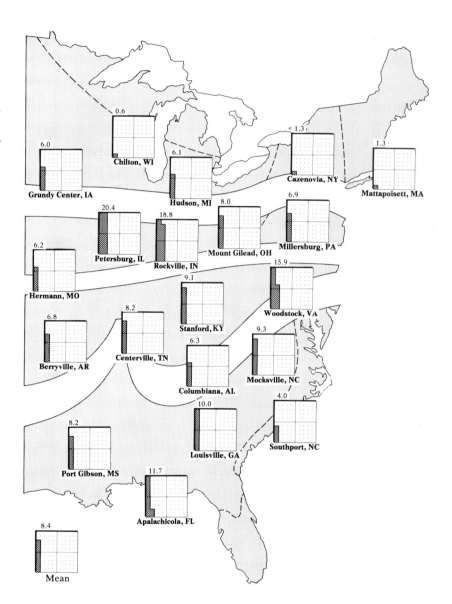

5.2　Single-Pile Dwellings (percent)

hypotheses. In recognition of the folk roots of single-pile dwellings each of the maps in this chapter portrays their frequency not only among all dwellings, but also among those built before 1920.

One-room deep structures comprised only 8.4 percent of all dwellings across the twenty study towns, but nearly one-fifth of those built before 1920 (Figures 5.2 and 5.3). We expected that single-pile housing would be common in the eastern seaboard towns owing to the English imprint. Nonetheless, we anticipated a slightly greater predominance of one-room deep dwellings across the South reflecting an economic depression and general lack of building activity from the Civil War to World War I. This was an era when irregularly massed dwellings became more common in the North. Except at Woodstock it is not in the South, but in the Lower Middle West, that single-pile dwellings prove most numerous today. However, among pre-1920 dwellings the single-pile variety consistently occurs at a high level of frequency only in the Upper South (Figure 5.3). One-room deep cottages and houses are nearly absent in the northern communities of Mattapoisett, Cazenovia, and Chilton (Figure 5.2).

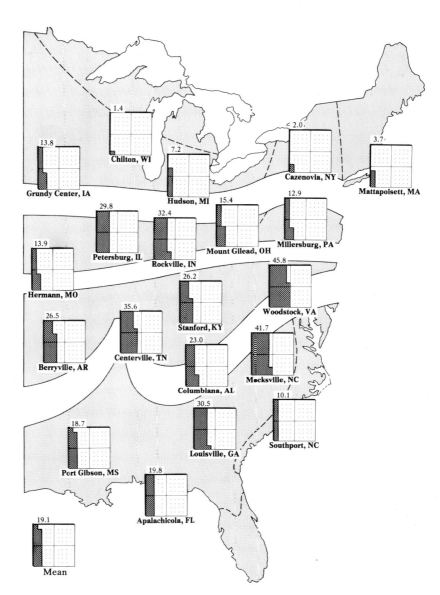

5.3 Pre-1920 Single-Pile Dwellings (percent)

Early on, New England and New England Extended were dominated by double-pile building traditions as we will subsequently describe. In addition, both Mattapoisett and Cazenovia are relatively affluent suburban places, a socio-economic fact discouraging survival of small worker housing, single-pile or otherwise. The Upper Middle West town of Chilton (0.6 percent) had the fewest single-pile dwellings of all towns. In both Hudson and Grundy Center a substantial 6 percent of the dwellings were single-pile, most built to house laborers at the beginning of the railroad era. The industrial nature of Hudson today, with its large blue-collar population, and Grundy Center's persisting agricultural orientation, with its large number of farm workers both active and retired, explains the frequency of single-pile dwellings in those places.

Today single-pile dwellings are most numerous in Rockville and Petersburg. Both towns were established early in the nineteenth century, grew rapidly and were settled by immigrants from Pennsylvania and the Upper South. Small one-room deep cottages with appendages met the housing requirements for working class people, especially as starter houses for young families and retirement homes for older

people. Whereas similar housing may have been removed in other towns it survives in these places, a function of slow growth between World War I and II. Although Hermann (with 6.2 percent single-pile homes) evolved within an area with a strong Upper South folk building tradition, its considerable German veneer explains a local inclination toward a two-room deep building tradition rather than a single-pile tradition. This preference is echoed in Pennsylvania's Millersburg with its strong German overlay. Thus the northern towns provide a curious mix of under-representation and over-representation related to the influence of ethnicity on local building preferences, the proportion of working class population in the community, and substantial variations in the level of construction of replacement housing in recent decades.

The southern one-room deep building tradition proves not as strong in our towns as expected (Figure 5.2). In three places, Columbiana, Centerville, and Berryville single-pile dwellings occur in less than average numbers. Woodstock has a strong single-pile tradition and appears more aligned with the Lower Middle West than with the remainder of the South. In the Lower South, only in Mocksville, Louisville, and Apalachicola were one-room deep dwellings built in numbers significantly above average.

Throughout the South, single-pile dwellings tended to be located in the poorer black neighborhoods or in other working class areas associated with railroads, warehousing, and manufacturing. Housing in many southern towns has been stripped from around the business districts and from along railroad tracks. In some places, like Louisville and Apalachicola, older cottages removed from the center appear in recently created peripheral subdivisions (especially black subdivisions). They are indicative of what once was predominant at the center. Considering only pre-1920 single-pile dwellings, southern towns have the highest frequencies. In Woodstock, Mocksville, and Centerville, vintage single-pile dwellings are more common than in Rockville or Petersburg (Figure 5.3). It is the preponderance of post-1945 dwellings in the South, mostly ranches, that makes the historic single-pile variety appear relatively insignificant (Figure 4.1).

Single-pile dwellings are primarily residuals of a previous century. Yet, for their simplicity and diminutive size, single-pile forms rooted in folk tradition remained popular in some localities until new national planforms totally superseded them after World War I.

Single-Pile Cottages and Houses

Regarding structure types, we make a distinction between "cottages" and "houses." Our criterion for differentiation is dwelling height. Residences lacking a full second story are labeled cottages. Those with two full stories are called houses. Three kinds of single-pile cottages predominated in the Eastern United States: the hall and parlor, the saddlebag, and the I. These three linear plan dwellings are often seen as variations on the same theme given similarity in shape, the number and common placement of doors and windows in each, and the frequent use of common L or T appendages. Although few of these dwellings exist, their inclusion is necessary given their significance in the literature (Figure 5.2). Concern with the I house (in its broadest sense, any single-pile structure with two full stories and a width of two rooms) has been especially important to the evolution of American scholarship focused on vernacular housing; however, we initially differentiate each type of house rather than deal with the types in the aggregate. Thus we use the term I house to refer only to those narrow houses where the two rooms are separated by a central hallway. Each single-pile cottage and house is treated individually to disclose distinctive regional patterns.

HALL AND PARLOR COTTAGES

The hall and parlor cottage features two rooms side by side without a separating central hallway (Figure 5.4). It has a gable roof and usually an end chimney (or chimneys) and is of one- or one-and-a-half stories, with the half-story usually finished into bedrooms. The hall and parlor cottage is the most numerous of the single-pile forms and, indeed, the most numerous cottage form (by a two to one margin over its nearest rival). We anticipated that this common American cottage would be widely distributed across the South given its importance in the Virginia and Carolina source areas and the evolving diffusion network created by settlers moving west in the early nineteenth century (Marshall 1981, 48). Today, the form is most numerous in the Lower Middle West. It ac-

5.4 This Rockville hall and parlor cottage survives as blue-collar rental housing, and may have been moved several times over the past century.

counts for a majority of the single-pile dwellings in Rockville and Petersburg (Figures 5.2 and 5.5). The survival of this folk dwelling in substantial numbers can probably be attributed to limited new home construction in both communities between 1900 and 1950. This was a period of population stability in Rockville and Petersburg.

In the northern tier of towns, the Yankee tendency to build double-pile dwellings is evident in a paucity of hall and parlor cottages (Figure 5.5). Hudson and Grundy Center prove somewhat exceptional, a function, perhaps, of their blue-collar nature even today. In the South, particularly in Mocksville and Port Gibson, this cottage type is associated with black neighborhoods located near once active railroads. Apalachicola in the Lower South has the greatest percentage of hall and parlor cottages of any southern town. Double-pen cottages were one of the structure types built there by housing speculators during the cotton and lumber eras. A depressed economy in the twentieth century has not only reduced the number of new dwellings constructed there, but encouraged retention of old dwellings or relic planforms, especially in poor black residential areas. Hall and parlor cottages are a common dwelling type among pre-1920 structures not only in Mocksville, Port Gibson, and Apalachicola, but also in Columbiana, Centerville, and Berryville. It is apparent that this kind of dwelling was formerly more widely built in the South than in the Lower Middle West (Figure 5.6).

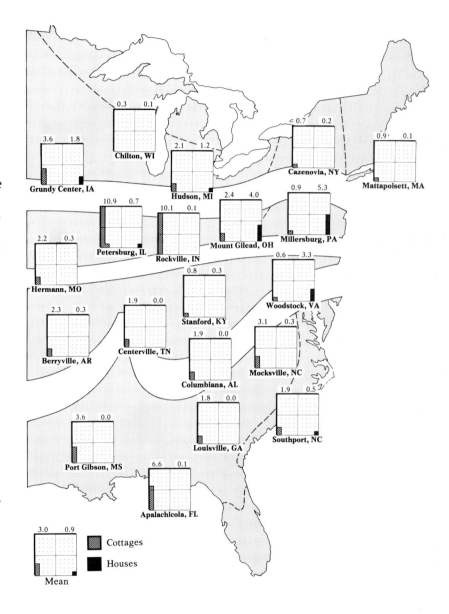

5.5 Hall and Parlor Cottages and Houses (percent)

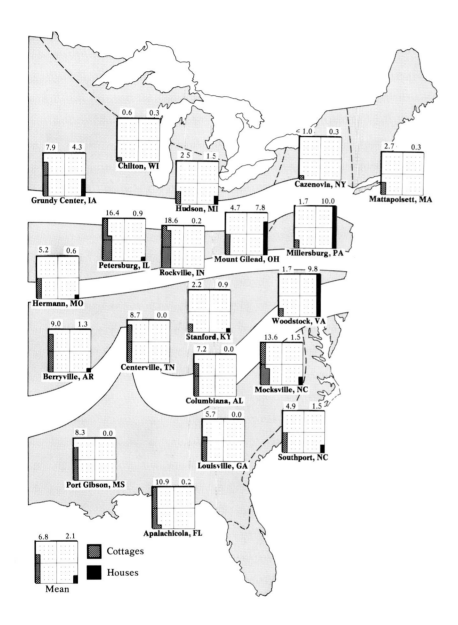

5.6   Pre-1920 Hall and Parlor Cottages and Houses (percent)

HALL AND PARLOR HOUSES

The hall and parlor house idea is clearly related to the hall and parlor cottage as it is organized with a similar room arrangement but with two full stories (Figure 5.7). L and T rear appendages are common as with other single-pile dwelling types. Rooms unequal in size, as indicated by the asymmetrical facades of early examples, reflect Old World origins (Swaim 1978, 36). The hall and parlor type is a part of the Midland and Upper South folk building tradition. Richard Pillsbury refers to this house in Southeast Pennsylvania as the pre-classic I house (Pillsbury 1977, 16–17). Many early hall and parlor houses in Pennsylvania and Virginia were of log. With the advent of balloon framing and associated standardized materials and decorative components, the hall and parlor plan remained popular in rural areas until the end of the nineteenth century. By then symmetry was introduced: equal-sized rooms, balanced window treatment, the pairing of end chimneys and sometimes the use of two front doors (Glassie 1968a, 68; Pillsbury 1977, 17; Swaim 1978, 36).

Hall and parlor houses are found in significant numbers only in Millersburg, Mount Gilead and Woodstock (Figure 5.5). Other towns were void or nearly void of this form, excepting Hudson and Grundy Center.

5.7 This Millersburg hall and parlor house sports a rear appendage as well as recent siding, both indicators of extended serviceability.

When the frequency of hall and parlor houses among pre-1920 dwellings is considered, Hudson becomes an insignificant location (Figure 5.6). Pennsylvanians and Ohioans did settle in Grundy Center, although not in Hudson. The hall and parlor house was associated with the early westward movement of Pennsylvanians. Apparent is a folk building tradition diffused from the Midland core of Southeast Pennsylvania southward through the Great Valley of Virginia and westward across Pennsylvania to Ohio. We find a clear regional implication which seems to validate Zelinsky's claim for Pennsylvania culture influences in a "Pennsylvania Extended" (Zelinsky 1973, 126).

SADDLEBAG COTTAGES

The oldest saddlebag cottages in many towns probably originated as hall cottages. Adding another pen beyond the side chimney of a single pen was one of the primary means of expanding such one-room dwellings. The efficiently placed central chimney is the primary characteristic of this structure which usually often has two front doors (Figure 5.8). Built originally of logs in many areas, it was widely replicated in balloon frame during the nineteenth century, and even into the present century. We anticipated widespread dispersal of this common cottage type in the Up-

5.8   This saddlebag cottage (or cabin) now houses renters on Louisville's near west side. Such housing was usually intended for laborers in the South's small towns.

per South. Introduced as part of the frontier log building tradition, it persisted as a housing form in poor agricultural areas. In the Lower South this structure often served as quarters for black farm laborers and appeared, according to Henry Glassie, as "unpainted rows in the Negro sections of the small towns" (Glassie 1968a, 102).

As anticipated, saddlebag cottages are not a part of the New England building tradition as evidenced by their general absence in the Massachusetts and Upstate New York towns. Nor are they found in the towns of the Upper Middle West (Figure 5.9). They are of some significance in Stanford and Centerville, but not in the numbers anticipated according to documented evidence for rural portions of Kentucky and Tennessee. The only Lower South town to have a substantial number of saddlebag cottages is Louisville. There saddlebag cottages are located predominantly in black neighborhoods and were built primarily in the later part of the past century. When we restrict our view to older dwellings, the significance of the saddlebag cottage as a southern cultural form becomes clearly apparent. More than 17 percent of the pre-1920 dwellings surviving in Centerville for example, are of the saddlebag cottage type. This type of dwelling also occurs with above average frequencies among early structures in Stanford and Berryville in the Upper South and in Louisville and Mocksville in the Lower South (Figure 5.10).

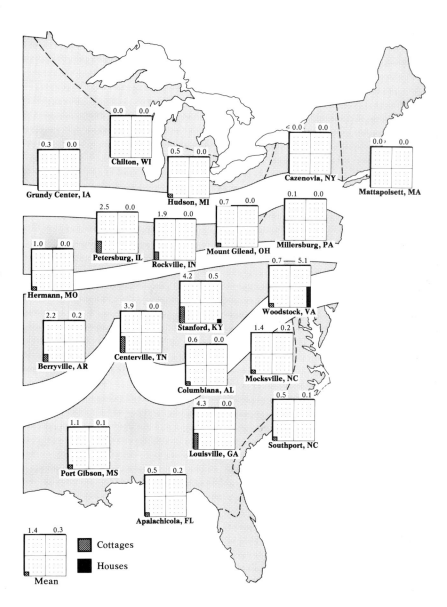

5.9 Saddlebag Cottages and Houses (percent)

SADDLEBAG HOUSES

Related to the saddlebag cottage by floor plan, this house is distinguished by its often unbalanced facade oriented to an off-center chimney (Figure 5.11). In colonial America the saddlebag planform was built by Pennsylvania Germans, but was rare in the Tidewater South (Glassie 1968a, 48–51, 124–25). By the nineteenth century, Georgian ideas, balloon framing and standardized materials combined to make this Old World derivative more symmetrical. As with saddlebag cottages, both the interior arrangement of living space and exterior front elevations were altered.

The saddlebag house is rare compared to the saddlebag cottage except at Woodstock (Figure 5.9). Thirteen of the twenty study towns have no saddlebag houses. Surprisingly, they do not appear with any frequency in the Midland culture region. However, at Woodstock they comprise more than 5 percent of all dwellings and one in six dwellings built before 1920 (Figure 5.10). Indeed, this house type makes a strong impression in the town, dominating the older streets. The early highway network used by German and Scots-Irish migrants linked Woodstock with Mocks-

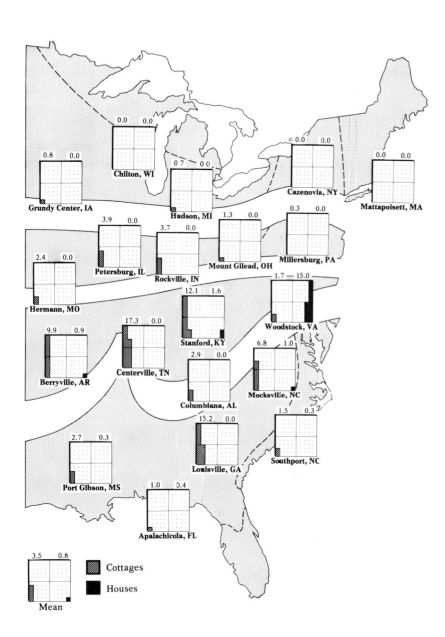

5.10 Pre-1920 Saddlebag Cottages and Houses (percent)

118

5.11 The saddlebag house in Woodstock traditionally carried middle-class aspirations.

ville and Stanford: specifically, the Great Wagon Road of the Great Valley and the Wilderness Road. Besides Woodstock, only in Mocksville and Stanford, among our sample towns, is this house form seen with any frequency today.

5.12 The rear appendage doubles the space in this 1830s I cottage in Rockville, but contributes little to the dwelling's public image as a distinctive structure type.

I COTTAGES

The I cottage is distinguished from the two previously discussed cottage forms by its Georgian influenced classical symmetry. Here we identify different types of single-pile cottages using the same criteria (absence or presence of a central hall and/or central chimney) that are applied to two story houses one room in depth. The I cottage, so named for its similarity to what we are calling the I house, is often characterized by a five bay facade (a central door with two sets of flanking windows), central hallway flanked by a hall and a parlor respectively, end chimneys and gable roof (Figure 5.12). Of all the small cottages inventoried in the study, this variety proved most likely to carry Federal, Greek Revival or Gothic Revival architectural decoration. Porches, appendages of the shed or L or T variety, and centered front-facing gables over front doors are also common features (Swaim 1978, 41). We anticipated the I cottage more in our southern towns (Glassie 1968a, 96; Montell and Morse 1976, 28).

I cottages barely comprise one percent of the total dwellings in the study towns (Figure 5.13). As expected, New England, the Upper Middle West and the Midland towns are virtually without I cottages. On the other hand, in the Lower Middle West towns of Petersburg and Rockville they survive in the largest numbers. Only half of the southern towns have higher than average numbers. Dwellings of this type are most numerous among the pre-1920 housing stock in Mocksville, Rockville, Petersburg, Centerville, and Louisville (Figure

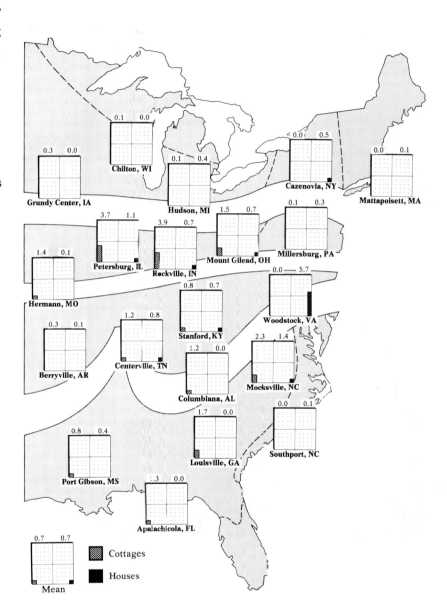

5.13   I Cottages and I Houses (percent)

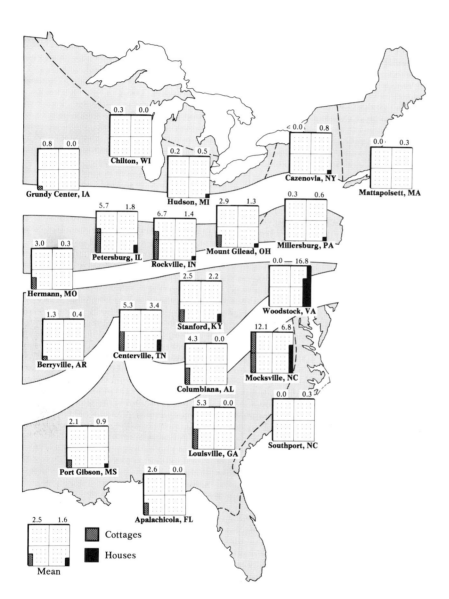

5.14 Pre-1920 I Cottages and I Houses (percent)

5.14). Historically, this dwelling type appears to have been most popular in interior locations in both the South and the Lower Middle West.

I HOUSES

In the rural Eastern United States the central hall I house is one of the more noticeable traditional house forms. During the nineteenth century it symbolized affluence born of the land. The I house was an Old World form inspired by Renaissance ideas. Essentially, it is a hall and parlor house with an added central hallway serving a centrally positioned front door. Irrespective of its use as interior space, (parlor, bedroom, or hallway), the central hall permitted symmetrical balance among facade openings on the exterior. The form is one-room deep with single rooms on either side of the hallway. It has two full stories with gable roof and, in older houses, end chimneys (Figure 5.15). By the early nineteenth century, variations with three or five bay facades had evolved, openings usually symmetrically arranged. The form spread westward into the TransAppalachian interior with Pennsylvanians and Upland Southerners and into the Lower South with southern coastal migrants (Kniffen 1965, Glassie 1968a, Glassie 1972, Pillsbury 1977, Southern 1978, Swaim 1978).

The strength of the form as a class or status symbol was maximized when facades faced public roads thus projecting an impressive front elevation wider than that of any other early house type except for the full double-pile Georgian house. Its popularity reflected a newly emerging democratic agrarian society. The I house symbolized prosperity and respectability both among farmers and among businessmen and professionals in the villages and towns. The rise of commercial agriculture associated with the development of regional railroad networks first accounted for the growing affluence. The strength of the I house as an icon of success was especially strong among Kentuckians and Tennesseans who carried the form into the Lower Middle West. The I house mirrored both folk and popular culture as it was picked up by builders almost everywhere in the Eastern United States in the mid to late nineteenth century. Ornament from various styles, Federal, Greek Revival, Gothic Revival, and Italianate, was attached. Age of the house, local or regional popularity of national style, and owner's status and tastes influenced the resultant style accumulations on facades. A centered gable in a variety of pitches and trim detail became a common feature on I houses in

5.15 I houses, such as this example in Woodstock, clearly symbolized middle-class respectability across the Upper South and Lower Middle West of the nineteenth century.

some sections. It probably evolved from the picturesque movement that was popularized in the pattern books and standardized plans featuring romantic Gothic dwellings (Southern 1978, 78). One variation, called the "Triple-A" house by students of North Carolina vernacular architecture, was a product of the standardized machine age of sawed "gingerbread" decoration (Southern 1978, 81). At the end of the nineteenth century and on into the early twentieth, the central gable was frequently attached to two-room and four-room cottages.

Despite its rural popularity, as described in the literature of vernacular architecture, we did not find large numbers of I houses in our study towns. They accounted for less than one percent of the total dwellings inventoried. In fact, they are absent altogether from five towns (Figure 5.13). The form is numerically significant in only three places: Woodstock with nearly 6 percent of the total dwellings so classified and both Mocksville and Petersburg with slightly over 1 percent. That the I house along with hall and parlor houses and saddlebag houses continue to enjoy popularity in Woodstock suggests a strong relationship between the three, perhaps the former evolving from the latter two. More importantly, these three rather similar house forms were perpetuated by commercial builders in Woodstock in the mid to late nineteenth century, each form undoubtedly reinforcing the others as symbols of domestic comfort. Curiously, only two-story single-pile dwellings are numerous in Woodstock as if to imply that comfort, if not social status, derived only from taller structures.

The I house is clearly a relic feature surviving from the nineteenth century. Considering only pre-1920 houses, however, the geographical patterns of distribution are somewhat broader (Figure 5.14). I houses are widespread among early dwellings in Woodstock and Mocksville and they account for respectable percentages in Centerville, Stanford, and Petersburg. Comprehending the I house across a sample of towns necessitates not only understanding cultural origins and diffusions, but the processes of planform persistence and continuity. All of the above towns were slow- or no-growth places through much of the twentieth century. Petersburg remains such today.

A problem arises in relating our findings concerning the geographical distribution of the I house to what is suggested in the literature. This occurs because of our strict definition of this type of dwelling. We classify a dwelling as an I house only if it has a central hall as well as one-room depth, two-room width, and two-story height. What Kniffen describes as I houses includes our version as well as what we label hall and parlor and saddlebag houses. He ig-

nores the presence or absence of a central hall. Nor is he concerned with chimney placement. "But these qualities all 'I' houses unfailingly had in common: gables to the side, at least two rooms in length, one room deep, and two full stories in height" (Kniffen 1965, 553, 555). In a diagram labeled "A range of 'I'-house floor plans" Kniffen illustrates the hall and parlor form (rooms of uneven size and no central hall), the saddlebag form (a central chimney shared by two rooms), and our symmetrical I type (a central hall separating two rooms of equal size) (Kniffen 1965, 556).

What sort of geographical distribution is revealed by our data if we combine frequencies of occurrence for the hall and parlor, saddlebag, and I house types? Among all dwellings we find them closely associated with the Pennsylvania culture area and its southward and westward extensions into Virginia and Ohio. These house types, in combination, are most common in the Shenandoah extension at Woodstock (Figure 5.5, 5.9, and 5.13). Among pre-1920 dwellings we found a similar, but more expansive area in which these types of dwellings, when combined, are common. This area extends onto the North Carolina Piedmont and into the Bluegrass Basin of Kentucky. Once again, the highest frequencies are encountered at Woodstock (Figure 5.16).

Mitchell suggests that the Shenandoah Valley was a secondary area from which diffusion advanced. He looks upon western Virginia as a zone in which culture traits from the southeastern Pennsylvania and Chesapeake hearths were fused. According to his interpretation, western Virginia (Woodstock), in turn, exerted a primary influence on central Kentucky (Stanford) and a secondary influence on northwestern North Carolina (Mocksville) (Mitchell 1978, 74–77).

OTHER SINGLE-PILE COTTAGES AND HOUSES

Several other single-pile cottages and houses are described in the Glossary. They were included in our inventory given their importance in the literature on vernacular housing. However, they prove too few in number to warrant mapping although we should note their general absence. Single-room cottages have already been mentioned. Only thirteen hall cottages or single pen cabins were counted. They are scattered across eleven towns in the Middle West and South. Nor is the dogtrot cabin common (only two examples). In this latter form, two rooms are separated by an open porch which usually gives access to a rear L appendage. Neither type were expected to be numerous in any of our sample towns being iden-

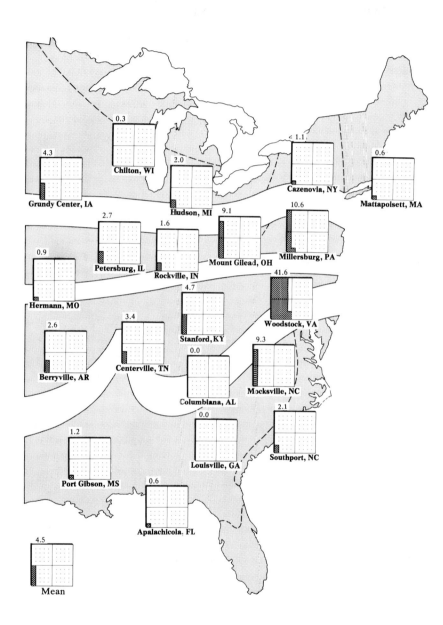

5.16 Pre-1920 Saddlebag, Hall and Parlor, and I Houses (percent)

tified in the literature almost exclusively as rural folk forms. Only eighteen two-thirds I houses (one room and hall on each floor) were counted in four towns, including nine examples in Stanford and seven in Woodstock. A relic folk form, it is clearly related in its limited geographical extent to both the I house and the hall and parlor house. Only eight one-over-one houses (sometimes called stack houses) were counted. These dwellings (essentially two rooms with one placed above the other) often have a single story L or T rear extension. It has been identified with late-eighteenth and early-nineteenth century Philadelphia and other eastern cities being appropriate to narrow city lots (Murtaugh 1957, 9). These houses also have been found in central Missouri (Marshall 1981, 41). Only one dogtrot house was inventoried. Clearly a rural form, it features pairs of stacked rooms separated on the first floor by an open porch, the space above the porch containing a fifth room.

Appendages

Single-pile dwellings are small because they are shallow in depth. Smallness has encouraged structural appendage either as part of original construction or as subsequent addition. We noted extensions in categorizing all dwellings, differentiating appendage types according to the overall perimeter configurations formed with primary units. We defined the primary unit as that part of a dwelling which contained the front facade and would remain inviolate should appendages be removed. The L appendage extends outward from either the left or the right rear of the primary unit whereas the T appendage is centered on the rear. Usually, their gabled roofs run perpendicular to the axis of the primary unit. The shed appendage abuts parallel to the rear wall of the main structure, a shed roof extending the primary roof rearward, but usually at a change of pitch or slope. Lateral appendages extend dwellings either to one or both sides where the axis of the primary unit is parallel to the street. Rear axial appendages extend dwellings rearward where the axis of the primary unit, itself, is perpendicular to the street. Of the total dwellings inventoried, only one-third have appendages. Of the total, 8.3 percent are lateral, 7.6 percent shed, 6.4 percent L, 3.5 percent rear axial, and 2.8 percent T.

We had hoped to find distinctive regional patterns by which different dwelling types are enlarged using different appendage configurations. No such patterns are evident. Regarding single-pile dwellings, L, T, and shed appendages are most common, but no more so in one culture region or in one town as opposed to another. To predict the popularity of different appendage forms, one only has to trace the popularity of various structure types. Ninety percent of all I cottages and I houses in the study towns have rear appendages. Nearly one-half are of the L variety, about one-fifth are of the T type, and one in six have a shed configuration. This pattern holds with little variation wherever I cottages or I houses are present.

Single-pile dwellings comprise only 1,446 of the 17,261 houses surveyed, and form the second smallest structure category after bungalows. In only five towns does one-room deep housing comprise 10 percent or more of the total; these towns are Petersburg, Rockville, Woodstock, Apalachicola, and Louisville (Figure 5.2). Cottages predominate in the towns of the Lower Middle West and South. In the Pennsylvania culture region (Millersburg), and its southward extension (Woodstock) houses are more important (Figures 5.5, 5.9, and 5.13). One might expect that where there are single-pile cottages there would also be single-pile houses in large numbers, and vice versa. Such is not the case. Single-pile houses and cottages have filled different niches traditionally, the former serving lower- and the latter middle-income people. A possible exception is the I cottage which in several southern towns appears to have been a "starter" home for upwardly bound young families. We expected that traditional folk houses would be more prevalent in the east than in the west. What we found is an association between single-pile houses and the Pennsylvania culture area and its extended zones of influence in Ohio, western Virginia, central Kentucky, and Piedmont North Carolina. However, the highest frequency of these houses occurs in Woodstock rather than Millersburg (Figure 5.16). Explicit patterns of cultural origin and diffusion are not apparent. Although relatively few in number, single-pile cottages and houses do make a rather

strong visual expression at least in the older parts of certain towns. Plain, simple, clapboarded housing persists along older residential streets, especially in neighborhoods associated with development in the railroad era. These streets are most visible in communities at the eastern and western ends of principal culture regions: Rockville, Petersburg, Woodstock, Stanford, Mocksville, Louisville, and Apalachicola (Figure 5.2). To the east there may have been larger numbers of these dwellings built. To the west dwellings are newer and although never as numerous have managed to survive on the basis of relative youth.

CHAPTER VI   DOUBLE-PILE DWELLINGS

The essential characteristic

of the double pile plan

is that it is entirely

two rooms in depth.

R. W. BRUNSKILL

Rearward extension of older single-pile plans produced the earliest dwellings in North America two rooms deep. Renaissance concepts of symmetry, carried from England during the Georgian era, ultimately led to front and back rooms of equal depth, and use of regular gable roofs rather than roofs with shed-like "salt box" profiles (Brunskill 1971, 112; Kniffen 1965, 558). Some double-pile dwellings, Cape Cod and square cottages for example, appear to have developed in a rural environment (Connally 1960, 48–49; Lewis 1975, 8). Others reflect urban origins. These include double-pile houses with symmetrical facades and those with temple-like gable fronts inspired by Greek Revival concepts of architectural design (McAlester and McAlester 1984, 90). The influence of narrow urban building lots is evident in gabled side-hall

dwellings, such as the two-thirds double-pile house: a plan brought from London to Philadelphia during the Colonial era (Murtaugh 1957, 10–11). Double-pile dwellings were built for both the humble and the proud as revealed, for example, in the contrasting forms of the shotgun cottage and the large two-story Georgian-plan house with four rooms upstairs and down. They were erected, on the one hand, by people guided by a utilitarian spirit and, on the other, by those seeking architectural fashion.

Geographical Distribution

Among our twenty study towns double-pile dwellings comprise the most numerous structure group: 6,890 dwellings or nearly 40 percent of all we surveyed. The relative frequency of double-pile structures varies widely from a high of more than 75 percent in Mattapoisett to a low of 25 percent in Berryville. Excepting Germanic Hermann, towns with above average frequencies

of double-pile dwellings are
found in the Northeast, New England Extended, and along the
southern seaboard (Figure 6.1).
In addition to Mattapoisett, these
towns include Cazenovia, Hudson, Millersburg, Southport, and
Apalachicola.

Double-Pile Dwelling Types

CAPE COD COTTAGES

The Cape Cod cottage (also
called the double-house Cape
Cod) is a one-and-one-half-story
gable-roofed dwelling (Figure
6.2). On the ground floor there
are two large rooms in front. In
early Cape Cods these rooms are
separated by a stairway and a
massive central chimney. To the
rear three smaller rooms are
common with the main bed-
rooms located in the upper half-
story. In twentieth century adap-
tations of the Cape Cod, room
arrangements usually deviate
from the traditional colonial
models. Revival versions often
reveal a bungalow-like interior
floor plan with attic dormers
sometimes front and back.

The early Cape Cod cottage
has been described as a dwelling
type found throughout New England, but one particularly common on Cape Cod itself and on
eastern Long Island (Glassie
1968a, 128–29). Presumably, it
began to evolve during the seventeenth century (Lewis 1975, 8),

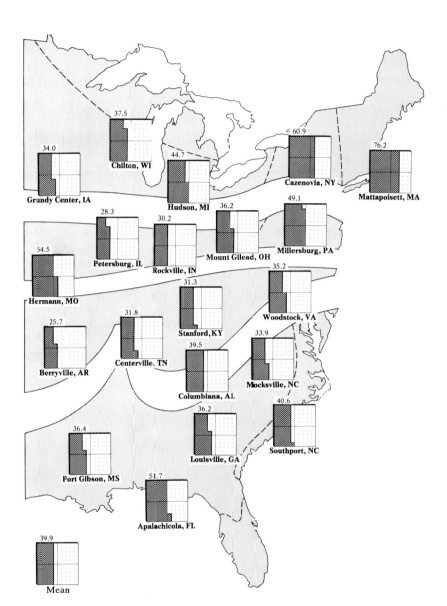

6.1   Double-Pile Dwellings (percent)

128

but only became fully developed as a distinctive form by the end of the eighteenth century (Connally 1960, 47). Its primary period of construction in New England extended from the late 1700s to the early 1800s (Glassie 1968a, 128). In twentieth-century revival form it has been described as "America's dream house" of the interwar and early postwar years (Foley 1980, 220).

How do the results of our survey compare with previously published descriptions of the geographical and chronological distribution of the Cape Cod cottage? Our findings do agree with the assertion that the Cape Cod cottage has a regional affiliation with New England (Figure 6.3). Among our study towns this type of structure comprises less

than 2 percent of the housing stock, but in Mattapoisett it amounts to 18.0 percent. In only one other place in New England's extended culture region does it occur with above average frequency: Chilton far to the interior. However, the other towns with exceptional numbers of Cape Cod cottages all have Pennsylvania ties: Millersburg, Mount Gilead, and Woodstock.

This apparent discrepancy can be explained by the relative age of Cape Cod cottages inventoried. Only in Mattapoisett do Cape Cod's survive both from the pre-1865 and 1865–1919 construction eras. However, its unusual frequency there is primarily the result of post World War II revival. Ninety-one of the

town's 151 Cape Cod cottages were built after 1945. Another thirty-four date from the interwar years with a mere twenty-seven erected during previous eras. In Chilton, Millersburg, and Woodstock, a majority of the Cape Cod cottages were built between 1920 and 1945. At Mount Gilead the majority were built after 1945 rather than during the previous era. Thus Cape Cods are revival dwellings rather than vintage folk forms. A northeastern bias in the distribution of these dwellings lends limited credence to the assertion that they embodied an American dream

6.2   This new Cape Cod cottage in Mattapoisett adheres strictly to traditional form: center chimney and stairway with four rooms down and two rooms up under the half-story.

house during the interwar and immediate postwar years. Their predominantly recent vintage also dispels any traditional association with the Pennsylvania culture area that might seem to be suggested by Figure 6.3.

Cape Cod cottage forms other than the double-house Cape Cod are rare, i.e., three-quarters Cape Cod cottages (also called house-and-a-half Cape Cods) and one-half Cape Cod cottages. Twenty-nine three-quarters Cape Cod cottages, comprised of two rooms, lobby entrance and chimney and staircase to one side, were inventoried (only 0.2 percent of the total dwellings). Twenty-two of these structures were found in Mattapoisett where they account for a mere 2.6 percent of the single family dwellings. Only nine one-half Cape Cod cottages, comprised of two rooms with fireplace and stair in one corner of the front room, were found, five of them in Mattapoisett. Most of these dwellings were revival cottages having been built after World War II. Although few in number, they do, like Cape Cod cottages, reinforce Mattapoisett's Yankee architectural roots through revivalism.

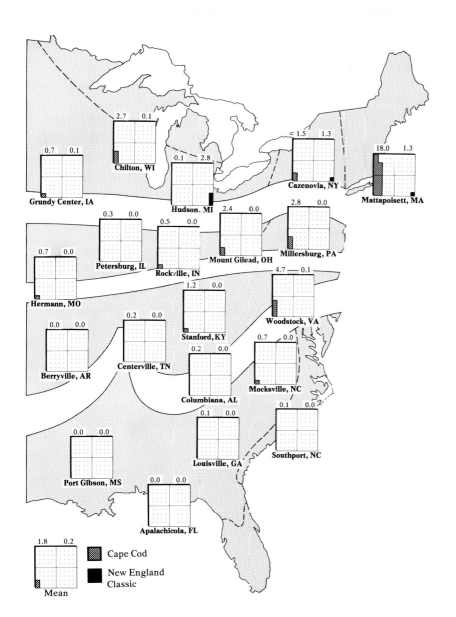

6.3   Cape Cod and New England Classic Cottages (percent)

NEW ENGLAND CLASSIC COTTAGES

The New England classic cottage is a Greek Revival era derivative of the Cape Cod cottage (Figure 6.4). It is a one-and-one-half-story gabled dwelling with two large front rooms and smaller rooms across the back. A central stairway giving access to two attic bedrooms is another feature inherited from the Cape Cod. Traits inspired by early nineteenth-century Greek Revival fashion include paired chimneys, either flanking the stairway or positioned in the end walls, and decorative entablature boards beneath the eaves. Many classic cottages have entablatures punctured by small rectangular "lie-on-your-stomach" windows. The New England classic cottage is described by most authors as a dwelling type common throughout New England, across Upstate New York, and westward along the southern margins of the Great Lakes (Kniffen 1965, 559; Glassie 1968a, 129; Lewis 1975, 10). It took form in the late eighteenth century (Kniffen 1965, 558–59) and became popular during the early decades of the nineteenth century (Connally 1960, 47, 55; Glassie 1968a, 129; Noble 1984, 104).

Are our findings consistent with the distribution and age of these structures as described in the literature? The reply to this question is clearly affirmative. Although the New England classic cottages comprise only 0.2 percent of the total housing stock in our twenty study towns, communities with substantially higher frequencies are located in the traditional New England culture region and its extension westward (Figure 6.3). These places include Mattapoisett, Cazenovia, and Hudson. Nearly one-half of the surviving New

England classic cottages were built before 1865. All but one of the remainder were erected during the 1865–1919 construction era. Considering the potentially high attrition rate among antebellum structures, our results seem to be in line with the period of popularity of these dwellings as previously described.

6.4 As its name implies, the New England Classic cottage often carried Greek Revival ornamentation. This example is from Mattapoisett.

DOUBLE-PILE COTTAGES

The double-pile cottage is a one-
or one-and-one-half-story dwelling with either a gable or hipped
roof, the ridge line running parallel to the facade (Figure 6.5).
Early double-pile cottages have
two rooms on each side of a central hallway and paired chimneys, often placed in an interior
position. In twentieth-century revivals the hallway is often eliminated with the front door
opening directly into a front
room. This kind of structure is
thought to have appeared at an
early date along the Carolina–
Georgia coast (Glassie 1968a,
109). Its form was remotely
related to that of the Cape Cod
cottage. It was built in New England and Pennsylvania as well
as in the South (Pillsbury 1977,
27). However, in the South numerous structures of this type acquired a visually commanding
attribute during the nineteenth
century when steeply pitched
hip or pyramidal roofs replaced
moderately pitched gable or hip
roofs. (Glassie 1968a, 112).

We found the double-pile cottage to be the most common
dwelling in the double-pile
group. It comprises more than 12
percent of the housing stock in
our study towns. It is encountered most frequently in Hermann (Figure 6.6) and least often

6.5   The double-pile cottage, such as
this example in Louisville with
screened portico porch, combines a
simple rectangular floor perimeter
with a simple gable roof.

6.6   The pitch of the roof, the dormers, and the portico porch establish
this nineteenth-century double-pile
cottage in Hermann as German-
American.

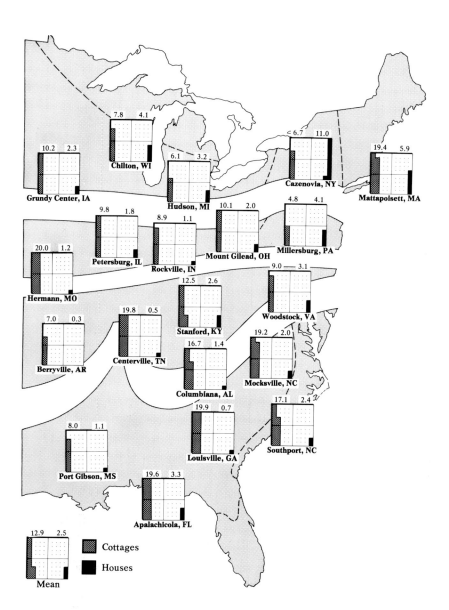

6.7 **Double-Pile Cottages and Houses (percent)**

in Millersburg. It clearly has a stronger association with the South than with other regions (Figure 6.7). Outside the South only Mattapoisett and Hermann had above average concentrations. In Mattapoisett, twentieth-century versions are most numerous and appear as oversized imitations of the Cape Cod cottage. At Hermann its popularity mirrors traditional, post-Renaissance cottage prototypes with French Creole ideas frequently apparent. Southern towns with exceptional concentrations of the double-pile cottage include Columbiana, Centerville, Southport, Mocksville, Louisville, and Apalachicola.

In Mattapoisett, both the double-pile cottage and the Cape Cod cottage, which it resembles in basic form and wood shingle siding, are primarily of postwar derivation. At Hermann, Southport, and Apalachicola, the largest numbers were built between 1865 and 1919. In the remainder of the southern towns most were built in the interwar period. By this time steeply pitched hip and pyramidal roofs were no longer in vogue and the moderately sloped gabled varieties had been revived.

Double-pile cottages with gambrel roofs are rare: only fifty-eight of the total dwellings inventoried. Most of these structures were of post–World War II origin scattered across recent subdivisions, especially in Mattapoisett (eighteen examples) and Chilton and Stanford (with six each). In each town the gambrel roof carries either Colonial Revival or Early American ornamentation. Although widely promoted in sales catalogues and plan books of the early to mid twentieth century, judging from our sample towns, gambrel-roofed dwellings were not widely adopted. These roofs were more difficult and more costly for builders to erect although they did serve to open up usable space in the half-story under the roof.

DOUBLE-PILE HOUSES

Double-pile houses are two- or two-and-one-half-stories high (Figure 6.8). Capped with either gable or low-pitched hip roofs. They commonly have paired chimneys placed internally or on the outside walls of the structure. Those built during the late eighteenth and early nineteenth centuries usually have a central hall separating two rooms to either side. This Renaissance plan-form may have been adopted somewhat later in the Georgian era than another typical trait, the symmetrical facade. At an early stage in the evolution of double-pile houses in New England, a centrally placed front door opened into a small lobby and often a stairway built against a central chimney (Kniffen 1965, 558–59). In twentieth-century revival forms the central hallway was often reduced in width or eliminated altogether.

Viewpoints on the geographical distribution of the double-pile house vary. It has been described as occurring throughout the Pennsylvania culture area in small numbers and across the Midwest south of the National Road (Pillsbury 1977, 26; Lewis 1975, 12). This dwelling form also has been associated with frontier New England and Upstate New York (Kniffen 1965, 559). In New England it was adopted by the wealthy early in the eighteenth century and by the middle class around mid-century (Morrison 1952, 473). A

6.8 Four rooms astride central hallways, both upstairs and down, mark the classic full Georgian floor plan of the double-pile house. This revival example of the 1920s is located on Chilton's gentry row.

similar date of adoption has been postulated for the Mid-Atlantic seaboard. In Pennsylvania and the Lower Middle West the traditional unadorned version of the double-pile house continued to be built until the early twentieth century (Lewis 1975, 4, 12). As the traditional variety was being abandoned a fashionable revival version of this dwelling type became popular in suburban settings as a modern link to America's colonial heritage (Foley 1980, 214).

The double-pile house is considerably less popular than the double-pile cottage. About one in fifty of the dwellings in our study towns are of this type. They are encountered most often in Cazenovia, and least frequently, in Berryville. Towns with above-average numbers are located primarily in the New England–Upper Middle West region (Figure 6.7). In addition to Cazenovia, these places include Mattapoisett, Hudson, and Chilton. Other places where they are common include Millersburg and Woodstock within the Pennsylvania culture area, and Stanford and Apalachicola in the South.

Our findings tend to support previous generalizations regarding the house's changing popularity: 1) it appeared early in New England, 2) it was a persistent nineteenth-century form in areas of Pennsylvania culture, and 3) it enjoyed an early twentieth-century revival. We also discovered a more recent postwar revival of this house type in our New England and Upstate New York study towns. In Mattapoisett the largest number of older double-pile houses were built before 1865 with a somewhat greater number erected since 1945. In Cazenovia a large majority of the vintage dwellings of this type were built between 1865 and 1919. A somewhat larger number also were

6.9 Colonial New England spawned a central chimney, lobby entrance version of the double-pile house. This early nineteenth-century example is located in one of Mattapoisett's new subdivisions.

constructed after 1945. In Millersburg and Woodstock a majority of the surviving double-pile houses were built between 1865 and 1919. Thus they may represent either persistence of a folk form through the late nineteenth century or its revival as a fashionable design during the early years of the twentieth century. Double-pile houses in Chilton and Apalachicola are of similar age. Both towns are far removed from the Pennsylvania culture area where folk influences endured longest. Neither place, however, was beyond the reach of popular revival influences that resurrected this house form early in the twentieth century. In Stanford the bulk of these structures date from the interwar years and reflect the persistent popularity of Colonial Revival architecture among builders during the 1920s (McAlester and McAlester 1984, 326).

The double-pile house with central chimney, an early New England structure organized around a lobby entrance, proved rare, represented by only thirteen of the total dwellings (Figure 6.9). However, nine of those houses are located in Mat-

tapoisett and date from the late colonial or early federal periods. Also uncommon is the salt box house with its distinctive "cat slide" roof (Figure 6.10). Yet again, seven of the ten structures inventoried are located in Mattapoisett, and they are post–World War II revival houses. Thus two traditional Yankee forms endure in our New England study town, both reflecting the gentry or upper middle class predilections to embrace the past architecturally: the one a result of careful preservation at the community center and the other a result of revival on the suburban fringe.

6.10 In recent years Mattapoisett builders have begun to revive late colonial dwelling types as, for example, this salt box house in one of the town's newer subdivisions.

DOUBLE-PILE COTTAGES
WITH FRONT EXTENSION

A variety of double-pile cottage appeared early in our inventory which was simply too distinctive and too frequently encountered not to be treated as a separate category. Named exactly as it appears, this double-pile cottage with gable roof has a perpendicular extension off the front, either to the left or to the right, and is covered by a small gable which hits the main roof at or below its ridge line (Figure 6.11). The extension produces, in most instances, an enlarged living room and sometimes contains the front door. It is not an appendage for its removal severs the remainder of the house asunder.

Of the total houses inventoried, 3 percent were double-pile cottages with front extensions. They occur at nearly three times the average at Hermann (Figure 6.12) and their exceptional popularity here appears associated with that of the ordinary double-pile cottage. Both forms are rooted in local nineteenth-century German building traditions with echoes of the colonial French Creole common in Missouri before German settlement. Both are plain, straightforward forms, usually covered with a brick veneer. In Hermann, most of these cottages were built just before or just after World War II. They represent a kind of continuity whereby traditional ideas, much modified, persist in a modern house form. Double-pile cottages with front extensions also appear with above average frequency in other

6.11 The double-pile cottage with front extension emerged in Hermann in the 1920s and continued to be popular through the 1940s.

towns which experienced growth in housing during the 1930s and 1940s: Millersburg, Woodstock, Chilton, Columbiana, and Mocksville. The form's popularity appears rooted in builder proclivities, town to town, to excite and serve a modest-priced market for middle class housing. Although a variation on a theme, it is an important variation with widespread visibility.

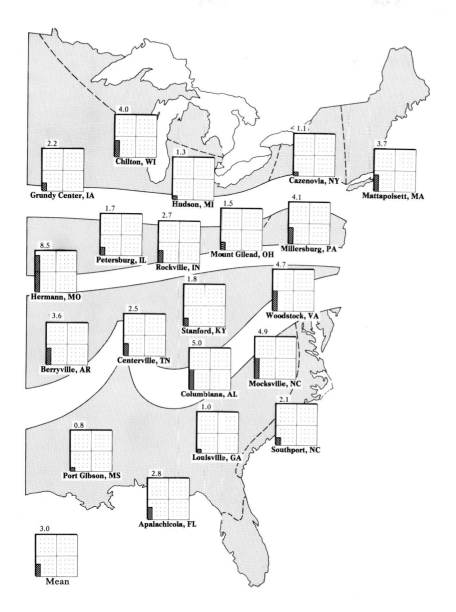

6.12   Double-Pile Cottages with Front Extension (percent)

138

SQUARE COTTAGES

Square cottages resemble the
double-pile cottage. They too are
of one- or one-and-one-half-sto-
ries with either a gable or hip
roof (Figure 6.13). The difference
between the two types results
from the absence of a central
hallway in the former. The
square cottage, therefore, has a
distinctive box-like form whereas
the double-pile cottage has a def-
inite rectangular shape. A less
obvious distinction involves
chimney numbers. The square
cottage usually has a single centrally placed chimney whereas
central hallways make paired
chimneys a necessity in double-
pile cottages. Square cottages
normally have four rooms on the
main floor, but of unequal size.
In terms of basic shape, room arrangement and chimney placement, the pyramid cottage, in
turn, resembles the square cot-

**6.13   Here is a very grand late nine-
teenth-century square cottage from Columbiana. The extensive porch and
steeply pitched hip roof helped shade
and ventilate during long Alabama
summers.**

**6.14   The pyramidal cottage is a vari-
ant of the square cottage. However, it
sports a pyramid-shaped roof, and
hence its name. Shown here from Columbiana is an unusual example with
an incised porch.**

tage, its prominent pyramid-shaped roof being the distinguishing feature (Figure 6.14). Generally, pyramidal cottages have been associated with the South, the tall steeply pitched pyramid roof serving to vent hot air up and out of living space below. This roof is seen as especially suited to long, hot summers (Lewis 1975, 20).

Square cottages are not widespread. They comprise less than 1 percent of the housing stock in our study towns, the highest concentration in Columbiana (Figure 6.15). None are to be found in Cazenovia, Millersburg, and Woodstock. The towns with a substantially above average number of dwellings display no pronounced regional clustering. They do share westward locations within their respective culture regions where utilitarian builder designs would be expected to overshadow traditional folk designs. These towns include Grundy Center in the Upper Middle West, Rockville and Petersburg in the Lower Middle west, Berryville and Columbiana in the Upper South, and Apalachicola and Port Gibson in the Lower South. A majority of the square cottages in each of these towns was built between 1865 and 1919. Their age as well as their occurrence among interior

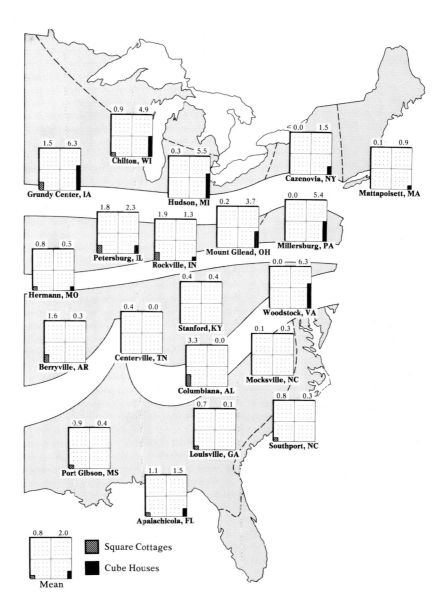

6.15   Square Cottages and Cube Houses (percent)

towns suggests that most were built on speculation for humble households. They were built at a time when stock materials first became abundantly available. Circumstances responsible for the selection of gable as opposed to hip roofs merit additional attention. The pyramidal cottage, for its part, was also infrequently encountered, making up only thirty-nine of the total houses. None were observed in New England or New England Extended, except for Grundy Center far to the west. All the remaining examples were scattered across the Lower Middle West and South with the highest frequencies in Rockville, Columbiana, Berryville, and Apalachicola. From our evidence the pyramidal cottage appears to be a builder form having a modest affinity with the South.

CUBE HOUSES

A more common dwelling type sporting a pyramidal or peaked-hip roof is the cube house. It is a two- or two-and-one-half-story box-like structure with a square or nearly square perimeter plan which contains three or four rooms on each floor (Figure 6.16). Attic dormers, at least on the front slope of the roof, are a common feature. As in square cottages, central hallways are frequently absent. Partial central hallways or entry ways are more common and incorporate the second floor stairs. This house has been associated with the central Corn Belt, specifically, and the Middle West and Northeast, generally (Kniffen 1965, 577; McAlester and McAlester 1984, 100; Noble 1984, 125). Chronologically, it has been assigned to the late nineteenth and early twentieth centuries (Kniffen 1965, 576–77; Rickert 1967, 229; McAlester

6.16 The cube house (sometimes called the four-square house) stands as a giant square box, usually capped by a hip roof as shown here in Woodstock.

and McAlester 1984, 100). Although many are catalog houses, having been sold prefabricated by Sears, Roebuck, and Company, and other firms in the twentieth century, they resemble earlier nineteenth-century square-shaped houses which were usually decorated in Italianate style.

Cube houses are encountered more frequently than square cottages in our study towns, comprising 2 percent of the total housing stock. Interestingly, they are most common in Grundy Center and Woodstock. There are no cube houses in either Columbiana or Centerville (Figure 6.15). Other towns which have higher than average concentrations include Hudson and Chilton in the Upper Middle West and Millersburg, Mount Gilead, and Petersburg in the Midland–Lower Middle West. This is a peculiar pattern where the highest frequencies occur in an area of Pennsylvania culture on the one hand and in the Yankee influenced Upper Middle West on the other. In every town the vast majority, if not all, of these structures were built between 1865 and 1919. This was a time when mass produced stock materials became abundant and widespread and utilitarian design triumphed in small towns, especially in the newer Middle West. In Millersburg and Woodstock these plain-looking structures may have appealed to the architecturally conservative spirit attributed to inhabitants of the Pennsylvania culture area (Lewis 1975, 12).

GABLE-FRONT DOUBLE-PILE COTTAGES

Here the gable faces forward and contains the front entrance, the axis of the dwelling being perpendicular to the street. These one- or one-and-a-half-story dwellings are two rooms wide and two or more rooms deep (Figure 6.17). Nearly all of the gable-front cottages inventoried were three bays wide, a bay being a space containing either a window or a door. Those of nineteenth-century vintage often have a side hallway so common in Greek Revival design while twentieth-century gable-front cottages have a centrally located door, but no hallway. Their floor plans resemble those of the bungalow group. However, they lack the depth of the gable-front southern bungalow to which they are similar in appearance.

Scholars have not made clear distinction between gable-front cottages and houses. Both forms are associated with nuclear New England and its extensions to the north and west (Finley and Scott 1940, 416; Hubka 1979, 219; McAlester and McAlester 1984, 78, 80, 90). Each is assumed to have become popular by the second quarter of the nineteenth century when Greek Revival design was so much in fashion (McAlester and McAlester 1984, 78, 90). Since little reference is made to gable-front cottages built in other areas during the early twentieth century, they were probably not recognized as a separate type because of their close resemblance to the southern bungalow.

6.17   **Three gable-front double-pile cottages stand in Hermann, possibly the work of a single builder-speculator of the 1920s.**

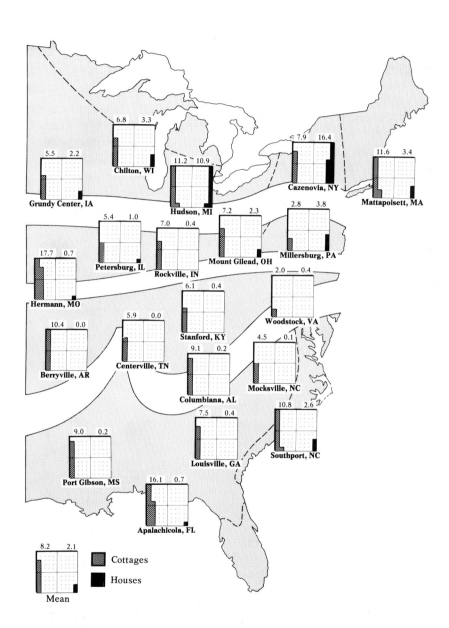

6.18 Gable-Front Double-Pile Cottages and Houses (percent)

Within the double-pile structure group the gable-front cottage is the second most frequently encountered dwelling. It comprises more than 8 percent of the housing stock in our study towns. It reaches its highest frequency in Hermann, and is least common in Woodstock (Figure 6.18). Towns other than Hermann with higher than average concentrations are Mattapoisett and Hudson in the North, and Columbiana, Berryville, Southport, Apalachicola, and Port Gibson in the South.

Their occurrence today in our study towns suggests a Greek Revival inspiration in the North and a potential association with the southern bungalow at Hermann and in the South. At German-influenced Hermann, the popular gable-front cottages may reflect a simple adaptation: rotating a double-pile cottage to fit it to a narrow lot. At both Mattapoisett and Hudson a majority of these cottages were built between 1865 and 1919. However, a substantial number in each community survive from antebellum years and are clearly Greek Revival inspired. At Columbiana, Berryville, Southport, Apalachicola, and Port Gibson in the South, and also at Hermann in the Lower Middle West, large numbers of gable-front cottages survive from both the 1865–1919 and 1920–1945 building eras, especially from the bungalow period. Thus it is probable that many of these gable-front cottages originated as scaled-down imitations of similar looking but more spacious southern bungalows.

Gambrel-front double-pile cottages are a variation on the theme (Figure 6.19). Only forty-three of the total dwellings surveyed fall into this category. All are builder houses dating from the 1890s through the 1920s. Use of this variant roof-type is most common in Chilton, Hermann, Millersburg, and Mocksville. There is no apparent regional pattern, the form resulting from local builder preferences and client tastes. Gambrel roofs are clearly pattern-book or catalog inspired.

6.19 Gambrel-front double-pile cottages, like their gable-front cousins, were appropriate to narrow lots on traditional street grids. This example is from Chilton.

GABLE-FRONT DOUBLE-PILE HOUSES

In the gable-front double-pile house, the gable faces the street and the structure rises to a height of two- or two-and-one-half stories (Figure 6.20). It is also two rooms wide and two or more rooms deep. Those of nineteenth-century vintage usually feature a side hall serving a front door set to one side. Gable front houses built during the present century have irregular bungalow-like room arrangements. This type of floor plan allowed for greater latitude in front door placement. Scholars have associated these dwellings with New England, adjacent parts of the Northeast, and the Upper Middle West. Chronologically they have been placed in

the Greek Revival era of the early nineteenth century (Finley and Scott 1940, 416; Lewis 1975, 17; Hubka 1979, 219; McAlester and McAlester 1984, 78, 80, 90).

We encountered gable-front houses much less frequently than gable-front cottages; gable-front houses comprise little more than 2 percent of the dwellings of our study towns. They are most numerous in Cazenovia and are altogether absent in two southern towns, Centerville and Berryville (Figure 6.18). Towns other than Cazenovia with well above average numbers include

6.20 Gable-front double-pile houses lent themselves easily to classical revival decoration in the early nineteenth century. Later, other styles were applied. A trace of the Queen Anne can be seen on this house in Cazenovia. Once appropriate to Cazenovia's gentry, this form, diminished in size and reduced in ornamentation, filtered down to less affluent classes.

Mattapoisett, Hudson, and Chilton in the North, and Millersburg in Pennsylvania. In each of these towns the majority of gable-front houses were built between 1865 and 1919. In Cazenovia, Mattapoisett, and Hudson a substantial number also survive from the pre-1865 era. This distribution pattern supports previous contention that the gable-front house appeared early in New England and diffused into the adjacent Northeast inspired by Greek Revival fashion. By the early twentieth century the gable-front house was widely available as both a stock builder form and a prefabricated catalog house. It received a national acceptance unbound by regional heritage as a dwelling type suitable to narrow city lots.

Only four gambrel-front houses were counted. Tall two-story structures with gambrel roofs are rare given their awkward vertical configuration. Most so-called "Dutch colonial houses" with gambrel roofs are, in fact, one-and-one-half-story cottages with half stories configured under gambrel roofs.

SHOTGUN COTTAGES

Shotgun dwellings are included in this chapter as a matter of convenience. We do not mean to imply that shotguns are related genetically to other types of double-pile housing. Shotgun cottages are slender one-story dwellings with an orientation perpendicular to the street. They have a very narrow facade and are well suited to blue-collar neighborhoods where residential lots of modest width prevail (Figure 6.21). Other traits include a front gable or hip roof, and a ridge line leading away from the street. This long linear cottage is one room wide, but two or more rooms deep with each room connecting one to another. Internal hallways are absent although in deeper versions a middle room often has an exterior side door.

The shotgun cottage has been described as a southern dwelling form that is common along the waterways of the Lower Mississippi Valley, in Southeast Texas, and along the Gulf Coast. New Orleans has been singled out as the North American focus of development. This type of structure is closely associated with blacks (Kniffen 1936, 168; Finley and Scott 1940, 413, 417; Glassie 1968a, 218, 220; Vlach 1976, 49, 69). Shotgun cottages appeared in New Orleans during the first quarter of the nineteenth century and may be Haitian or even west African in origin. They came to dominate modest neighborhoods in southern towns between 1880 and 1930 (McAlester and McAlester 1984, 90).

As expected, shotgun cottages are rare in most of our study towns. Although they comprise less than 1 percent of all dwellings, their association with southern towns is pronounced (Figure 6.22). None are found in the northern-most places (excepting one counted in Grundy Center). Nor are there any in Petersburg in the Lower Middle West, or even in Centerville and Mocksville in the Upper South. Southern towns with higher than average numbers include Port Gibson, Apalachicola, Louisville, and Stanford. The extraordinary concentrations in Apalachicola and Port Gibson reinforce previous assertions that the form is primarily a Lower Mississippi Valley and Gulf Coast type, although, obviously, it has diffused beyond. The vast majority of shotgun cottages were built between 1865 and 1919, with most constructed in the 1880s. A regional railroad network was evolving in the South during this period.

6.21 Shotgun cottages are associated traditionally with blacks in the South. Here a black quarter, with structures dating back to the past century, persists close to Port Gibson's courthouse.

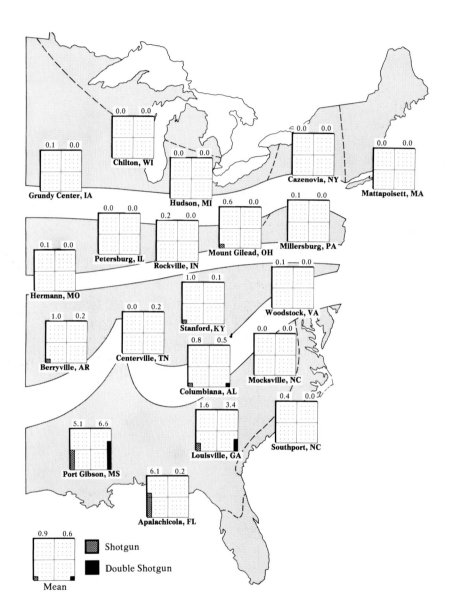

6.22 Shotgun and Double Shotgun Cottages (percent)

This dwelling type consists of two shotgun floor plans placed side by side beneath a single front gable or hip roof (Figure 6.23). The result is a structure with two front doors, a two room width, and a depth of two to three rooms. In cities such as New Orleans the double shotgun cottage frequently functions as a duplex providing separate shelter for two households. In small towns double shotguns usually serve single households. They represent for poorer families a substantial upgrading of available floor plan area and of apparent social status.

The double shotgun cottage has been ignored by scholars, the form described only as common in New Orleans (Lewis 1976, 59–60). Its distribution among the study towns is more limited than the shotgun cottage itself. It is absent in thirteen communities, primarily in the North (Figure 6.22). It is most common in Port Gibson, but also occurs in above average numbers in Louisville. Port Gibson's location suggests an upriver diffusion from New Orleans. So also might the large concentration of double shotguns in the port city of Augusta explain their unusual numbers in nearby Louisville. Their resemblance to southern bungalows and gable-front cottages suggests a mutual reinforc-

6.23   Double shotgun cottages with their two front doors have traditionally housed less affluent families in Louisville, both black and white.

ing, each form encouraging the popularity of the others. Indeed, southern bungalows and gable-front cottages may have evolved from double shotguns in some places. While a majority of the double shotguns in Port Gibson and Louisville were built before 1920 a substantial number in both communities date from the interwar years. It was before and after 1920 that large numbers of gable-front cottages were also built in these towns. The double shotgun has enjoyed a persisting social acceptance among blue-collar families.

No camelback houses, a shotgun variant common to New Orleans and the city of Louisville, Kentucky, were recorded for any of the study towns. The camelback has a two-story unit attached to the back of the shotgun's one-story room array. The form evidently derives from taxing policy whereby houses were assessed according to height along front lot lines. Tax savings came from consigning any two-story enlargements to the rear. It is an urban form not expected in small towns.

TWO-THIRDS DOUBLE-PILE HOUSES

Two-thirds double-pile houses are two- or two-and-one-half-stories high and generally have gable roofs. They are two rooms deep, but have sufficient width for only one room and a side hallway containing a staircase (Figure 6.24). The term "half-house" is sometimes used. Houses of this sort, built for the middle class, are well suited to narrow city lots, but were also erected in small towns and on farms where they were sometimes enlarged by means of lateral extensions.

Two-thirds double-pile houses are described as row-type dwellings common to cities and the crowded centers of towns in the Eastern United States. Refer-

6.24 In nineteenth-century Cazenovia, two-thirds double-pile houses were closely related in floor plan to gable-front houses. The gable-front roof was dropped in favor of a flat hip, and Italianate decoration substituted for Greek Revival.

ences have also been made to freestanding rural versions of this form of dwelling (Hamlin 1944, 125; Glassie 1968a, 54; Lewis 1975, 7; Pillsbury 1977, 25). It has been asserted that this house was built less frequently in rural areas after the middle of the nineteenth century, but that it continued to be built in urban settings as row houses until the end of the Victorian era (Pillsbury 1977, 26).

Two-thirds double-pile houses account for less than 1 percent of the dwelling structures in our study towns. They are most numerous in Cazenovia. There are none in four southern study towns: Columbiana, Centerville, Berryville, and Louisville (Figure 6.25). Outside of Cazenovia, above average frequencies occur in Hudson, Millersburg, Mount Gilead, and Woodstock. Their close association with the communities in the extended Pennsylvania culture area was expected. Closely spaced dwellings are, according to Wilbur Zelinsky, a distinguishing characteristic or signature of Southeast Pennsylvania towns (Zelinsky 1977, 131). The side hallway plan may explain the popularity of the two-thirds double-pile house in Cazenovia. This type of floor plan also typified the gable-front dwellings which were and are very popular there. In this Upstate New York community a majority of the gable-front and two-thirds double-pile houses were built between 1865 and 1919 although substantial numbers of each also predate the Civil War. This supports the probability of Greek Revival influence even on side hall dwellings without front gable roofs. Two-thirds double-pile houses built after the Civil War for the affluent middle class often carried Italianate ornamentation.

The two-thirds double-pile cottage is a related dwelling organized around the same floor plan, but with only one- or one-and-one-half stories. Only thirty were inventoried, being most numerous in Woodstock, Hermann, Mattapoisett, and Cazenovia. It appears to be a late eighteenth century form which fell out of popularity by the mid nineteenth century in most urban places. Unlike its larger two-story relative, it did not re-emerge as a revival form in the twentieth century.

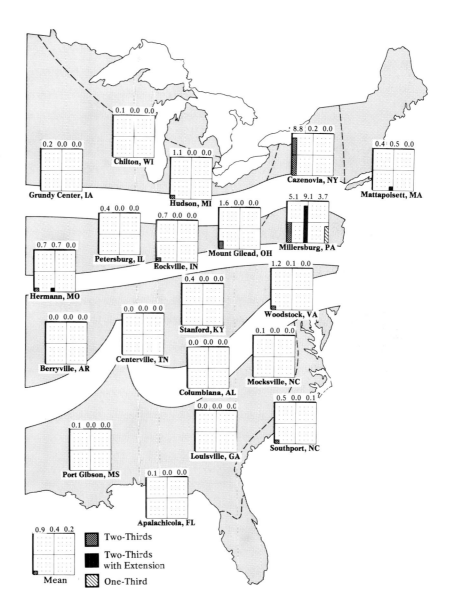

6.25   Two-Thirds Double-Pile, Two-Thirds Double-Pile with Rear Extension, and One-Third Double-Pile Houses (percent)

TWO-THIRDS DOUBLE-PILE HOUSES WITH REAR EXTENSION

When a two-thirds double-pile house occupied a narrow city lot, particularly as a unit of a contiguous row, it could most easily be enlarged by rearward extension (Figure 6.26). These rear extensions were usually narrower than the main part of the house, and positioned to one side of the lot rather than down its center. Such ells were either of one or two stories. The two-thirds double-pile house with rear extension is almost ignored in the literature, being described primarily as a form built in Colonial Philadelphia. Labelled a "town house," its origin was attributed to London (Murtaugh 1957, 10–11; Brunskill 1971, 112–13).

In our survey, the two-thirds double-pile house with rear extension is less common and has had a more restricted range than the unextended variety. It contributes less than 1 percent of the total housing stock in our study towns and is found in but five communities (Figure 6.25). It is unusually common in Millersburg as a detached house rather than a row house. Town houses of this sort, along with the ordinary two-thirds double-pile variety, account for nearly one in six dwellings in Millersburg. In other towns, the numbers of rearward-extended two-thirds double-pile houses pale in comparison. Such places include Mattapoisett and Hermann. The majority of these structures in each community predate 1865, although in Millersburg they continued to be built until the beginning of the twentieth century. Being substantially constructed, large, and close to the town center they persist primarily as rental housing today.

6.26 A comfortable middle class dwelling with Italianate trim, this two-thirds double-pile house with rear extension sits flush with the sidewalk of Millersburg's Pine Street.

cent of the single-family dwellings in Millersburg. Here, indeed, is the typical Pennsylvania town so far as central area character is concerned (Zelinsky 1977, 131).

Closely related is the one-third double-pile cottage. Only fifteen were encountered across the various towns, seven of those in Mattapoisett. It is a relic early nineteenth-century form which would be expected in older eastern seaport towns, although it is missing from both Southport and Apalachicola.

Our findings regarding double-pile dwellings generally support previous assertion. We encountered older Cape Cod and New England classic cottages and double-pile and gable-front houses primarily in the Northeast as expected. Shotgun cottages are most numerous in the Lower South as anticipated. Two-thirds double-pile houses with rear extensions occur primarily in the historic core of Millersburg where there are narrow residential lots similar to those in older parts of Philadelphia and other cities where row houses prevail. Cube houses, however, are not concentrated in the Corn

ONE-THIRD DOUBLE-PILE HOUSES AND COTTAGES

The one-third double-pile house is a two-story, two-room deep structure pared down to an even narrower width than the two-thirds double-pile variety (Figure 6.27). With a rear extension it has been called a "city house" and tended originally to house lower middle-class and lower class families. It lacks an internal hallway although in some Philadelphia examples the front room is protected from the street by a shallow hall leading directly to a

6.27   A working class home without ornamentation, this one-third double-pile house also sits on Millersburg's North Street.

larger back room (Murtaugh 1957, 10). In our twenty towns, the one-third double-pile house is rare outside of Millersburg (Figure 6.25). It comprises well below 1 percent of the housing stock in our study towns. In Millersburg the majority of these structures were built before 1865 as were most of the two-thirds double-pile houses. In combination, the various types of two-thirds and one-third double-pile houses account for almost 18 per-

Belt or even in the Middle West as expected. High frequencies characterize the Pennsylvania and Pennsylvania-influenced towns as well. We expected a large number of double shotgun cottages in Port Gibson given the popularity of this dwelling type in nearby New Orleans. A second notable cluster of double shotguns in Louisville, rather than in Apalachicola on the Gulf Coast, must be attributed to builder proclivities, the form varying substantially from place to place as a southern type. The popularity of the two-thirds double-pile house in Millersburg reflected high density construction on narrow lots as typical of Pennsylvania towns. Its even higher rate of frequency in Cazenovia, was not anticipated and may be attributed to a Greek Revival influence involving similar gable-front houses.

Three dwelling types displayed traits and regional associations that have not been described previously. The double-pile cottage had widespread acceptance as a building industry form. It is even common in the South where it is generally covered by a gable roof. Gable-front cottages that resemble southern bungalows are also widespread in our southern towns. Cottages with square plans, on the other hand, have been characterized as a southern house type, especially those with pyramidal roofs. Their regional affiliation is not so much with the South, however, as with the western or the interior study towns of North and South. Here we have a clear example of a plan book type of dwelling gaining strength away from the older seaboard towns. The hypothesized association of folk forms, such as the Cape Cod cottage, New England classic cottage, and double-pile house, with older towns located farther east was confirmed.

CHAPTER VII IRREGULARLY MASSED DWELLINGS

The great charm in

the forms of natural

landscape lies in its

well-balanced

irregularity.

CALVERT VAUX

As a category, irregular massing may seem at first thought little more than a miscellany into which a diversity of structure types not classifiable elsewhere might be conveniently lumped. However, irregularly massed structures do carry common, easily recognizable characteristics which provide more than adequate rationale for evaluating them as a family of structure types. As architectural historian Wilbur Peat expresses it, all of these structures are comprised of "irregular masses" and "asymmetrical planning." They involve "combining masses or blocks of different sizes in an informal way" (Peat 1962, 121). In the discussion which follows, as in preceding chapters, we seek to define this class of dwellings, briefly describe the evolution of the principal types as described in the literature, and outline their geographical distribution in the Eastern United States as reflected in our twenty study towns.

Irregular Massing

Most scholars have seen irregular massing only as a characteristic of such architectural styles as Gothic Revival, Italianate, and Queen Anne. They have treated irregular massing as eclectic or as following few established patterns of form. In actuality, beneath the profuse ornamentation of late nineteenth-century dwellings, standardization was a reality, especially in form. As social historian Gwendolyn Wright establishes, even the builders knew this, despite their appeal for individualized architecture. "Simple economics dictated building from similar floor plans, so that carpenters and masons would be familiar with the arrangement and so that materials could be ordered with greater accuracy" (Wright 1980, 26). In addition, lot sizes in most places, standard rectangular plats in a gridiron of streets, invited standardized shapes and sizes in dwellings. Equally important, Wright continues, was the need to have a clear code of meaning. The Victorian middle-class home had to be based upon a readily understood symbolic language which included "a precise vocabulary of forms" so that it could be easily read and understood as a social statement (Wright 1980, 26).

Irregular massing symbolized modernity, a breaking away from the formal symmetry of traditional dwelling design. The irregular shape of each dwelling also was intended as a sign of natural complexity. Andrew Jackson Downing first introduced simple, L-shaped forms in his promotion of Gothic Revival cottages or villas (Downing 1842). Downing advocated the picturesque which he found "always to depend upon the opposite conditions of matter: irregularity, and a partial want of proportion and symmetry" (Downing 1850, 29). Calvert Vaux, Downing's partner and business successor, promoted the picturesque by attacking frontally the "meagre, monotonous, unartistic buildings" of the past, especially those associated with the Greek Revival style. "Square boxes, small and large," Vaux wrote, "are springing up in every direction, constructed without any attempt at proportion, or the slightest apparent desire to make them agreeable objects in the landscape." Each of these "bare, bald, white cubes," he wrote, tells a "monotonous story" (Vaux 1864, 47–48).

Irregularity of shape connotated nature. Builder-architect George Garnsey advised readers in the *National Builder* (one of the myriad of builder magazines to appear after Congress lowered postal rates in 1879) to be imaginative by avoiding the "dry-goods box" look of a plain square house. "Don't be afraid to introduce breaks, jogs and angles, the more the better," he wrote, for "an irregular plan breaks the skyline at the roof and lends picturesque beauty to exterior corners." Such a natural house appeared to grow out of the earth's irregularities, he added (Garnsey 1885, 4). The "natural house," so constructed, opened wide to the out-of-doors. According to Gwendolyn Wright, designs emphasized openness between interior and exterior, between the built environment and the natural. "Houses usually had large bay windows, with wide panes of glass to let in sunlight and fresh air, while offering . . . a pleasant view" (Wright 1980, 28). A broad rambling porch offered further mingling between inside and out for summer living.

Rooms, at least at ground level, were also open to one another with circulation facilitated by broad arches, sliding doors, and connecting hallways. Dwellings were organized into three distinct kinds of spaces: 1) formal spaces for presenting the home ideal to guests and to the family (the formal parlor and dining room for example), 2) utility spaces for domestic service (the kitchen), and 3) private spaces (bed chambers) (Wright 1980, 34). It was the formal space that seemed to flow together and then relate directly to the out-of-doors. Space was also used to assign people social roles in keeping with the increased affluence and leisure time available. As Wright notes, even the modest middle-class residence segregated the various groups that used the house—visitors and residents, women and men, adults and children, family and servants—in distinct rooms. "Each had its particular furnishings, materials, even shapes of rooms" (Wright 1980, 34). Irregular massing lent itself to the defining of distinctive social spaces within the Victorian home.

Irregularity crept into cottage and house design by stages. Simple L-shaped dwellings, rectangular blocks with a projection toward the street, dominated in the Gothic Revival era (Figure 7.1). Virginia and Lee McAlester speculate that approximately one-third of all Gothic Revival houses displayed such a "compound" plan (McAlester and McAlester 1984, 197). With Italianate styling there evolved, in addition, cruciform or crossplan designs (Figure 7.2). With Queen Anne ornamentation truly compound configurations evolved which we label composite cottages and houses (Figure 7.3). Wilbur Peat described the Queen Anne as follows: "Projecting sections give exteriors a complex and plastic character . . . a com-

7.1   Irregular massing rendered
dwellings with more visual character
than the simple rectangular and square
boxes previously popular. This L-
shaped cottage is located close to Stanford's downtown.

7.2   Although the combining of geometries was intended to suggest innovation through informality, most
irregularly massed dwellings, in fact,
were of one or two standardized arrangements: L-shaped and crossplan.
An example of the latter is pictured
here in Petersburg.

7.3   The wealthy could afford truly
eclectic dwellings. As with this house
in Mount Gilead, shallow wings were
added, the whole adorned with towers
or turrets and other decorative devices.

plexity which is heightened, as seen from the outside, by the variety of openings and the diversity of wall treatments. Added to this is the irregular contour of the roof with its many gables, dormers, and prominent chimneys" (Peat 1962, 150). Key to the Queen Anne, according to architectural historian Sadayoshi Omoto, was "irregularity both in plan and in silhouette" (Omoto 1964, 31).

So apparent are the associations between various styles and various irregularly massed forms that it is logical that scholars in the past saw the one as necessarily a function of the other. Nevertheless, it is important to emphasize the separation of the two. Even Calvert Vaux, perhaps the nineteenth century's leading proponent of the picturesque, wrote of the necessity "to make the ornament secondary to the construction, and not the construction secondary to the ornament" (Steese 1947, 11). Popular styles gave impetus to the construction of irregularly massed forms, but the forms themselves had an independent raison d'être rooted in certain technological innovations. It is important to realize that the vast majority of irregularly massed houses built were never ornamented in any style.

Irregular massing (and the social symbolisms of modernism, naturalness, and family organization it was meant to convey) rode the crests of two important enabling technologies. First, cast iron stoves, new heating devices vented with metal stovepipes, permitted the wider use of longer, less regular floor plans (McAlester and McAlester 1984, 28). Central heating reduced further the need to arrange rooms symmetrically relative to chimney columns. It was no longer necessary to radiate warmth outward from a central chimney core, or inward from lateral chimney columns.

Balloon framing was the other technological breakthrough. First developed in Chicago in the 1830s, balloon framing facilitated the massing of different shapes and forms to produce complex silhouettes (Sprague 1981, 311). As Virginia and Lee McAlester note, masonry is especially susceptible to erosion and failure at corner junctions and usually requires carefully shaped stones or strengthened brick-bonding to make walls secure. Also, heavy timbers of post-and-girt corners require the special treatment of complex hand-hewn corner joints and braces to provide rigidity. Thus in traditional construction, unnecessary outside corners were generally avoided and simple, geometrical dwelling forms preferred. By contrast, secure corners in balloon framing were readily constructed of light boards and wire nails. Balloon framing thus helped to free domestic architecture from its "plane-walled patterns" (McAlester and McAlester 1984, 30).

Geographical Distribution

Irregularly massed dwellings reveal clear regional differentiation. Before turning to individual structure types, let us examine the general geographical patterns which irregular massing displays in our study towns across the Eastern United States. We hypothesized that irregular massing would be widespread in towns which experienced rapid economic growth in the decades after the Civil War. Thus we expected the greatest concentration of houses in the Middle West, especially in the Upper Middle West. The South, we anticipated, would be noticeably lacking in irregularly massed structures given the general economic stagnation of the region's post-war "Reconstruction."

These expectations appear to be substantiated, but not without some surprising exceptions (Figure 7.4). The Middle West is, indeed, the predominant area for irregularly massed dwellings although both the Upper and Lower Middle West appear equally important. Unexpectedly, Stanford aligns with the Middle West while the remainder of the South, along with Hermann, displays a general lack of irregularly massed cottages and houses. Cazenovia is clearly linked with the Middle West through one distinctive type of structure, the upright and wing house. The vast majority of the irregularly

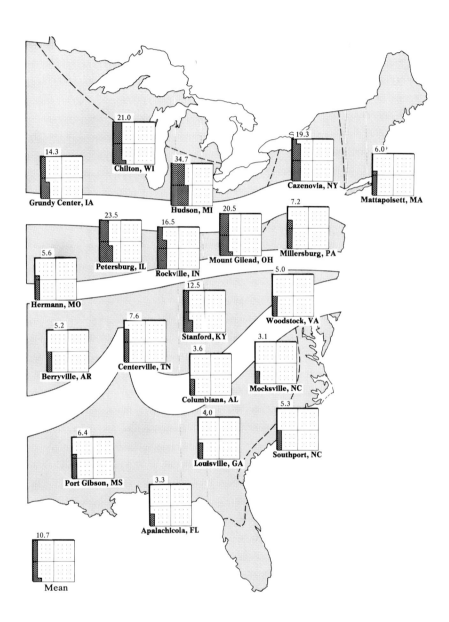

7.4   **Irregularly Massed Dwellings (percent)**

massed houses dates from the nineteenth and early twentieth centuries. However, it is important to note that irregularly massed dwellings in some towns, notably those of the Middle West, survive in remarkable numbers. In Hudson with its depressed economy in recent decades, irregularly massed cottages and houses still account for over one-third of the total dwellings.

THE UPRIGHT AND WING

The upright and wing house was the first of the irregularly massed forms to evolve. Its place of origin was Upstate New York and from there it was spread westward across the Upper Middle West (Lewis 1975, 14). The upright and wing derives from the combining of traditional double-pile forms: the New England Classic Cottage or double-pile cottage and either the two-story gable-front house or the one-and-a-half-story gable-front cottage. Architectural historians see it as a vernacular simplification of the formal Greek Revival "Temple and Wing House" (Foley 1980, 138; McAlester and McAlester 1984, 92). Geographer Peirce Lewis writes: "If a Connecticut Yankee moved to New York and built a traditional New England one-and-a-half . . . and then grew affluent selling wheat . . . during the early Greek Revival, what would be more reasonable than to attach a

7.5 The upright and wing originated as a middle class and gentry form in Upstate New York after 1800. A logical purveyor of Greek Revival decoration, the form filtered to lower classes with little or no ornamentation. On this example from Cazenovia, the "wing" strikes the "upright" under its eave.

Greek temple to one's original one-and-a-half naturally placing it to the front of and higher than the older, *déclassé* one-and-one-half" (Lewis 1975, 14). A Michigan resident writing to the *Genesee Farmer* in 1857 noted: "The houses recently built in this vicinity [Oakland County], though individually dissimilar have generally a strong family resemblance, viz: Main building, gable end to the road, story and a half, about 18 x 26 feet, nice rooms, bedroom stairway with cellar stairs underneath, about two rooms above, cellar whole size. . . . Front door ornamental,

seldom opened except on wedding and funeral occasions. Wing, one story, containing living room, bedroom, frequently a bed recess, pantry and woodroom" (Cooley 1857, 115).

Robert Bastian has recognized two chronologically distinctive varieties of the upright and wing in Northern Indiana (Bastian 1977, 116). The oldest version has small-paned (six over six) windows, the ridge of the wing's roof extending outward from beneath the eave of the upright's roof (Figure 7.5). The later variety has taller windows with larger panes (four over four), the roof ridge of the wing extending from an intermediate position on the roof slope of the upright (Figure 7.6). In both versions the front door may be located either in the upright or in the wing. When the front door is in the wing, the upright usually does not have a door. However, when the front door is in the upright a subsidiary entrance is usually found in the wing as well.

Many upright and wing dwellings were built in stages. As Lewis suggests, the upright section is usually the addition. Even in dwellings where both the upright and the wing were built at the same time, both parts retain their own identities as distinct units. The floor plans of each section are quite separate, rooms belonging either to one or the other section but not to both. Thus both sections can be pulled apart and each continues to function as a separate entity.

Given its origin, we hypothesized that the upright and wing would be important in our Upstate New York town and in the towns of the Upper Middle West. The upright and wing should neatly outline "New England Extended." In addition, there should be some evidence of the upright and wing in New England, the result of a secondary eastward cultural diffusion in the nineteenth century linked to the popularity of Greek Revival styling. The upright and wing would be totally absent, we predicted, from the South.

Distribution of the upright and wing across the twenty study towns confirms our expectations (Figure 7.7). It is a common type of dwelling in Cazenovia, Hudson, and Chilton. However, we did not expect that this house type would occur with highest frequency in Hudson. The fact that it is much less common in Cazenovia might be explained by the prevalence of the closely related gable-front house in the

7.6 On this upright and wing house in Hudson, the "wing" strikes the "upright" at midroof.

New York town. We are surprised that the upright and wing is so rare in Mattapoisett. Perhaps, the eastward spread of the upright and wing was less substantial than previously thought, it being less a simplification of a Greek Revival high style form and more a vernacular form of the frontier with its own integrity and history. Surprisingly, the upright and wing falls off so abruptly in Grundy Center. Yankee influence was clearly diluted in this westernmost town of the Upper Middle West.

The upright and wing is barely represented in the Lower Middle West and not represented at all in our Pennsylvania town of Millersburg nor in many towns of the South. Its occurrence in a few southern towns represents a very recent arrival. It is not the classical early nineteenth century house, as in New York and the Upper Middle West, but either a much simplified "residual" late nineteenth-century form or a very recent "revival" form of the twentieth century. "Revival" structures have been built at Stanford, Centerville, and Port Gibson as well as at Rockville in the past decade. Thus the upright and wing remains a clear regional indicator, although the form, once restricted primarily to "New England Extended," has recently reappeared as part of a "revival" design vocabulary with potential national implications.

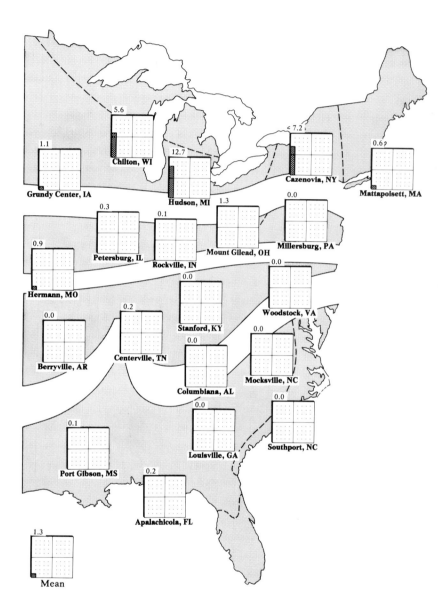

7.7   **Upright and Wing Houses (percent)**

L-SHAPED COTTAGES AND HOUSES

L-shaped dwellings bear a close resemblance to the upright and wing in that one part of the building thrusts forward, either on the left or on the right of the front facade. However, basic differences lie in both the roof and floorplan. In L-shaped cottages and houses a single multiple-gable roof covers the entire dwelling, although multiple-hip roofs are not uncommon (Figures 7.8 and 7.9). Thus, unlike the upright and wing, there are not the multiple roof levels. More importantly, in floor plan L-shaped dwellings comprise a single integrated whole. To separate the two sections of an L-shaped cottage or house is to pull rooms apart, severely disrupting interior space. The residual halves are not self-standing.

L-shaped cottages and houses are clearly creatures of the age of balloon frame construction and improved stoves. As building industry dwellings promoted in the plan books of the middle and late nineteenth century and the house catalogs of the early twentieth century, they are not "folk" derived. Consequently, cultural geographers and folklorists have paid little attention to these very common dwelling forms. Geographers Robert Finley and Elizabeth Scott did note the L-shaped cottage as more impor-

7.8   The L-shaped cottage viewed from above strikes either an "L" or a "T" outline, the "T" lying on its side. This Petersburg example built in the 1890s has a rear addition.

7.9   L-shaped houses served both middle- and lower-class families, varying in size accordingly. This middle-class Rockville home dates from the 1880s.

tant in the Lower Middle West and the South when they undertook their north/south traverse from Wisconsin to Texas in 1939. The L-house, on the other hand, they found more important in the Upper Middle West (Finley and Scott 1940, 415–16). It has been suggested that the L-shaped house, given its close resemblance to the upright and wing, has a "New England Extended" connotation. Indeed, Howard Marshall notes that in the Little Dixie region of Central Missouri the L-shaped house is called the "Yankee house" (Marshall 1981, 35).

We hypothesized that L-shaped cottages and houses would have a close association with Yankee culture. We also expected that they would be more numerous in the expansive towns of the immediate post–Civil War era, especially those of the Middle West. Largely due to the region's state of economic depression following the Civil War, we did not expect L-shaped dwellings to be important in the South. Assuming that the upright and wing as a folk form might have encouraged construction of the L-shaped house as a builder form, we expected to see this two-story version of the L-shaped plan strong in the western Middle West in approximate reverse proportion to the number of upright and wings extant there.

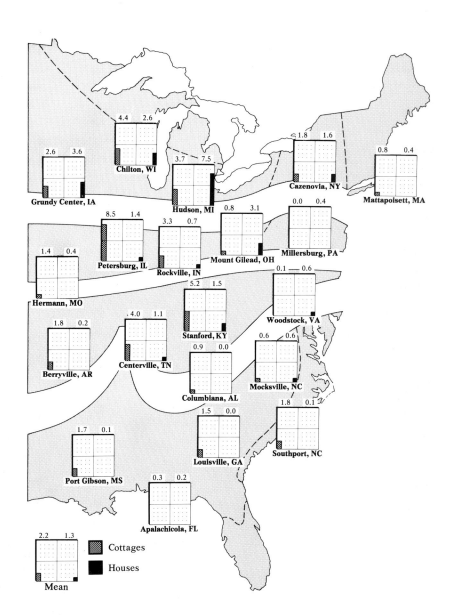

7.10   L-Shaped Cottages and Houses (percent)

Important departures from these expectations are evident (Figure 7.10). Indeed, the L-shaped house is most important in the towns of "New England Extended" (Hudson, Chilton, and Grundy Center) although not in the numbers anticipated. Only in Hudson is there clear association with the upright and wing. This suggests, at least for selected towns, that traditional folk forms may have influenced the local adoption of related builder forms. Too few L-shaped houses are found in Chilton and Grundy Center to support the idea that this type of dwelling is a successor to the upright and wing as a symbol of Yankee culture in the interior.

The geographical distribution of the L-shaped cottage across the twenty study towns is not easily interpreted. Not only is it important in the towns of the Middle West (especially Petersburg), but so also is it significant in the towns of the Upper South (especially Stanford and Centerville). The distribution of L-shaped cottages appears to re-flect the idiosyncracies of individual town growth in the late nineteenth century. Those towns that grew vigorously in the 1880s and 1890s as a result of an improved railroad network required substantial numbers of working class dwellings. In addition, the popularity of the L-shaped cottage from town to town certainly reflects the predilections of individual builders in the past who widely replicated selected plan types in their communities, the L-shaped cottage being one of the more favored in this instance. Thus there is a strong regional clustering of L-shaped cottages from the towns of Wisconsin, Michigan, Illinois, and Indiana through those of Kentucky and Tennessee, a peculiar clustering not fully anticipated and not fully explained.

CROSSPLAN COTTAGES AND HOUSES

In a crossplan dwelling, the principal axis of the structure is perpendicular to the street with one or two wings forming a cross section midway back from the street (Figures 7.11 and 7.12). The positioning of the front door varies. In many crossplan dwellings it is located in one of the crossing arms and is approached along a side porch. In other dwellings it is located in the front facade. Although houses built in this form are numerous

7.11   Small crossplan cottages, like this example in Rockville, made excellent speculative housing for working-class families of the late nineteenth and early twentieth centuries.

7.12 Crossplan houses almost always housed middle-class or gentry families before World War I. This example is from Chilton.

in the plan books and house catalogs of the late nineteenth and early twentieth centuries, scholars have taken little note of them (Vaux 1864, 247; Chicago Millwork Supply Co. 1913, 32). Where crossplan dwellings have appeared in scholarly literature they have been combined with and thus confused with L-shaped plans (Noble 1984, 56). The crossplan arrangement reflects builder attempts to fit irregular massing (with all of its symbolic connotations) on the narrow urban lot typical of most towns and cities.

Since the crossplan cottages and crossplan houses are clearly builder forms, we did not anticipate that they would reflect the folk traditions of any culture region. Rather, we hypothesized that they would be found primarily in those towns which experienced growth in the 1880s and 1890s, and in the early decade of the twentieth century. The survey substantiates this hypothesis (Figure 7.13). Taken together both structure types outline a distinct region comprising the towns of the eastern Middle West, New York and Pennsylvania. Taken individually, however, the pattern is partially obscured. The crossplan cottage is important in Rockville and Chilton. The crossplan house, on the other hand, appears with some frequency in Hudson, Mount Gilead, Cazenovia, and Millersburg. Beyond Stanford neither form appears with any frequency in either the Upper South or the Lower South.

COMPOSITE COTTAGES AND HOUSES WITH IRREGULAR MASSING

Composite cottages and houses with irregular massing display substantial diversity as to floor plan although the general visual effect of extreme asymmetry and informality strikes most eyes with a general consistency dwelling to dwelling (Figures 7.14 and 7.15). So varied are they that the mind easily generalizes the intended variety as a single category of structural meaning. In many of these cottages and houses the Queen Anne impulse, as well as other eclectic styles of the 1880s and 1890s, play out their artful extravagance. However, the vast majority of these dwellings were not ornamented, and most of those once ornamented are no longer so.

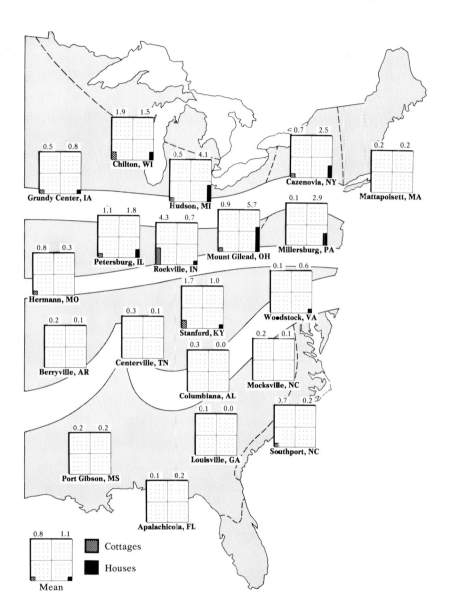

7.13   Crossplan Cottages and Houses (percent)

7.14   **The composite cottage with irregular massing is very eclectic and less a precise form repeated consistently by builders than a convenient descriptive category for scholars. As such, it is closely associated with Queen Anne ornamentation, although most examples visible today, as here at Rockville, have been stripped of decoration.**

7.15   **The composite house with irregular massing, as this one at Grundy Center, is reminiscent of a small town "gilded age" in the Middle West if not elsewhere in the United States. Although builders embraced eclecticism by attempting to make every house unique, in actuality they produced structures very much alike for their excesses.**

Geographical distribution of the composite cottage and the composite house was expected to follow closely that of the crossplan forms, i.e., to be prevalent in the growth towns of the late nineteenth and early twentieth centuries. The cottage was expected to be the more widely distributed and to be prominent in selected southern as well as northern towns. A distinctive pyramidal-roofed composite cottage has been documented for the South (Figure 7.16). Lewis describes it as a "veritable haystack of interlocking pyramids, facets, dormers" (Lewis 1975, 20). The composite house was expected to be less widely distributed and to be confined largely to the Northeast and Middle West given the greater af-

fluence of those areas relative to the Upper and Lower South during the period of irregular massing's popularity in the 1880s and 1890s.

The composite cottage with irregular massing appears with some frequency in the towns of the Lower Middle West: Mount Gilead, Rockville, and Petersburg (Figure 7.17). The pyramidal roof version of the composite cottage is important in Port Gibson, but not elsewhere in the South much to our surprise. The composite cottage with irregular massing is noticeably absent in northeastern towns, yet it occurs with slightly higher than average frequencies as expected in most Upper South towns. Builder predilection from town to town undoubtedly accounted for its popularity in only selected places. The larger size of the composite cottage, when compared to other cottage types, made it more desirable to the middle class, especially when decorated stylishly.

7.16 The steeply pitched pyramidal roof, or the hip which approximates a pyramid, has been closely associated with the South. Pictured is a composite cottage with irregular massing and pyramidal roof in Port Gibson.

The composite house with irregular massing, on the other hand, displays the anticipated geographical pattern. With the exception of Mattapoisett, it is significant in the Northeastern and Middle Western towns accounting for more than 5 percent of the total housing at both Mount Gilead and Petersburg. Whereas the composite house is weak in Rockville the composite cottage, discussed above, seems to replace it. With the exception of Woodstock the composite house with irregular massing, as expected, is not significant across the South, although it is found in every town in at least token numbers. The composite house with its spacious two-story plan was attractive to both middle-class and upper-middle-class buyers. It could be plainly configured for the unpretentious or extravagantly decorated for the status conscious.

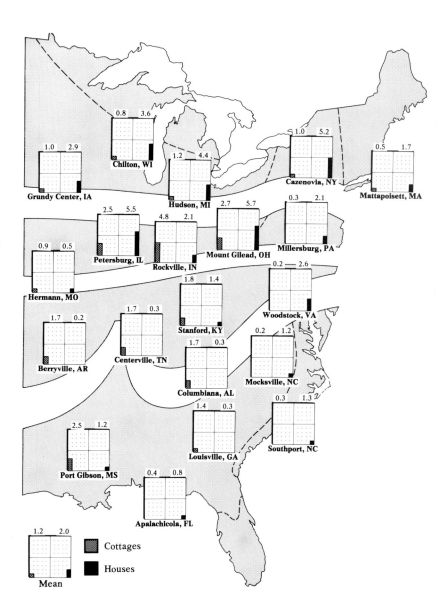

7.17 Composite Cottages and Houses with Irregular Massing (percent)

Although irregularly massed dwellings accounted for only 1,847 or nearly 11 percent of the 17,261 houses surveyed, in certain towns, such as Hudson, Petersburg, Chilton, and Mount Gilead, they comprise over 20 percent of the existing houses (Figure 7.4). In most places only two specific structure types in combination account for the vast majority of irregularly massed dwellings. At Cazenovia it is the upright and wing and composite house, and not the upright and wing and L-shaped house as hypothesized. At Hudson on the other hand, the upright and wing and the L-shaped house do combine as expected. At Mount Gilead the L-shaped cottage and composite house dominate whereas at Petersburg it is the L-shaped house and composite house.

Considering irregularly massed dwellings as a set, the hypothesis that folk forms tend to invite similarly structured builder forms cannot be supported. It is also apparent that the most similar dwellings do not combine town to town. In other words, structure types do not tend to group place to place on the basis of visual similarity. The hypothesis that irregularly massed dwellings, products of the post–Civil War and pre–World War I building era, characterize towns in the more expansive growth areas during that era is sus-

tained. Indeed, the towns of the Northeast, the Upper Middle West, and the Lower Middle West carry a heavy imprint of irregularly massed forms surviving from this building era.

A stamp of the picturesque has been left on the Middle Western towns: an impress which even subsequent building eras have little obscured, at least in traditional town centers. Thus the image of the Middle Western small town, especially in its older core, remains one of white clapboarded or red brick cottages and houses fancifully arranged in the eclecticism of a "gilded age." Despite the builders of the period having promoted "unique" expression in dwelling construction, these cottages and houses of the picturesque era are not excessively diverse. To the contrary, most irregularly massed dwellings can be identified as belonging to one of seven structure categories. The origin of these structural types in the builder's repertoire, and the regional patterns formed by surviving examples, begs additional investigation.

CHAPTER VIII   BUNGALOWS

Our little love nest

Beside a stream

Where red, red roses grow

Our bungalow of dreams.

BIX BEIDERBECKE

The term "bungalow" derives from the eighteenth-century British presence in India, particularly in that area which is now Bangladesh. It first referred to a kind of temporary shelter along India's highways, low-roofed cottages built of unbaked brick and covered with a tile or thatch roof surrounded by a wide porch or verandah (Lancaster 1958, 239; Mattson 1981, 76; King 1984, 14). As an indigenous Asian mode of shelter adapted for European living, it was clearly a product of cultures in contact. Various spellings such as "bungalo," "bungelow," and "bangalloa," gave way to "bungalow" in the nineteenth century when the term came to be indiscriminately applied to any kind of small European house in India (King 1984, 37). Carried to England, the word was first used to describe small resort cottages and, thereby, became a symbol of "Bohemian" or unconventional lifestyles.

American Bungalows

The term was first affixed in the United States to a Massachusetts "stick-style" beachfront house designed by architect William G. Preston and publicized by him in the *American Architect and Building News* in 1880 (Lancaster 1958, 239). Historian Anthony King speculates that the word was borrowed from English architects through the pages of such English publications as the *Building News* and *The Studio* (King 1984, 130). As in England, the bungalow idea was first attached to vacation dwellings at the beach, and also at the mountains. Soon it was linked to suburban houses where builders sought to promote images of recreation and health. As Lancaster points out, the word presented a "euphony and vagueness of meaning, which made application elastic" (Lancaster 1958, 239).

Eventually, the term "bungalow" replaced the word "cottage," to mean simply a small, single-story (or at most story-and-a-half) dwelling. Bungalows did not have the demeaning class connotation attached to cottages, especially in England. But, between approximately 1905 and 1925, the term also had explicit structural and stylistic implication in the United States. Bungalows were distinctive dwellings significantly different from other kinds of residences. They were low-slung structures, although often built on high basements, with wide projecting eaves, exposed brackets and other supports, a large front porch, a prominent chimney, and many windows (Mattson 1981, 77). They featured large simple roofs which seemed to sweep out beyond the walls in an attempt to hug the ground. Porch and house under one roof emphasized the broad, low silhouette characteristics of the building (Dole 1974, 239). Natural materials were emphasized including cobblestones and rough stones for foundations, and unsurfaced boards and rough split shakes for wall cladding. Bungalows made of wood were to be stained to give them a simple natural beauty (Mattson 1981, 78).

Bungalows were intended to blend indoor and outdoor spaces as much as possible and the use of natural materials was a step in this direction (Figure 8.1). Emphasis on the porch was another. Bungalow porches were often depicted in plan book illustrations enhanced by trellises covered with climbing roses or other vines. Massive porch columns framed views of the outdoors as the eye was invited out into a landscaped lawn and garden. As in many of the irregularly massed houses, the more public spaces indoors were designed not only to flow together, but to flow out onto the porch which now became, more than ever, outdoor living space. On entering, the front door usually gave way directly into the living room which connected along one side of the dwelling through a broad arch to the dining room. The

8.1 Bungalows with their peculiar room arrangements come in varied shapes and sizes. Usually visible on the outside, however, is a low silhouette and the use of extended eaves often bracketed as if to expose superstructure. This cottage bungalow is in Rockville.

dining room, in turn, was connected, sometimes by small pantry, with the kitchen. Bedrooms were arrayed down the other side of the structure with a minimum of hallway space connecting.

Bungalow plans stressed simple, informal planning with emphasis on utility and convenience (Mattson 1981, 90). They represented a kind of "minimal house" which articulated not only a "blending with nature," which the picturesque era of irregular massing had done, but, as well, a quest for the economical and efficient. No longer could the American middle class afford extravagant houses. The costs of building materials and construction labor were soaring, as were heating costs and the costs of domestic help. As social historian Gwendolyn Wright notes: "The ideal middle class dwelling underwent a major transformation: from an exuberant, highly personalized display of irregular shapes, picturesque contrasts, and varieties of ornament, supposedly symbolizing the uniqueness of the family, to a restrained and simple dwelling" (Wright 1980, 3). Architectural simplicity and the rational organization of the household became the new order.

The Arts and Crafts Movement aided and abetted the popularity of bungalows. English architect William Morris gathered around him in the 1890s a following devoted to a return to natural materials, craft skills, and architectural simplicity. Carried to the United States, the movement took hold on both coasts and in the Middle West. From New York, designer and furniture manufacturer Gustav Stickley published *The Craftsman*. In Chicago Frank Lloyd Wright and other architects evolved a "Prairie Style" of architecture based substantially on craftsman ideals. In California architects Charles and Henry Greene developed their own distinctive architectural statements accentuating simplicity of form as generated by the active participation of the worker/artisan in the design process. The Greenes are credited with bringing the bungalow to a high state of art in a region ripe for the bungalow idea (McAlester and McAlester 1984, 454).

California, with its mild Mediterranean-like climate, was a place infinitely suited for informal, pleasurable outdoor-oriented living. Los Angeles, experiencing an economic boom rooted in oil, movies, and aircraft, experienced a housing explosion. The small, efficiently built bungalow with all of its symbolism proved the ideal dwelling to house the multitudes of migrants swarming in from the Middle West and the Southeast (Brown 1964). Architects David Gebhard and Robert Winter write: "Here a young family on the make, a sick family on the mend, or an old family on meagre savings could build a woodsy place in the sun with palm trees and a rose garden" (Gebhard and Winter 1977, 19). Quickly, the word "California" was attached to the bungalow designation. Soon "California styles" enticed potential buyers to "put a little California in your home" in various parts of the country (Mattson 1981, 76). Even in the Middle West the place image "California" dominated. Sears, Roebuck and Company's Honorbilt Homes offered "The Hollywood"; Lewis-Built Homes offered "The Pasadena," "The Alameda," and "The San Fernando" (*Honorbilt Modern Homes 1920*, 91; *Lewis-Built Homes 1918*, 13, 16, 56).

The prefabricated houses produced by the milling companies (lumber cut to specification and shipped to local contractors) departed substantially from the ideals of the Arts and Crafts Movement. Morris, Stickley, and the others had encouraged craftsmanship as an alternative to machine-made things. Paradoxically the bungalow popularized by the movement came to epitomize the very essence of machine-made housing. Even the semblance of hand-craftsmanship was retained in the look of the factory-made bookcases, fireplaces, window-seats and other "built-ins" supplied by catalog. Most of these bungalows were quite small, but some models were very large. But even the largest looked small. As one bungalow proponent wrote, they look as if they "had been built for less money than it actually cost" (Saylor 1913, 5). The proliferation of cheap bungalows and the fact that even the expensive ones looked cheap undoubtedly hastened the end of the bungalow's popularity.

The bungalow idea manifested itself both as a style statement and in distinctive structural forms. The style, as we have previously discussed was implicit in distinctive ornamentation, especially the use of "natural" building materials and their hand crafting. Such ornamentation (sometimes termed "bungaloid" or "western stick style") was applied to a limited set of structure types. The principal distinguishing feature between types was the kind of roof, gable, front gable, and multiple gable being the principal forms. Geographer Richard Mattson argues that there was no single bungalow type. He writes: "The American bungalow followed no comprehensive tenets of design. Typical traits were merely points of departure for architectural inspiration" (Mattson 1981, 83). Nonetheless, builders did restrict themselves to a very limited set of structural forms in pursuing the bungalow idea. Like irregular massing, the potential variety in dwellings was theoretically infinite, but in reality constricted. Consistent attributes included a basically rectangular outline and an informal arrangement of rooms.

Geographical Distribution

The bungalow idea, spread primarily from California, is viewed by Anthony King as America's first "distinctively national type." He writes: "The American bungalow marks a clear watershed in the domestic architecture of the nineteenth and twentieth centuries. On the one hand, the vertical, formal, cluttered and historically derived styles of the Victorians; on the other, the low, horizontal, informal, 'open plan' and functional design which has come to characterize 'modern' architecture of today" (King 1984, 154). It was, according to King, one of the first common house ideas to break regional boundaries and gain acceptance virtually everywhere. Its popularity was carried through the national media, especially in such magazines as *The American Architect*, *Good Housekeeping*, *Architectural Record*, *Country Life*, and *Ladies Home Journal*.

Although bungalows were expected in every study town, an uneven representation was assumed. Bungalows, we hypothesized, would be more common in the South. Save for California and the Southwest, perhaps no other region in the United States is more suited climatically to the bungalow idea than the Southeast. Short winters make for more outdoor living and before the days of air conditioning hot summers made extended eaves and broad porches very practical as sunshades. We also expected to find bungalows more numerous in the Middle West than in the Northeast given the influence of the prefabricated house manufacturers there. Furthermore, the continued prosperity of most Middle Western towns in the first two decades of the twentieth century would have contributed to greater bungalow construction there.

Our southern towns, in fact, do have more bungalows (Figure 8.2). For some, Apalachicola, Southport, and Columbiana, the frequencies are indeed very high. What seems to be an exceptionally high frequency in Port Gibson is the net result of including incised-porch cottages in the bungalow structure group. When these are removed the bungalow numbers are consistent with those in other towns in the Lower South. However, we suspected the number of bungalows in the southern towns would be even larger. Clearly, prosperity in the teens and twenties was not sufficient to encouraging larger numbers. Bungalows were unexpectedly numerous in Millersburg which did enjoy prosperity during the bungalow era. Bungalows were also well represented in certain Middle Western towns, but, again, not in the frequencies expected. Most significant, so far as regional pattern is concerned, are the towns which generally lack bungalows: Cazenovia, Mattapoisett, and Hudson. The towns where Yankee influence was greatest seem to have had an aversion to the bungalow idea. Bungalows are everywhere, an early twentieth-century form bracketed in the decades either side of World War I.

INCISED-PORCH COTTAGES

Although the origin of the bungalow name is rooted in India, students of American bungalow forms have looked closer to home for structural origins. In 1958, architectural historian Clay Lancaster speculated that the bungalow with gable roof and incised-porch may have origi-

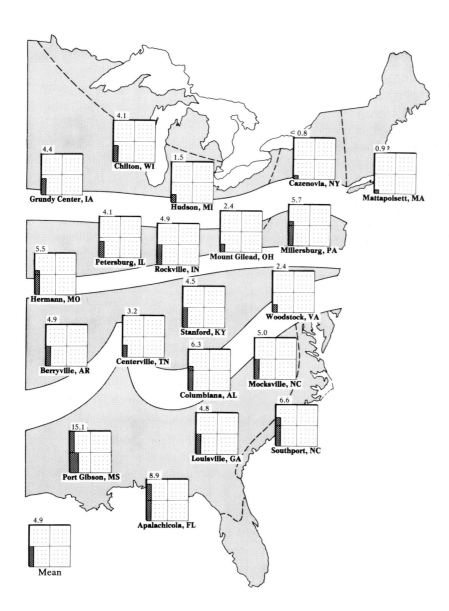

8.2 Bungalows (percent)

nated in the Caribbean area, an outgrowth of seventeenth-century Spanish colonial architecture. It was then carried by the French to the Lower Mississippi River in the eighteenth century. Lancaster writes of the Creole cottage and its "resemblances to the Cuban farmhouse in its gallery, double-pitched roof, plan, etc." (Lancaster 1958, 241). Mary Foley recently restated the case for the "French cottage of the American South" as the "logical prototype" for the bungalow (Foley 1980, 220). It was with these speculations in mind that the incised-porch cottage was included as a bungalow form.

The incised-porch cottage, including the Creole Cottage, is a double-pile dwelling with gable roof (Figure 8.3). It usually has two large front rooms and from two to three rooms arrayed across the back. The porch, as the term "incised" describes, dominated the front of the dwelling inset under the long sloping gallery roof. Many of these dwellings are raised to allow air-circulation through an open basement (Kniffen 1936, 182; Glassie 1968a, 118; Fricker 1984, 137). We expected to find incised-porch cottages across the Lower South in modest numbers with the highest concentration closest to the Mississippi River at Port Gibson.

8.3 **Given the configuration of its porch, some scholars have thought the incised porch cottage (often called the Creole cottage) to be the precursor of the incised porch bungalow. This example was found in Port Gibson.**

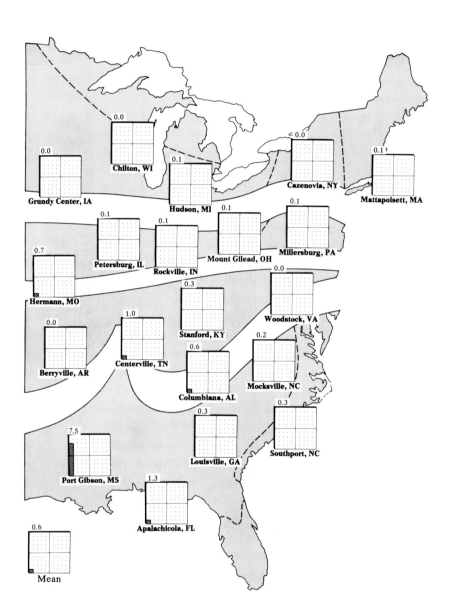

0.0
Chilton, WI

0.0
Grundy Center, IA

0.1
Hudson, MI

< 0.0
Cazenovia, NY

0.1 ?
Mattapoisett, MA

0.1
Petersburg, IL

0.1
Rockville, IN

0.1
Mount Gilead, OH

0.1
Millersburg, PA

0.7
Hermann, MO

0.3
Stanford, KY

0.0
Woodstock, VA

0.0
Berryville, AR

1.0
Centerville, TN

0.6
Columbiana, AL

0.2
Mocksville, NC

0.3
Louisville, GA

0.3
Southport, NC

7.5
Port Gibson, MS

1.3
Apalachicola, FL

0.6
Mean

8.4 Incised-Porch Cottages (percent)

Indeed, incised-porch cottages are significant in Port Gibson (Figure 8.4). However, numbers are surprisingly low elsewhere in the South as for example Apalachicola and Centerville. Outside the South, above average numbers of incised-porch cottages are confined to Hermann in an area of German settlement, the rural Germans having adopted incised-porch cottages and houses in the nineteenth century (Van Ravenswaay 1977, 153). Except for this unique occurrence, this structure form is rare to absent in the Middle West and the Northeast. At Hermann, the Creole tradition not only encouraged some incised-porch cottage construction in the nineteenth century, but, more importantly, the construction of double-pile cottages in the twentieth as discussed previously.

INCISED-PORCH AND COTTAGE BUNGALOWS

On the exterior, incised-porch bungalows are strikingly similar to incised-porch cottages. They are both somewhat square in floor plan perimeter, one- or one-and-one-half stories in height, and gable-roofed. It is, of course, the inset porch which offers the strongest resemblance (Figure 8.5). What is different about the incised-porch bungalow are the overhanging eaves, the chimney

to one side, the interior stair-
ways and the frequent use of
dormers. Older Creole type
incised-porch cottages frequently
have an exterior stairway placed
at one end of the front porch. Because incised-porch and cottage
bungalows proved to be few in
number, and since they are so
similar, we discuss them in aggregate (Figure 8.6).

We expected incised-porch and
cottage bungalows to be closely
associated geographically with
incised-porch cottages. This was
another instance of suspected relationship between an early folk
form and a later builder form, a
relationship expected to have

8.5   Wherever its origins, the incised-
porch bungalow, like this one in
Southport, became popular in the
early twentieth century across the nation, and not just the South.

8.6   The cottage bungalow has a shed
rather than an incised porch. Here, at
Mocksville, the porch has been partially enclosed.

clear regional connotation. It was quite a surprise, therefore, when we discovered not only a lack of positive correlation, but, indeed, an inverse correlation (Figure 8.7). Port Gibson, where folk-inspired incised-porch cottages are exceptionally numerous, does not have a single incised-porch or cottage bungalow. It is the only town of the twenty places studied not to have either of these builder forms.

Status implications appear to play an important role in relating folk and builder forms within a given town. Where a folk form carries high status implications, commercial builders may simulate it in new dwelling types. For example, in Cazenovia and Hudson the high status upright and wing house may have encouraged popularity of the L-shaped house. In Port Gibson, on the other hand, the incised-porch cottage carried low status implications. We should not be surprised that builders opted not to replicate it in bungalow form.

Towns with the largest number of incised-porch and cottage bungalows, Millersburg and Hermann, are not in the South. These two forms represent what most plan catalogs referred to as "California" bungalows. They are the bungalow planforms

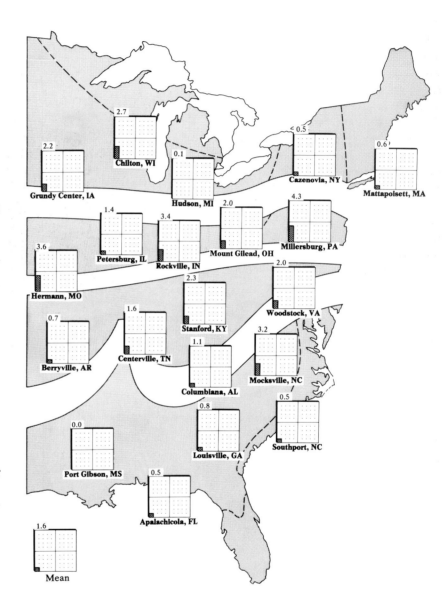

8.7   Incised-Porch Bungalows and Cottage Bungalows (percent)

most closely associated with the "craftsman" mystique. In retrospect we probably should not have expected these bungalow forms in the South in any frequency. Perhaps, we should have expected them in towns where carpentry and other craft traditions survive. It is interesting, therefore, to speculate about the role of the large German-American communities at both Millersburg and Hermann. Was this craft-oriented ethnic group responsible for the wide adoption of incised-porch and cottage bungalows in one or both of these places? We suspect so.

SOUTHERN BUNGALOWS

Southern bungalows differ from other bungalows in that a front-gable roof gives the building an axis clearly perpendicular to the street (Kniffen 1936, 188; Figure 8.8). The dwelling is one- or one-and-a-half stories with a low-pitch roof and projecting eaves in bungalow fashion. Although its interior floor plan (two sets of rooms aligned three deep along either side of the structure) remains the same, it appears to be elongated even when it is not. The form is closely related in floorplan to the double-shotgun cottage, previously discussed, except that it is given clear bungalow treatment and possesses a single front door (Newton 1971, 15). Robert Finley and Elizabeth

Scott found these bungalows more to the southern end of their Wisconsin to Texas transect (Finley and Scott 1940, 414). The form, however, is not exclusive to the South. It was built in the Middle West and is known in the Chicago area as the "Chicago Bungalow." Chicago bungalows are distinctive only in so far as the porch is partially enclosed to provide a front "sun room" (Legner 1979, 21).

We hypothesized that the southern bungalow would be most prevalent in the South as the name implies. This is clearly the case, the structure type accounting for more than 5 percent of the total dwellings in Port Gibson, Apalachicola, and Southport

8.8 The roofline of the southern bungalow runs perpendicular to the street rather than parallel. This form may have evolved from the double shotgun in the South. For example, all that visually distinguishes this bungalow in Apalachicola from a double shotgun (Figure 6.23) is its single door and greater building depth.

(Figure 8.9). No dominant regional pattern emerges across the South. There is a lack of southern bungalows in Centerville, Stanford, and Woodstock. However, Columbiana and Berryville also in the Upper South, do fit with their Lower South neighbors.

COMPOSITE BUNGALOWS WITH IRREGULAR MASSING

In conducting our inventory we not only identified incised-porch, cottage, and southern bungalows, but as well a complex bungalow form which we termed a "composite bungalow with irregular massing" (Figure 8.10). Highly irregular in floor plan and in roof shape, this category of bungalow appears in prefabricated house catalogs (for example: *Plan Book of Harris Homes* 1918, 17; *Honorbilt Modern Homes* 1920, 33). However, so few of these bungalows were inventoried (less than 1 percent of the houses) that we do not map its distribution here. Its scarcity is important since its lack of significance reinforces the notion that picturesque variety in builder forms, although frequently emphasized in advertising, did not necessarily translate into reality. Bungalows, like irregularly massed dwellings, were championed as unique expressions of family status and lifestyle. Customers were invited

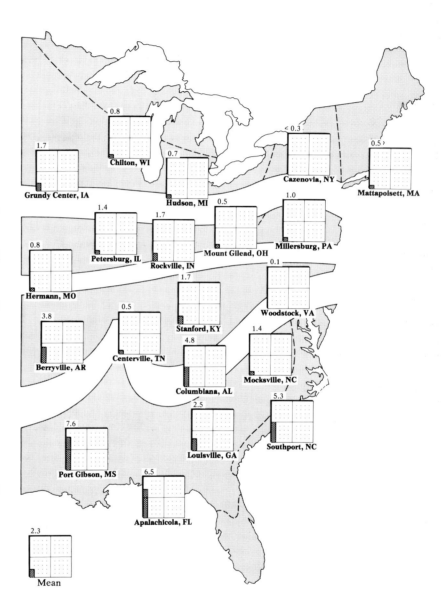

8.9   Southern Bungalows (percent)

to pick and choose features quite literally from catalogs. And yet, the variety obtained was constrained within narrow ranges of diversity. Difference in similarity reigned.

Bungalows represented the smallest of several structure groups. Only 844 bungalows were counted in the various study towns, or less than 5 percent of the total houses surveyed. This showing is not surprising given the bungalow's popularity during a brief twenty year period, approximately 1905 to 1925, which included a nationwide construction hiatus during World War I. Nonetheless, the southern towns, as a group, carry a significant bungalow stamp in their older sections, especially Apalachicola, Port Gibson, and Southport (Figure 8.2). The majority of the bungalows in most southern towns are of the southern bungalow variety. Mocksville, Stanford, and Woodstock are exceptions. In these towns, as in the Middle West, incised-porch and cottage bungalows prevail.

As with the irregularly massed group of dwellings, hypotheses linking folk and builder forms were examined. The suspected relationship between the incised-porch cottage, the incised-porch bungalow, and the cottage bungalow, proved to be inverse. It might be inferred that builder forms when introduced into a community are often intended to

8.10 Eclecticism carried over into bungalow design although the irregularities involved seem minor when compared with the excesses of the Queen Anne era. This composite bungalow with irregular massing is in Louisville.

be departures from traditional building ideas, perhaps deliberately intended to submerge folk forms. On the other hand, the widespread popularity of the southern bungalow in the South appears to be closely related to the popularity of earlier double shotgun cottages. That the southern bungalow also appears in the Middle West and the Northeast suggests that it is not merely a regional form but a national form, although it is rooted more in the South due to earlier housing traditions there.

CHAPTER IX   RANCH "HOUSES"

Little boxes on the hillside

Little boxes made of ticky tacky

Little boxes on the hillside

Little boxes all the same

MALVINA REYNOLDS

The single-story ranch "house" has spread everywhere in the United States to dominate America's sense of home. Never before has an architectural idea spread so rapidly and proved so influential in American housing. The ranch idea originated in California in the 1930s, especially in the San Francisco Bay Area. Cliff May, among others, is credited with developing the ranch as a distinctive idea (Gebhard and Winter 1977, 26, 704; Walker 1981, 235). May not only designed dwellings using construction methods and building materials common to vernacular farm houses, barns and "woodsmen's cabins" of the region, but he also widely publicized his houses in plan books (for example, May 1950). May and his contemporaries used several historical analogies to identify and promote their creations. Inspiration was said to have come from the Spanish rancho of early nineteenth-century Southern California. Built of adobe bricks, these houses had been organized around inner courtyards or patios. But primary inspiration actually derived not from colonial but from American ranches of late nineteenth-century Northern California. Thus cedar-shake roofs, rubble-stone chimneys, board and batten walls, and knotty-pine interiors figured prominently from the beginning (May 1950, 25).

The Ranch

The ranch movement was rooted in the bungalow craze. The term "ranch bungalow" was often used to describe bungalows with a clear "western" regional decorative motif (Lancaster 1958, 239; King 1984, 150). Architects Charles and Henry Greene may have set precedent in both the Arturo Bandino House, built in 1903 at Pasadena, and the Charles Hollister House, built a year later in Hollywood (Makinson 1977, 70). The Bandino House, called a bungalow, was a series of rooms arranged around three sides of a central court, the two side wings containing bedrooms and the rear section containing the living, dining and kitchen area. Each room opened onto a covered verandah. The exterior walls were sheathed with vertical redwood boards; the roof was of shingle. In the Hollister house the architects reversed the U-shaped plan with the main portion of the house facing toward the street rather than into the courtyard. Viewed from the street the Hollister house appeared very much like a post–World War II ranch home. But these Greene and Greene experiments, despite their originality, did not stimulate replication. Nor was the term "ranch" coined.

The Depression and World War II set the stage for the ranch's popularity. Clearly, the nation awaited something new: a dwelling that symbolized a fresh start for a nation wracked first by economic collapse and then by war. The sense of a "new dawn" after 1945, unmet housing demand, and the pent up buying power that accompanied it, let loose a torrent of housing innovation. The automobile, an integral part of most evolving American lifestyles, encouraged new, spread-out city and town morphologies. Curvilinear streets with wide lots reflected American preferences for more pastoral and less urban living. The automobile enabled builders to erect houses which seemed to sprawl across large lots with clear social status implication.

What to call this new structural form was at first a problem. The term "ranch" competed with other words such as "western," "Northwestern," "Puget Sound," "California ranch," "Texas ranch," "contractor modern," and even "California bungalow" (Sleeper and Sleeper 1948, 146; Walker 1981, 234). By 1950, however, the ranch term, used without qualifiers, universally described the new subdivision tract houses. Cliff May writes: "Most of us describe any one-story house with a low, close-to-the-ground silhouette as a ranch house. When a long, wide porch is added to this form, almost everyone accepts the name. And when wings are added and the house seems to ramble all over the site, the name is established beyond dispute" (May 1950, ix).

Ranch "houses" differed from bungalows in their low, sprawling appearance. The elevated basement disappeared, permitting this new type of dwelling to truly hug the ground. The only antecedent for this type is found in rather rare dwellings designed or inspired by the Prairie School architects. Whereas the eaves were extended, no longer were brackets and other supports visible. Roof slopes were of much lower pitch. In interior plan, rooms continued to flow one to another; however, rooms were now arrayed parallel and not perpendicular to the street. The ranch dwelling spread out laterally across its wide lot. It appeared to "ramble" and, indeed, the term "rambler" was widely used as a descriptor (McAlester and McAlester 1984, 479). Even small dwellings appeared big when turned lengthwise and the ranch, even the smallest, carried much pretense to affluence for all social class levels. Indoor and outdoor spaces continued to blend except that now large "picture" windows and sliding glass doors facing rear patios (as opposed to front porches) dominated the linkage (Gebhard and Winter 1977, 704–5).

The rationales presented for single-floor living were many. Savings derived from shorter plumbing lines, electric lines, and heat ducts, less height in chimneys and sidewalls, and lack of staging during construction. All load-bearing partitions could be eliminated when trussed roofs were used, giving complete freedom for partition changes within the shell of the structure. Savings in building costs also resulted from not having to build a stairway to a second floor. Lack of stairs removed a hazard said to account for one-quarter of all household accidents (Wills 1955, 12). Likewise the homeowner could make house repairs without the need to climb tall ladders. According to promoter Barry Wills: "House for house the low, contour-fitting form of the one level design best fulfills the esthetic and inherent demand for houses that are knit into the landscape" (Wills 1955, 13).

Whatever the perceived benefits from ranch living, a million ranches were constructed in the United States each year between 1948 and 1955 (Walker 1981, 25). The popularity of the ranch was promoted in such trade journals as *American Builder,* and by popular magazines such as *House Beautiful.* Prefabricated housing was produced as never before. Ranch dwellings dominated the plan books and the sales catalogs of the 1950s (for example, Group 1946, *Garlinghouse Ranch and Suburban Homes* 1950, Johnson 1958).

Geographical Distribution

Since the ranch is now found virtually everywhere in the United States, we hypothesized that ranch "houses" would be important in every study town. The southern towns, however, for their more vigorous economic growth over recent decades, were expected to be more clearly dominated by this structure form. Although our expectations were validated in basic outline, the distribution of ranch "houses" proves more complex than anticipated (Figure 9.1). Ranches clearly dominate most southern towns: Berryville, Centerville, Mocksville, Louisville, Columbiana, Stanford, Woodstock, and Southport. Only in old river towns in the Lower South such as Port Gibson and Apalachicola are ranches substantially less numerous. These latter towns have not experienced an economic boom in recent decades, but have, instead, declined in population.

For the northern towns, three regional groupings are apparent. From Pennsylvania across the Lower Middle West percentages cluster around 30 percent, for example in Mount Gilead and Hermann. In the Upper Middle West, the westernmost towns of Grundy Center and Chilton have substantially higher percentages than Hudson, Cazenovia, and Mattapoisett. At Hudson, a depressed economy in recent decades underlies a decided lack of ranches. In Cazenovia and Mattapoisett, the continued preference for more traditional house forms (for example, the Cape Cod cottage in the latter) accounts for the ranch's relative lack of popularity.

Ranch structures across the various study towns are overwhelmingly of post–World War II construction. In several towns primarily in the South, such as Louisville, Centerville, Mocksville, and Stanford, some 2 percent of the ranches were built before the war. This fact suggests that the ranch spread more rapidly nationwide than previous commentators have been wont to admit. The "ranch revolution" was clearly well underway before World War II.

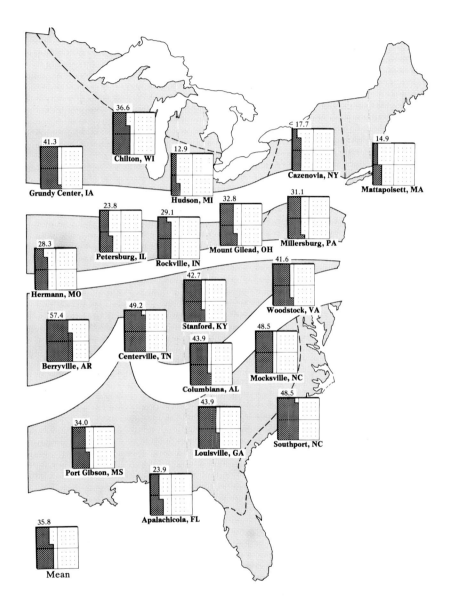

9.1   Ranch Dwellings (percent)

186

The standard ranch "house" is a box-like, one-story structure with a very low-pitched gable or hip roof. In the perimeter outline it is a strict rectangle, the garage usually attached or integrated as part of the overall plan. With a minimum of six rooms it personifies the ranch idea as symbolic of affluent middle-class families. Set off from the street by a wide lawn and broad driveway, the standard ranch presents a clear "suburban" image, especially in post–World War II subdivisions (Figures 9.2 and 9.3). It is what most Americans probably consider a "typical" ranch to be. We expected them in large numbers everywhere.

The standard ranch is not evenly distributed across the study towns (Figure 9.4). It is important in the South, as is the ranch form generally. Those southern towns experiencing rapid growth in the past two decades (for example, Berryville, Centerville, and Mocksville) have significant numbers. Given its simplicity of plan, it is a structure form rapidly replicated by builders, a replication which brings to new subdivisions a clear sense of sameness. Standardization facilitates and speeds construction, resulting in reduced costs.

The towns of the extreme Northeast, Mattapoisett, Cazenovia, and Hudson, clearly have been affected less by this most popular of ranch designs.

9.2 Whole sections of cities and towns are now given exclusively to ranches as here in Mount Gilead's northwest quadrant.

9.3 Most Americans today use the word ranch easily and freely to describe various kinds of dwellings made universally popular across the United States after World War II. This ranch is in one of the newest subdivisions in Centerville.

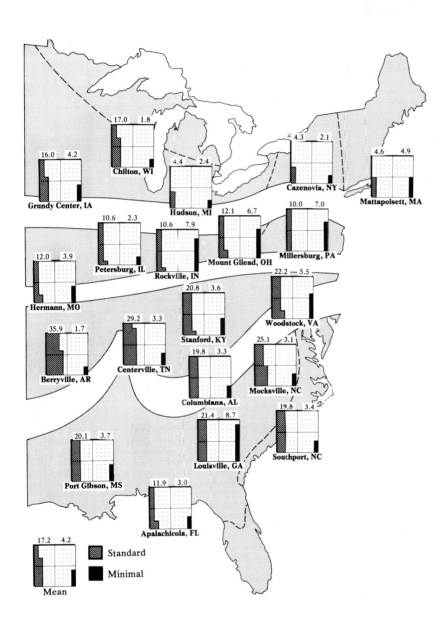

9.4   **Standard and Minimal Ranches (percent)**

In Mattapoisett traditional forms have continued to dominate builder activity over recent decades as previously discussed. Mattapoisett is unique among the towns in this regard, in part a function of its upper middle class suburban status. In Cazenovia another ranch form, the composite ranch, predominates as discussed below. In Hudson economic stagnation has discouraged residential construction over the past three decades thus reducing the number of ranches of all types.

THE MINIMAL RANCH

The minimal ranch, like the standard ranch, is a simple one-story rectangular box. Unlike the standard ranch, garages are not attached or integrated, but are self-standing structures when they exist. A small dwelling of five rooms or less, the minimal ranch is just that, "minimal." Looking very much like an elongated double-pile cottage, there is very little on the outside to suggest the ranch motif (Figure 9.5). Window treatment, especially the use of picture windows and/or horizontal bands of more traditional window frames, conveys the ranch allusion. The low pitch of the gable or hip roof is another indicator. Interior room

9.5 The minimal ranch is a return to the basic rectangular box with gable roof except that floor space is organized differently than in the double-pile cottage for example (Figure 6.5). Nothing could be more basic than this minimal ranch in Rockville.

arrangements are definitely ranch-like, the front door usually placed off-center accordingly. We expected the minimal ranch to be more prevalent in the less viable study towns of recent decades, especially the towns with large lower-middle-class or blue-collar populations.

The minimal ranch appears in every town, but with little geographical regularity between them (Figure 9.4). Its above average adoption in Mattapoisett probably relates to the popularity of the double-pile cottage there. The unexpected popularity of this form in an affluent community seems to refute the "blue-collar" hypothesis. However, its adoption in Louisville is a function of subdividers replicating small minimal ranches in black

suburban "quarters" thus supporting our hypothesized lower class association (Figure 9.6). Although there is some consistency to its popularity in Millersburg, Mount Gilead, and Rockville, we are not prepared to suggest that these towns are linked regionally. Rather, the predilections of builders seem to explain this form's popularity town to town. Once a form is accepted in a place, it may be replicated over and over as a measure of buyer satisfaction.

9.6 Ranches house families of all income levels today. Here, beyond Louisville's town limits to the east, is a low-income black quarter comprised of renter-occupied ranches.

THE COMPOSITE RANCH

Composite ranches feature irregular perimeter outlines. Thus they are characterized by degrees of irregular massing with L- and T-shapes the most prevalent forms (Figures 9.7 and 9.8). Like other ranches, roofs are low-pitched except that multiple-gables, multiple-hip, and combined gable and hip roofs predominate. Generally, composite ranches are as large if not larger than standard ranches. Certainly, they are more complicated to construct and materials are more costly. Composite ranches reflect builder attempts to break the standardization of simple box shapes and thus to provide some eccentricity in subdivisions. Composite ranches were expected to be ubiquitously distributed across the various study towns, but to be more important in the affluent, recent-growth communities.

9.7 A T-shaped composite ranch with multiple-gable roof is located in one of Woodstock's new subdivisions.
9.8 Larger ranch dwellings usually have integrated or attached garages, with the garages contributing substantially to the appearance of size. In this composite ranch at Mocksville, the garage is reduced to a carport.

Composite ranches are found everywhere; however, no apparent relationship exists between affluence and this particular ranch form (Figure 9.9). Only in Cazenovia do composite ranches seem to reflect wealth. There they outnumber standard ranches nearly two to one, a reflection of the town's "exurban" status with respect to nearby Syracuse. In every other town standard ranches are the predominant ranch form. However, even in less affluent towns characterized by lack of economic growth and/or accompanying population loss in recent decades, composite ranches prove relatively numerous; Hudson, Petersburg, Apalachicola, and Port Gibson are examples of such towns. Again, builder biases and their interpretation of buyer preferences seem to offer the only explanation for the greater popularity of composite ranches in some places as opposed to others.

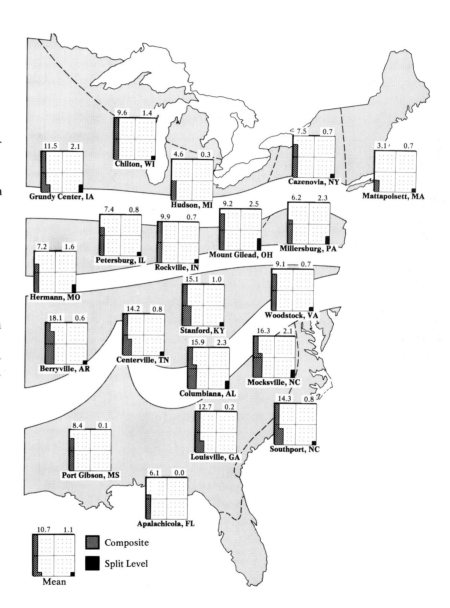

9.9 **Composite and Split-Level Ranches (percent)**

9.10 **From the single-story ranch, multilevel varieties evolved. This split-level ranch is in Columbiana.**

THE SPLIT-LEVEL RANCH

The split-level ranch has figured prominently in builder magazines and plan books since the 1950s. It is a multi-story variation on the ranch theme. Retaining the horizontal lines, low-pitched roof, and overhanging eaves, it combines a two-story unit intercepted at mid-height with a one-story wing to create three floor levels of interior space (Figure 9.10). An elaborate theory of interior planning developed around this form. Families were thought to need three types of interior space (quiet living areas, noisy living and service areas, and sleeping areas). The split-level form made it possible to locate these spaces on separate levels (McAlester and McAlester 1984, 480). Thus the lower level usually contains the garage and the informal family room with its television set; the mid-level wing houses the kitchen and more formal dining room and living room; the upper level contains the bedrooms (Walker 1981, 260). Virginia and Lee McAlester believe the form to be more important in the North than in the South (McAlester and McAlester 1984, 481). We expected to find it both in the North and the South, but more in places with recent growth.

The split-level ranch is least popular in the towns of the extreme Lower South and the extreme Northeast (Figure 9.9). Only one or two houses appear in Port Gibson and Louisville, and none at all in Apalachicola. Few split-level ranches are found in Mattapoisett, Cazenovia, and Hudson. Where the split-level does occur in some numbers, for example Mount Gilead, Millersburg, and Columbiana, builder proclivity appears to provide the only explanation. Nowhere, however, did its adoption match its currency in the trade journals and plan books of recent decades.

THE RAISED RANCH

The raised ranch, sometimes called the "split entry" ranch and the "bi-level" ranch, is a variation on the split-level theme (Stith and Meyer 1974, 6; Walker 1981, 261). It is a story-and-a-half dwelling, the lower story usually set into a partial basement. This arrangement permits the ground level entry to be located midway between the main and lower levels. Flights of stairs in a two-story entrance hall give access up and down (Figure 9.11). Beyond the entrance foyer, the house functions as a two-story structure with living room, dining room, kitchen and master bedroom upstairs, and family room and remaining bedrooms, utility space, and a garage downstairs. As with the split-level ranches, we expected to find raised ranches in the rapid growth towns of recent decades.

Like the split-level ranch, the raised ranch is least popular across the extreme Lower South (Figure 9.12). But its frequency elsewhere reveals little geographical clustering. Its popularity in Millersburg, Grundy Center, and Woodstock would seem to reflect builder prerogatives more than any other factor. Here is another form that might be found anywhere given its promotion in the national media of the building industry. But, in fact, it appears only in selected places where local builders were particularly receptive. Builders in Millersburg and Woodstock may have been inclined to popularize this form given the rolling topography of the town's newer subdivisions. Raised ranches fit nicely into hillside sites. Such was definitely not the case, however, for Grundy Center with its flat terrain.

9.11 Raised ranches, like this one in Millersburg, offer efficiently organized floor plans that separate distinct household activities on different levels.

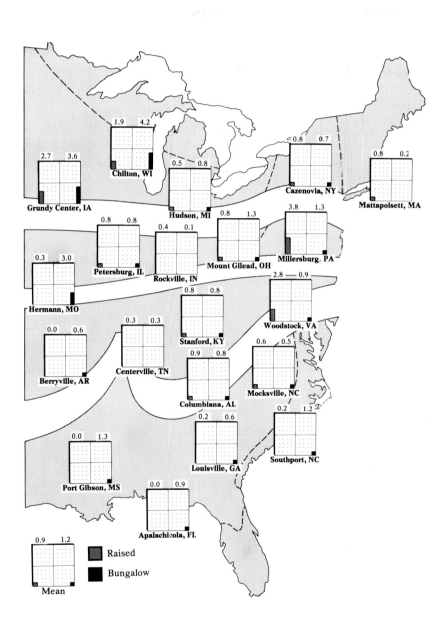

9.12   **Raised and Bungalow Ranches (percent)**

THE RANCH BUNGALOW

The term "ranch bungalow" is applied to ranch dwellings with narrow end turned to the street and interior space organized not unlike a bungalow's. The form derives from builders wanting to place ranch "houses" on narrow lots (Figure 9.13). This form appears infrequently in plan books of the 1940s and 1950s (for example, Group 1946, 3). We expected to find these dwellings in the towns which grew rapidly during the late 1940s and early 1950s.

To our surprise the ranch bungalow does have a regional popularity in extreme western towns of the Middle West: Chilton, Grundy Center, and Hermann (Figure 9.12). Most of these ranches have been built primarily on lots in the older sections of each town. Often the ranch bungalow reflects growth by means of replacement: old houses giving way to new ones on lots near a town center. Again, builder proclivity seems to offer the only explanation for their popularity town to town. Why the builders of one town adopted a given form that was nationally in vogue whereas the builders of another did not, remains a significant question demanding further study. For Chilton, Grundy Center, and Hermann, the availability of these houses from manufacturers and/or building supply wholesalers in the region may offer some explanation.

9.13 Standard ranch dwellings are inappropriate to narrow lots in old neighborhoods. This problem is solved by turning the ranch and placing its front door in one narrow end facing the street. Once established as a distinctive form, however, ranch bungalows appeared on wide lots in new subdivisions as pictured here in Chilton.

We might speculate as to why certain builder houses become popular in a place. A builder is obviously attracted to a particular form based on what he has seen in trade journals, in the popular media, or through first-hand experience elsewhere. Perhaps he is attracted to a sense of difference or uniqueness relative to what has been previously built. Perhaps there is a similarity to what has gone before, but enough of a difference to suggest innovation, a basis for meeting the local market in a highly visible way. Given estimated costs of materials and labor, he moves forward to build on speculation. Or, perhaps, he has sold his idea to a customer who through his purchase will subsidize the new experiment. Perhaps, the client is the innovator and driving force. Success breeds imitation as other builders move to take advantage of the new opportunity. Most innovations will go by the board and will not be replicated in large numbers. A few will succeed. Popularity will probably be based on cost and ease of construction as well as the sense of newness which an innovation imbibes.

As the second largest of the structure groups, the 6,188 ranches account for more than 35 percent of the total dwellings surveyed across the various towns. In some fifty years the ranches have almost supplanted double-pile cottages and houses as the most popular domestic forms in our towns. Of course, much of this growth has come only in the past twenty-five years. Ranch houses clearly dominate in the South, in such towns as Berryville and Center-ville (Figure 9.1). Only in the towns of the extreme Northeast (Hudson, for example) are ranches relatively unimportant.

Ranch dwellings, especially the standard ranch and the composite ranch, have become symbols of modernity and middle-class affluence. In the South recent economic vitality is clearly reflected in the numerous streets lined with new ranches. Large ranch-dominated peripheral subdivisions contrast sharply with older streets at town centers. Southern towns not only have a split personality in this regard, but the new, personified by the ranch idea, clearly dominates the old. In places with slow growth or no growth in recent decades, especially in Cazenovia, Hudson, Petersburg, and Apalachicola, the subdivisions are of very modest scale or nonexistent. There the ranch intrudes on the traditional plat of streets, not to dominate but to blend as one dwelling type among many. Given the lack of ranch dominance these places take on an antiquated or "historical" image. Visually they are "older" places as traditional folk and early builder forms assert themselves in defining place character.

The ranch house in its peripheral subdivision tract is probably the order of the future for the majority of the study towns.

A new sprawling sort of townscape has emerged quite in the image of big city suburbs. The "rambler" on its big lot is matched by decentralized retail trade and factory employment strung out in sprawling buildings of their own along peripheral roads, the whole scene totally automobile oriented. The ranch not only fits this contemporary technological scheme of things, particularly as it complements the automobile, but it borrows substantially from past housing traditions. It pretends to be rooted in a folk vernacular of the western frontier. It seeks to strike relationships to the land deemed picturesque in the era of irregular massing. It attempts to blend indoors and outdoors through a social informality which the bungalow accelerated. Geographically, the ranch has become ubiquitous in the American landscape, and likely will remain so with regional diversity being more a matter of frequency than of kind.

CHAPTER X   CONCLUSION

For now we see through

a glass, darkly . . .

ST. PAUL

Always a nation of highly mobile residents, America reflects that mobility in its common houses. The roots of restlessness lie in the oldest dwellings, in culture hearths of the Seaboard configured before national independence. Migrations westward to the Mississippi and beyond brought diffusion of diverse house building ideas as new cultural regions emerged. Many traditional house types survived the transplantation, but new types also emerged, weakly rooted in the traditional. In most houses visible in the landscape today (those of the late nineteenth and twentieth centuries) the sense of change has been more deliberately contrived. Fads and fashions have been promoted by a commercial building industry at once advocating new forms, materials, and building techniques while frequently reflecting the past, particularly in ornamentation. The construction of each

succeeding decade carries a distinctive stamp. The housing of every small town offers evidence of its community's roots in time.

Americans have never built for permanence. Most dwellings in the United States are constructed of wood. Balloon framing makes them easy to renovate, to expand, to alter. And yet, most American houses are not reworked save superficially through recladding. Americans tend not to improve their old residences but rather to move to new residences in search of improvement. This restlessness leaves most dwellings remarkably unchanged and clearly reflective of their place in time, a kind of paradox—permanence in impermanence. In a relatively affluent society with money to spend on new housing, the middle and upper classes aspire to new dwellings and allow old dwellings to filter down to the less well-to-do. Only occasionally do old houses play to status consciousness. Irrespective, the look of the typical American dwelling changes relatively little between construction and demolition.

In cities the pressures on residential neighborhoods are often times immense. The flight to the suburbs accelerated after 1960 with whole neighborhoods abandoned seemingly overnight in many American cities in the 1970s and 1980s. In contrast, the small town subdivision with its ranch houses strung along curving streets is not so distant from the bungalows of the traditional street grid. In small towns the filtering of people through houses of varying character is by its scale more comprehensible. It is, therefore, to the small towns of America that we have turned to assess the character of common dwellings. Like a motion picture played in slow motion, the small town scene enables one to grasp the peculiar American penchant for impermanence. As a key element of material culture the single-family dwellings of small towns speak with some implicit stability of the American penchant for mobility.

How do Americans in the small towns between the Atlantic Seaboard and the Mississippi Valley house themselves? With this question we began our work. Our first challenge was to assemble through review of scholarly and other writings a nomenclature or lexicon descriptive of vernacular dwellings com-

mon to the eastern half of the nation. Our typology of sixty-seven dwelling types proved adequate to the identification of some 96 percent of the structures inventoried. We believe this to be one of the primary contributions of our research. Scholars and other surveyors of dwelling types can now approach their work with greater confidence. No longer should they be content to assign plain or sparsely decorated structures, other than clearly recognized folk varieties, to such obscure categories as "vernacular" or "carpenter builder." By observing the configuration of a dwelling's outer perimeter, the form and orientation of its roof and the number of stories it contains, they can recognize its individuality and assign it to a specific rather than a vague category. The recognition of diverse types is a necessary prerequisite to meaningful interpretations of common dwelling forms in America.

Although our dwelling typology proved very useful, refinement is in order. Many of our dwelling types break down into clear subtypes. For example, the upright-and-wing house varies according to the height of the "upright" with respect to the "wing": a difference reflected in roof configuration. In perimeter cutline, some upright-and-wing houses display a T form when viewed from above, others are L-shaped. In some of these houses the front door is in the "wing," in others it is in the "upright." Where and when did such variations evolve? Where are they distributed today? For many dwellings, there are clear regional variations related to size or scale. Especially important are differences in width. For example, gable-front houses and cottages vary from two to four bays, a bay being defined as a space containing either a door or window on the first story level. The vast majority of our gable-front dwellings are three-bay structures. Most of the two-bay front-gabled dwellings are shotgun cottages and have been so identified in this study. But what of the exceptions? How might they have evolved? How are they distributed?

The answers to such questions demand finer-tuned surveys not only embracing refined typology, but embracing a finer grid of sample places. For our undertaking a sample of forty rather than twenty towns might have enabled us to use a refined typology; sixty towns would have been even more desirable. We were constrained by the limited financial resources for this type of survey. Nevertheless, we have created a unique data base. Our generalizations derived from this factual body of information stand on firmer ground than previously suggested geographical patterns as derived from casual observation. We anticipate that other scholars will refine further the patterns we have observed.

We have posed hypotheses based on our reading of the common house literature. We have tested these expectations against our findings. Did our findings confirm our basic hypotheses? We expected to find variations in dwelling forms and dwelling characteristics both between and within culture regions from the Atlantic to the Mississippi Valley.

Our study towns were selected to reflect differences and similarities across and between principal culture regions. For example, we anticipated differences in residual folk dwelling forms between seaboard "hearth" areas. A westward replacement of folk dwellings by national builder types promoted by the media of the building industry also was expected. Although our hypotheses provided an intellectual framework for analyzing and presenting results, they were but partially confirmed. It is evident that future study should focus more on commercial builders and the building industry. How is it that planforms are presented and popularized through various media? On what basis is an innovation introduced into a community? Under what circumstances is it copied, or largely ignored? At what point does a planform lose popularity?

Another primary contribution of our research relates to the regional patterns discovered among dwelling types in small towns. One principal generalization, based on regional variations in rural folk architecture, was not confirmed. Regarding common houses, we did not encounter four distinctive zones as anticipated: i.e., (1) New England–Upper Middle West, (2) Pennsylvania–Lower Middle West, (3) Upper South, and (4) Lower South. What we observed, instead, is a single pronounced

cleavage between North and South (Figure 10.1). This basic regional variation among dwelling types parallels that which we also found among individual structural traits such as facade material, roof form, and building height (Figure 4.52).

In terms of small town dwelling types, the only consistent linkage from east to west occurs among our northern tier of survey communities from Mattapoisett to Grundy Center. These ties reach their highest intensity between Cazenovia, Hudson, and Chilton. Similar associations do not exist among towns in the Lower Middle West. For example, Mount Gilead is most like Hudson and Petersburg is most like Chilton and Hudson. Rockville and Hermann stand alone. Rockville is a transitional community in terms of domestic architecture. Its older dwellings include southern folk types, but these are not sufficient in number to link the community to towns in the South. German heritage is clearly at work in Hermann giving the town its peculiar mix of dwelling types. The linkages between Millersburg and both Woodstock and Mount Gilead are suggestive of a Pennsylvania culture tie. However, the distinctiveness of this latter region is compromised by equally close links between Millersburg and Chilton and between Mount Gilead and Hudson. The basic North–South

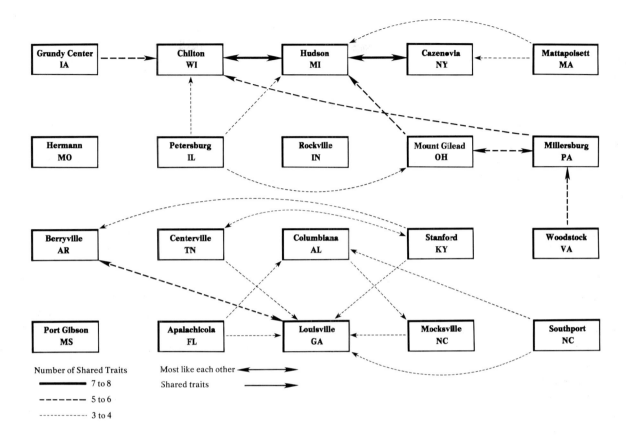

10.1 Most Similar Towns: Common Dwelling Types

dichotomy is not diminished by Woodstock's similarity to Millersburg. Woodstock more closely resembles this Pennsylvania community than any southern town. Hudson is the most typical town in the North as it shares a number of common dwelling types with five other northern study towns.

In the South, small-town dwelling types provide only one rather limited east to west linkage of relatively low intensity. This occurs within the Lower South between Mocksville, Louisville, and Apalachicola. Nevertheless, these towns are as similar to others in the Upper South as to one another. The primary focus of the ties between places in the Upper and Lower South makes Louisville the most typical of southern towns. Like Hermann and Rockville, Port Gibson stands alone as a unique place in terms of dwelling types. This is our only well preserved southern town with an abundance of antebellum residences.

Which dwelling types provide the linkages, North and South? To answer this question we looked separately at the ties provided by folk, nineteenth-century plan book, and twentieth-century ranch dwellings. Beginning with folk dwelling types we found greater continuity in the North than in the South (Figure 10.2). In this figure and the diagrams that follow, each line represents one dwelling type held in common, from town to town. There are particularly strong ties between Mattapoisett, Cazenovia, Hudson, and Chilton on the one hand and Millersburg and Woodstock on the other. The first group of towns is tied together by the common occurrence of such dwelling types as the New England Classic cottage, the double-pile house, and the upright and wing house. The unusual intensity of the tie between Cazenovia and Hudson suggests that the most consistent westward transfer of folk architecture occurred across an area between upstate New York and lower Michigan. Millersburg and Woodstock share large numbers of hall and parlor, double-pile, and two-thirds double-pile houses. These folk dwelling types provide more of the linkage between the two communities than subsequently built houses. This fact reflects the early southward migration from Pennsylvania into the Shenandoah Valley and the remarkable survival of historical architecture in both towns. Millersburg has weaker folk dwelling ties with Mount Gilead and Chilton. Mount Gilead and Petersburg resemble Hudson with a similarly diminished intensity. Hudson shares multiple folk dwelling

10.2 Most Similar Towns: Folk Type Dwellings

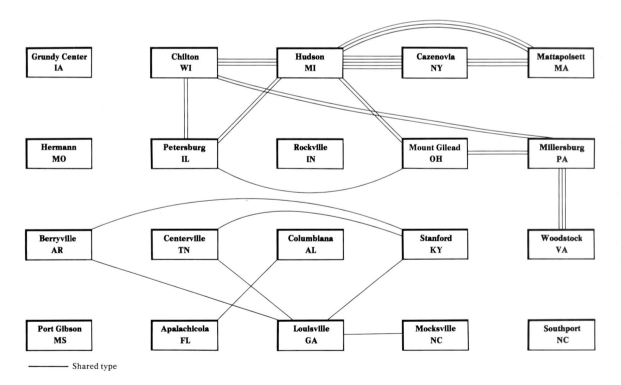

———— Shared type

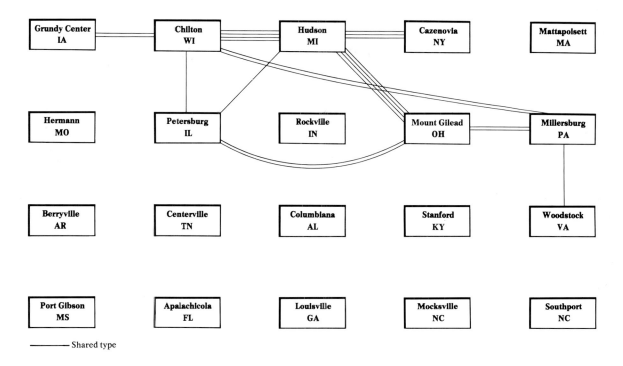

10.3   Most Similar Towns: Builder House Types

types with five other towns in the North. Its traditional domestic architecture epitomizes what has survived in small northern communities.

Folk dwelling types provide relatively weak ties among towns in the South. In the country, folk houses and cottages may differ substantially from the Upper to the Lower South. In towns, too few have survived to demonstrate any subregional continuity between places. While limited in number, the folk dwellings of Louisville are the most typical of the entire South. They resemble those found in four other communities.

Two-story "builder" houses, made popular in the late nineteenth century by the wide circulation of plan books, define a northern cluster of towns (Figure 10.3). Houses of the crossplan, L-shaped, cube, and irregularly massed composite varieties provide much of the linkage. These dwelling types give the closest ties to Hudson and Chilton on the one hand and Hudson and Mount Gilead on the other. Only slightly less intense is the tie between Hudson and Cazenovia. The size of these plan book houses and their frequency in all four communities makes it clear that these were prosperous places receptive to new design trends during the late nineteenth century. As with folk dwelling types, Hudson is the most typical town in terms of late nineteenth century plan book houses.

Popular one-story or one-and-one-half story "builder" cottages of the late nineteenth century are somewhat common in southern towns, but nearly absent in the North (Figure 10.4). Consistently important in the South are the double-pile cottage and the southern bungalow. Plan book cottages provide the strongest tie between Louisville and Apalachicola. They also provide a modest linkage between Louisville and both Southport and Berryville. Ties of similar strength exist between Columbiana and both Southport and

Apalachicola. Once again no separation between towns in the Upper and Lower South is apparent. As with folk dwelling types, Louisville is the most typical of the southern towns. The modest size of common late nineteenth century dwellings in the South reflects a less prosperous regional economy than in the North.

As with builder cottages, town linkages based on ranch-type dwellings are strongest in the South (Figure 10.5). Since 1945 new house construction has been much more important in southern towns than in northern

towns. For example, Mocksville and Columbiana resemble one another more since there are large numbers of composite, raised, and split level ranch dwellings in both towns. However, Louisville remains the most typical town in the South. It shares a high frequency of ranch-type dwellings with Mocksville, Stanford, Centerville, and Berryville. Louisville reflects both a vanishing Old South and an emergent New South. Hudson, however, reflects a relatively well preserved North, but one that is stagnant.

10.4   Most Similar Towns: Builder Cottage Types

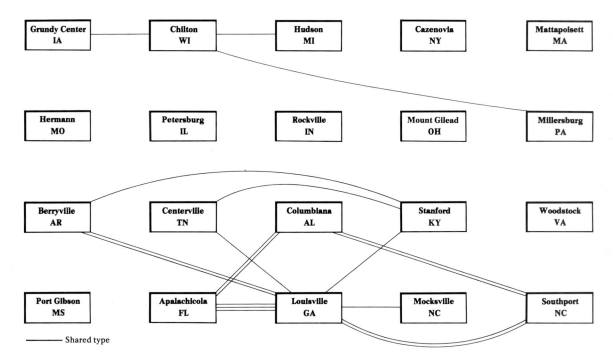

————— Shared type

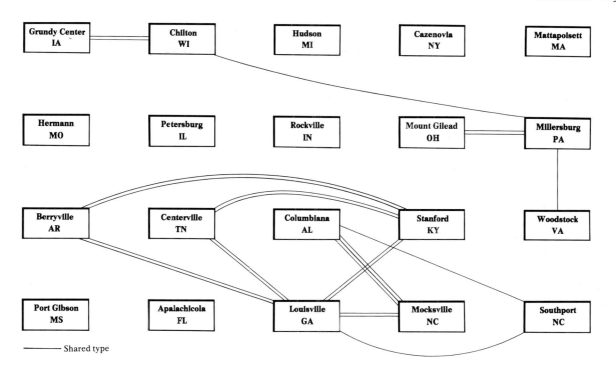

10.5   Most Similar Towns: Ranch Dwelling Types

Each of our towns generates a distinctive visual impression reflecting its peculiar mix of dwelling types. It is not only local grid peculiarities and the look of principal retail streets that give towns distinctive visual personalities. The different ways in which small towners house themselves helps define a sense of overall community character. For most towns several dwelling types are conspicuous, occurring in numbers far in excess of the norm. Apparent to even casual visitors to Cazenovia are older dwellings, such as the gable-front and upright-and-wing houses concentrated on the town's older streets. Visually prominent in Louisville and Centerville are the recently built standard ranches and minimal ranches that predominate in new subdivisions. At Stanford late nineteenth-century cottages and houses as well as bungalows of the early twentieth century blend at the center, and spill into the countryside along major arterials.

As we have established above, similarities exist town to town, as places are clearly linked through a sharing of specific cottage and house forms. We have focused on the towns that share three or more dwelling types in numbers that substantially exceed the average for all towns. However, the questions asked in our inventorying of dwellings suggest only partial answers to why these similarities define a pronounced North–South dichotomy (Figures 4.52 and 10.1). Concern with cultural origins and diffusions offers only a partial explanation for the similarities observed town to town. Scholars need to focus much more on local builders, who under the influence of national trends replicated popular dwelling types in town after town. Thus it was coincidences of economic and population growth that explain many of the similarities observed place to place.

Important also are processes of survival. The common dwellings surviving over time have been those adaptable to the behavioral patterns of later generations. The preferred or dominant common house forms of earlier times are not necessarily the cultural artifacts or relics in the present cultural landscape. Why is it (and how is it?) that dwellings survive in large numbers in some places and not in others? What are the processes of selection by which some cottages and houses endure here and not there? Clearly, the Civil War brought destruction to most of our southern towns eliminating from them early nineteenth-century folk dwellings. But, what else has been eliminated? How wide is the gap between former circumstances and the realities of contemporary extant material culture? Reconstructing past realities in small towns may be impossible for most places. For only four of our towns (Cazenovia, Hudson, Chilton, and Hermann) is the historical record adequate to any retrospection, and then only through the limited offices of bird's-eye views of the 1870s

upon which houses, though depicted, appear highly generalized. It is very doubtful if retrospective study can be accomplished across a wide array of towns reflecting various culture regions. Focus on specific dwelling types across very limited areas might be possible, and ought to be encouraged. For example, an analysis of upright-and-wing, gable front, and L-shaped houses of upstate New York and the Upper Middle West has been undertaken with substantive results (Mattson, 1988).

What we have provided is a base-line inventory for comprehending selection processes as they operate in decades to come. Small towns long in hiatus, may be experiencing a revival in the United States: a reaction, perhaps, to problems of metropolitan living. Small-town revival is especially apparent across the South in places like Stanford, Centerville, Columbiana, Southport, and Mocksville. Older housing gives way rapidly to new as traditional town centers decline in favor of peripheral subdivisions. Older housing is also vulnerable to natural hazards. At Port Gibson, periods of profound cold immediately prior to our inventory in January 1984 left upwards of a half-dozen houses reduced to ruined foundations, victims of overheated stoves. Both Southport and Apalachicola were twice struck by hurricanes in the two years subsequent to

our surveying, with extensive damage to the latter place. Culling processes operate unabated with the old giving way to the new as reflects economic change, nature providing a helping hand. Such change heightens awareness that small towns, even the most conservative of them, are truly fluid places.

It is clear from our looking at common dwellings that a new regional landscape is fast emerging. Since World War II most southern towns have been remade in the image of the ranch dwelling and all that it implies. Traditional housing is rapidly being replaced, much of it flimsily built and lacking resistance to the decay of subtropical climes. Northern towns would keep pace, but find themselves unable to match southern economic expansion except where affluent commuters abound as at Mattapoisett and Cazenovia. Traditional housing in the North is proving necessarily more permanent. Thus the growing towns of the South are drifting toward new kinds of landscape expression implicit not only in new kinds of houses, but in new morphologies where modern subdivisions sprawl outward to completely ring and dominate the old.

Common houses in small towns display diversity from the single-pile and double-pile folk-inspired forms to the irregularly massed, bungalow, and ranch types that are more clearly builder-derived. Ours was a search for diversity and we are not surprised to have found it: much of it regionally configured in interesting ways. Nonetheless, there is much that all towns hold in common. Not the similarity of dwelling types shared town to town as we have established, but a ubiquity of selected forms. The American building vocabulary predominant in small towns shows a pervasive homogeneity: a preference for simple rectangular floor plan perimeters, a preference for one-story or one-and-one-half-story dwellings, and a preference for simple gable roofs. Consider the dwelling types so characterized: hall and parlor cottages, saddlebag cottages, I cottages, Cape Cod cottages, New England classic cottages, double-pile cottages, square cottages, cottage bungalows, standard ranches, minimal ranches, and raised ranches. Although plan books bristled with irregularly massed dwellings in the late nineteenth century and with split-level and other exotic ranch forms in the mid-twentieth, what Americans built in small towns appears highly standardized at all times.

Floor plan, arrangement of facade openings, use of porches, and facade materials all varied with changing fads and fashions. Nevertheless, local builders appear, in retrospect, wonderfully unimaginative with their single story or one-and-one-half-story rectangular boxes with gable roofs.

In the North in the nineteenth century, two-story dwellings suggested affluence and high status. Again, the rectangular floor plan and the gable roof prevailed in both full double-pile and two-thirds double-pile houses. Closely related was the gable-front double-pile house, the double-pile form with narrow end turned toward the public way. In the South after the Civil War, both climate and economic recession encouraged one-story and one-and-one-half-story structures at least in small towns. Thus gable-front dwellings were exclusively cottages there. This propensity in the South to build dwellings of low profile or silhouette was reinforced first by bungalow and then by ranch impulses. Now this inclination predominates on small town peripheries everywhere, North and South, through the ranch idea.

Although Americans have grown away from the single-room building modular (they no longer combine rooms toward hall and parlor and other simple planforms), the exterior shape of their typical dwellings remain rectangular, defined by right angles. This situation reflects the continued reliance on wood both in balloon frame and in modern post and beam construction. Certainly, builders long have relied on standardized plans which, through familiarity, could be rapidly executed. A further encouragement to simplicity was the drive to reduce the quantities of lumber and other materials used by eliminating structural complexity. Most houses found in our study towns were built on speculation. Reliance on common denominators of planform and appearance undoubtedly enhanced house marketability. Future study should focus on this pervasive sameness which, at the broadest levels of generalization, appears to subsume a wide spectrum of dwelling types. Specifically, attention should be paid to the builders' determination to embrace limited ranges of structural form in the defining and servicing of local housing markets.

Detached dwellings have come to symbolize certain key national virtues (Wright 1981, 89). At the individual level, common dwellings represent personal independence for ordinary people.

206

Socially, they symbolize family pride and self-sufficiency. Politically, vernacular architecture expresses democratic freedom of choice and equality. Economically, the vernacular dwellings of small towns mirror predominant patterns of private enterprise, housing packaged and sold commercially as commodity. The intentional austerity of most common houses in small towns reflects not only adherence to mainstream social values and tastes, but a necessary orientation to market realities. Difference in sameness, as a kind of social conformity, generally facilitates the buying and selling of houses as housing. This fact, more than any other, probably underlies standardization tendencies in dwellings evident nationwide.

We have focused on the American small town. Continued emphasis on small-town people and their housing inclinations is certainly appropriate. But the vast majority of Americans now live in big cities. How does metropolitan America house itself? What are the prevailing dwelling types? How do they relate to rural and small-town experiences? Every metropolis has some distinctive house and cottage forms. How do they relate to national and regional norms? How did they develop as local traditions? The metropolises, es-

pecially at their suburban peripheries, are the fashion leaders in domestic architecture today. Here, a new building industry is forming around large corporations. The builder as small businessman has lost importance. It is to urban neighborhoods that the search for dwelling types and the outlining of the geography of American common houses must ultimately turn.

Ours has been a modern exploration. Not an adventure into totally uncharted reaches, but an examination of everyday places focused on everyday features of common houses or dwellings. Ours is an attempt at rediscovery by clearly classifying dwellings according to form in order to see them as structure types variously repetitive from place to place. We have sketched the outlines of that geographical variation in a set of small towns from the Atlantic Seaboard to the Mississippi Valley. We have posited numerous questions, some of which we have tentatively answered. Above all, ours is an invitation to further exploring and questioning by scholars and lay people alike. What is required is a curiosity about common houses and a striving to understand them in a landscape context. Look

around. There are few houses that will not tell a story either of folk origins and diffusions or of a national building industry. Every house says something about its inhabitants, and as houses accumulate in a place they collectively say something about community and regional and historical consciousness. Learning to read these messages can be rewarding intellectually, and entertaining as curiosity resolves into understanding.

GLOSSARY OF STRUCTURAL FORMS

In our study of common houses we emphasize form or structure. Separate dwelling types are identified in terms of floor plan (especially perimeter outline and room arrangement), height (the number of occupied stories), and roof type. Described here are the sixty-seven structures inventoried. The diagrams are suggestive only since floor plans portray idealized room arrangements and door locations. Although front and side elevations illustrate height and roof shape, they are not descriptive of any specific dwelling. Readers should be warned of specific word usage. The term "house" refers to a structure of two or more floors (unless otherwise indicated). The terms "cottage" and "cabin" always refer to structures of either one- or one-and-a-half stories, a half-story defined as habitable space immediately under a roof. The cita-tions in each annotation refer to the accompanying bibliography. Readers will find additional descriptions in the references cited.

Camelback House

This version of the shotgun cottage, a single story structure one room wide and two or more rooms deep, has a two-story enlargement at the rear: either (a) a second story added above the back two rooms, preserving the strict linearity of the house, or (b) a separate two-story section perpendicular to the front of the structure. Chimney placement varies. This peculiar form is a response to property tax laws in New Orleans; Louisville, Kentucky; and other cities which assessed houses according to the size of front facades.

Newton 1971, 16; Vlach 1976, 51; Noble 1984, 98.

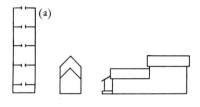

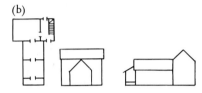

Cape Cod Cottage (Double-House Cape Cod Cottage)

This structure, common in late eighteenth- and early nineteenth-century New England, is derived from the hall and parlor cottage. This compact dwelling usually contains two rooms in front with three smaller rooms across the rear. A half-story is reached by a staircase set between central chimney columns (a). Twentieth-century revival versions (commercial builders' Cape Cod cot-

tages) retain the traditional exterior form, although interior floor plans are much changed (b). Roofs on revival cottages are frequently interrupted by attic dormers.

For traditional Cape Cod cottages, see Connally 1960, 51; Cummings 1979, 23; Hubka 1979, 220; Rifkind 1980, 14. For twentieth-century revival versions, see Stith and Meyer 1974, 4; Walker 1981, 88; McAlester and McAlester 1984, 78; Noble 1984, 23.

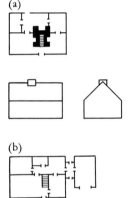

Carolina I House

This structure is a common variation of the basic I house, a two-story structure that is one room deep and two rooms wide with a central hallway. This version has an attached single-story shed-style porch across the front and a matching single-story shed-like extension across the rear. It is common to the Carolinas but is not restricted to that region.

Kniffen 1965, 554; Newton 1971, 11; Swaim 1978, 38; McAlester and McAlester 1984, 80.

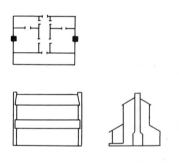

Composite Bungalow with Irregular Massing

An elaboration of either the cottage bungalow or the shotgun bungalow, this 1- or 1½-story structure displays geometric complexity with a highly irregular perimeter outline. Floor plans display considerable variation, although, as in other bungalows, rooms generally connect without use of large hallways, and the front door commonly opens directly into the living room. Broad eaves and a low pitch characterize roofs that are most frequently multiple-hip or multiple-gable. These structures first appeared at the very end of the nineteenth century as part of the bungalow fashion popularized by commercial builders.

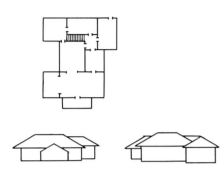

Composite Cottage with Irregular Massing

This 1- or 1½-story structure is geometrically complex and has a highly irregular perimeter outline. Multiple-gable, multiple-hip, or combined multiple–gable and hip roofs predominate. Floors plans display extreme variation. Bays, pavilions, dormers, and multiple porches and chimneys make the larger cottages eclectic architectural displays. Composite cottages were popular between 1890 and 1910.

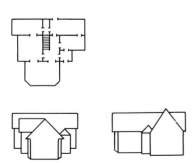

Composite Cottage with Irregular Massing and Pyramid Roof (Southern Pyramid)

This 1- or 1½-story structure features a steeply pitched pyramidal roof (sometimes truncated at the very top), making it an important variation of the composite cottage with irregular massing. The form originated in the South and appears to have been an elaboration of the pyramidal cottage. It was popular between 1890 and 1910.

Lewis 1975, 21.

Composite House with Irregular Massing

This 2- or 2½-story structure is a composite of geometric forms with a highly irregular outline. Multiple-gable, multiple-hip, or combined multiple–gable and hip roofs predominate. Floor plans vary substantially. Towers, bays, pavilions, dormers, and multiple porches and chimneys may produce eclectic architectural displays. Late nineteenth-century houses tend to have open floor plans with hallways and principal rooms separated only by wide arches with sliding doors. Early twentieth-century houses are much reduced in scale.

For late nineteenth-century houses, see Peat 1962, 91; Handlin 1979, 353; Rifkind 1980, 56, 69, 82; Wright 1980, 26; Walker 1981, 149, 153, 163. For early twentieth-century houses, see McAlester and McAlester 1984, 262.

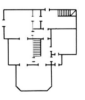

210

Composite Ranch "House"

An elaboration of the ranch "house," this 1- or 1½-story structure is geometrically complex and has an irregular outline. L, T, and lateral protuberances are most common requiring use of multiple-gable, multiple-hip, or combined multiple–gable and hip roofs. Floor plans vary considerably. First introduced immediately prior to World War II, its popularity continues today.

Walker 1981, 234, 252.

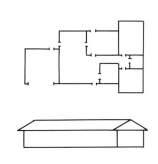

Continental Plan Cottage (or Cabin)

This 1- or 1½-story dwelling is divided into three rooms. A kitchen extends through the full depth of the dwelling along one side. A front room (or parlor) and a rear bedroom occupy the other side. The fireplace and chimney column are located on the interior wall of the kitchen (with a five-plate stove in older structures sometimes built into the rear of the fireplace to warm the parlor beyond). The continental plan, introduced by Germans into Pennsylvania in the eighteenth century, was modified in the nineteenth century to embrace English building ideas and thus appears in many variations.

Glassie 1968a, 48; Pillsbury and Kardos c. 1970, 49; Rifkind 1980, 12; Walker 1981, 72; McAlester and McAlester 1984, 83; Noble 1984, 43.

Continental Plan House (including the Penn Plan House or Quaker Plan House)

The continental plan, with its three-room first-floor arrangement, was used in 2- or 2½-story structures in the eighteenth century, especially in Pennsylvania (a). Quaker migrants to the Carolinas introduced a variant of the house there (b). Continental plan houses are very similar in exterior appearance to two-thirds double-pile houses. Only the off-center placement of the chimneys and front doors suggests German or German-Swiss origins. Internal gable-end chimneys are common in nineteenth-century houses which, on the exterior, embrace English building ideas (c).

Bucher 1962, 14; Glassie 1968a, 54; Glassie 1972, 41; Swaim 1978, 34; Herman 1978, 162; Foley 1980, 63; Patrick 1981, 62; Walker 1981, 73, 77; Noble 1984, 45.

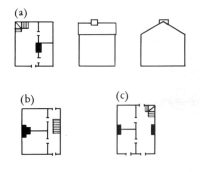

Cottage Bungalow

This 1- or 1½-story structure (usually with a gable roof) is similar to the incised-porch bungalow except that the porch is added-on and not built-in. Eaves of the low- to moderately-pitched roof are extended outward on all sides. Dormers, front and back, are common, providing additional space in the half-story. Floor plans vary as do chimney arrangements. Generally, rooms have access to one another without the use of large hallways: the front door commonly opening into the living room. Bungalows, promoted by commercial builders, reached their height of popularity just prior to World War I.

Finley and Scott 1940, 414; Lancaster 1958, 239; Mattson 1981, 75.

Crossplan Cottage

The floor plan perimeter is cross-shaped in this irregularly massed 1- or 1½-story structure with multiple-gable roof. The longer axis is usually perpendicular to the street, and the shorter cross-axis parallel. Floor plans and chimney placements vary in what is a late nineteenth- and

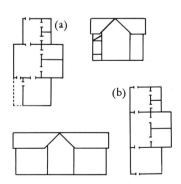

early twentieth-century form. Shed-like front and/or side porches are common (a). The shorter cross-axis is not always fully developed (b). These structures, often built on speculation by builders, were most popular just prior to World War I.

Crossplan Cottage with Multiple Gambrel Roof

This crossplan cottage, popular in the first decade of the twentieth century, has a multiple-gambrel rather than a multiple-gable roof. The roof, by its size and unusual configuration, clearly dominates the structure. Shed roof porches are common.

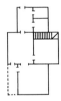

Crossplan House

The floor-plan perimeter is cross-shaped in this irregularly massed, 2- or 2½-story structure with multiple-gable roof. The longer axis is usually perpendicular to the street, the shorter cross-axis parallel. Floor plans and chimney placements vary in what is a late nineteenth- and early twentieth-century builder form. L-shaped shed-like front and side porches are common. The cross-axis is not always fully developed.

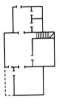

Crossplan House with Multiple Gambrel Roof

This early twentieth-century crossplan form has a multiple-gambrel rather than a multiple-gable roof. The roof, by its size and atypical configuration, clearly dominates the structure giving it a sense of vertical exaggeration. Shed-roof porches are typical.

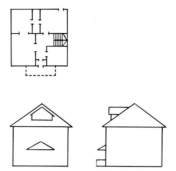

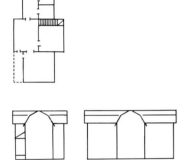

Cube House (Cubic House, Two-Story Square House, Cornbelt Cube House, or Four-Square House)

This structure is a square or nearly square box with peaked-hip roof (sometimes truncated at the very top). Being two rooms wide and two rooms deep, it is essentially a 2- or 2½-story version of the pyramidal cottage. However, most cube houses provide substantially greater floor space than pyramid cottages. This form type was popular throughout the first three decades of the twentieth century.

Finley and Scott 1940, 415; Kniffen 1965, 577; Rickert 1967, 229; Stith and Meyer 1974, 5; Walker 1981, 138; Noble 1984, 125.

Dogtrot Cabin or Cottage (Open Passage Cottage)

A widely used method of building a two-room 1- or 1½-story log dwelling in the early nineteenth century was to separate two log pens (each approximately sixteen feet square) by an open central hall (usually half the width of a pen). The whole was covered by a common gable roof (a). In the mid- and late nineteenth century, the plan was widely replicated in frame construction, with shed-like porches both front and back and an L-extension (b).

Kniffen 1936, 187; Morrison 1952, 169; Glassie 1968a, 94; Newton 1971, 8; Jeane and Purcell 1978, 8, 16; Marshall 1981, 41; McAlester and McAlester 1984, 83; Noble 1984, 117.

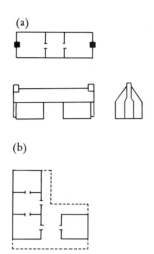

Dogtrot House

The dogtrot plan was occasionally used in two-story houses in the nineteenth century, although rear L-extensions were usually only one story. This resulted in separate gable roofs for the main structure and addition. The open passage was frequently enclosed at a later date.

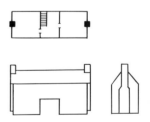

Double-Pile Central Chimney House (including the New England Large House)

A house with a salt-box floor plan (with lobby entrance facing a central chimney and smaller rooms in back), this structure has a symmetrical gable roof when viewed in side profile. Thus it has a full second story across the rear rather than a lean-to extension.

Kelly 1924, 14; Morrison 1952, 474; Williams and Williams 1957, 67; Pillsbury and Kardos c. 1970, 25; Hubka 1979, 220; Walker 1981, 78; Noble 1984, 26.

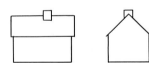

Double-Pile Cottage (including the Georgian Plan Cottage)

A double-pile, 1- or 1½-story dwelling with gable roof, most eighteenth- and early nineteenth-century versions have two rooms paired on either side of a central hallway (a). Chimney placement varies, with paired interior chimneys common. A flat hipped roof version of this cottage was also popular. Twentieth-century

structures only approximate traditional prototypes. The central hallway is reduced or eliminated, the front door frequently opening into the living room (b).

For eighteenth- and early nineteenth-century versions, see Swaim 1978, 40; Jeane and Purcell 1978, 53, 70. For twentieth-century structures, see Walker 1981, 113; McAlester and McAlester 1984, 98.

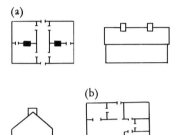

Double-Pile Cottage with Front Extension

A double-pile structure of 1 or 1½ stories, its roof form is a function of the size of the front extension placed to one side on the facade. Large extensions invite use of multiple-gable roofs as opposed to gables with dormers. A twentieth-century form, it derives from the traditional Double-pile Cottage.

Walker 1981, 91.

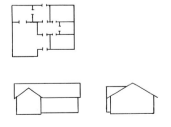

Double-Pile Cottage with Gambrel Roof

A double-pile, 1- or 1½-story cottage with gambrel roof, most eighteenth- and nineteenth-century examples have paired rooms on either side of a central hallway. Twentieth-century structures only approximate this floor plan. In "Dutch Colonial" 1½-story cottages, gambrel roofs are usually dominated by large dormers which create a two story effect.

For eighteenth- and nineteenth-century examples, see Morrison 1952, 128; Rifkind 1980, 13. For twentieth-century structures, see Embury 1913, 1; Stump 1981, 44; Walker 1981, 59; McAlester and McAlester 1984, 322.

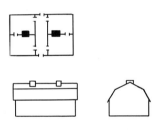

Double-Pile House (including the Georgian Plan or Four-Over-Four House)

A double-pile, 2- or 2½-story structure with gable roof, most eighteenth- and nineteenth-century versions have paired

214

rooms on either side of a central hallway on both floors (a). Chimney placement varies with paired gable-end chimneys typical, but flat-hipped roofs with paired interior chimneys are common also. Twentieth-century houses (Builders' Colonial Houses) only approximate this traditional prototype. Central hallways are reduced or eliminated with the front door often opening directly into the living room which commonly occupies the full depth of the house on one side (b).

For eighteenth- and nineteenth-century versions, see Glassie 1968a, 49; Pillsbury and Kardos c. 1970, 56; Glassie 1972, 37; Lewis 1975, 5; Noble 1975, 290; Rifkind 1980, 21. For twentieth-century houses, see Stith and Meyer 1974, 4; Foley 1980, 214; Walker 1981, 75, 96, 173; McAlester and McAlester 1984, 78; Noble 1984, 47, 103.

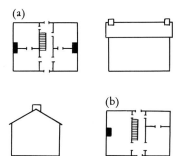

(a)

(b)

Double-Pile House with Gambrel Roof

Double-pile, 2- or 2½-story structures with gambrel roofs, most eighteenth- and nineteenth-century examples have paired rooms on either side of a central hallway on both floors. Twentieth-century houses only approximate this floor plan.

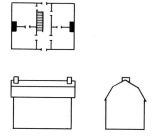

Double Shotgun Cottage (Double Bungalow)

This one-story structure, built primarily between 1890 and 1910, is comprised of two single shotgun plans built side by side under a common front-gable or hip roof. Front shed-roof porches are a typical feature, but chimney placement varies.

Lewis 1976, 59; Vlach 1976, 49.

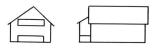

Double Shotgun House

This two-story structure, built primarily between 1890 and 1910, is comprised of two shotgun plans built side by side under a single front-gable or hip roof.

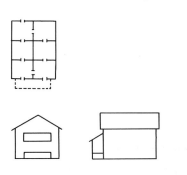

Gable-Front Double-Pile Cottage

A gabled, 1- or 1½-story structure two rooms wide and two or more rooms deep, this cottage retains only the outward form of the double-pile cottage. With the front door in a gabled end facing the street, the realigned floor plans of this cottage lack the classical symmetry of the central hallway cottage. Side-hall floor plans are common to nineteenth-century structures (a). In twentieth-century structures, space is usually arranged as in bungalows with rooms back to back down each side of the dwelling (b). One or more large side dormers are frequently used to enlarge space in the half-story. Chimney placement varies.

For gable-front double-pile cottage,

see McAlester and McAlester 1984, 90. For nineteenth-century structures, see Hubka 1979, 220.

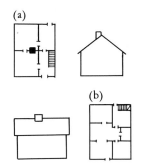

Gable-Front Double-Pile House

A gabled, 2- or 2½-story structure two rooms wide and two or more rooms deep, this house retains only the outward form of the double-pile house. Having a front door in one gable end facing the street, the varied floor plans of this house are substantial departures from the Georgian plan. Side-hall floor plans are common to nineteenth-century houses (a). Bungalow-related floor plans typify the twentieth century (b). Chimney placement varies.

Williams and Williams 1957, 80; Pil-

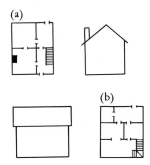

lsbury and Kardos c. 1970, 28; Handlin 1979, 358; Hubka 1979, 220; McAlester and McAlester 1984, 78, 90; Noble 1984, 108.

Gambrel-Front Double-Pile Cottage

A gambrel-roofed, 1- or 1½-story dwelling two rooms wide and two or more rooms deep, this structure is a variant of the gable-front double-pile cottage. It appears in the late eighteenth and early nineteenth centuries, and again as a twentieth-century revival.

Gambrel-Front Double-Pile House

A gambrel-roofed, 1- or 1½-story dwelling two rooms wide and two or more rooms deep, this structure is a variant of the gable-front double-pile house. Although based on early nineteenth-century precedents, it was most popular as an early twentieth-century revival.

Hall and Parlor Cottage (Double-Pen Cabin)

Elemental extension of the hall cottage (or single-pen cabin) through the addition of a second room or parlor produces a 1- or 1½-story structure that is two rooms wide and one room deep with a gable roof. Regional variation in chimney placement affected the appearance of these cottages during the colonial period. A central chimney and lobby entrance arrangement was typical in New England (a) whereas end-gable chimneys (either inside or outside) prevailed elsewhere (b). This form continued to be built until the end of the nineteenth century.

Finley and Scott 1940, 416; Morrison 1952, 162; Pillsbury and Kardos c. 1970, 27; Newton 1971, 7; Bastian 1977, 124; Swaim 1978, 33; Hubka 1979, 222; Foley 1980, 16; Marshall 1981, 41; Patrick 1981, 62; Walker 1981, 40, 60, 62, 77; McAlester and McAlester 1984, 78, 80, 83, 94; Noble 1984, 49.

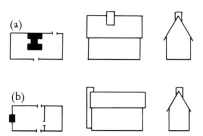

Hall and Parlor House (Pre-Classic I House or Early I House)

The plan of the hall and parlor cottage (or double-pen cabin) was commonly used in two-story houses in the nineteenth century (a). Structures were frequently enlarged with rear extensions which gave houses an overall L or T shape (b).

Glassie 1968a, 68; Glassie 1972, 45; Marshall 1981, 41; Patrick 1981, 64; Walker 1981, 53; McAlester and McAlester 1984, 78.

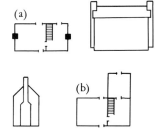

Hall Cottage (including the Single-Pen Cabin)

A simple one-room module with gable roof (often with a loft or half-story) and a fireplace and chimney at one end, this structure was built of heavy framing by the earliest English colonists. Dwellings of this form were constructed along routes of migration outward from the Delaware Valley. This basic house type persisted after the adoption of balloon frame construction well into the nineteenth century. Floor outlines typically approximated 16 by 16 feet: the size of space comfortably warmed by a single fireplace. These dimensions (the standard bay) may have deeper roots in European culture as the traditional size of building used for stabling oxen.

Kelly 1924, 6; Williams and Williams 1957, 71; Glassie 1968a, 53; Pillsbury and Kardos c. 1970, 24; Newton 1971, 6; Jeane and Purcell 1978, 8; Swaim 1978, 29; Hubka 1979, 222; Marshall 1981, 41; Walker 1981, 42, 46, 50, 56, 66, 74; McAlester and McAlester 1984, 80, 83; Noble 1984, 44.

I Cottage

A 1- or 1½-story version of the I house, this structure is one room deep and two rooms wide with a central hallway. Gabled roofs predominate. End chimneys are prevalent in nineteenth-century cottages (a). I cottages are commonly enlarged with rear extensions which gave them an overall L or T shape (b).

Swaim 1978, 41; Jeane and Purcell 1978, 8; Marshall 1981, 41; Walker 1981, 121.

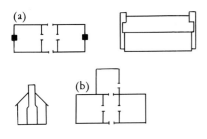

I House

This 2- or 2½-story structure is one room deep with two rooms wide with a central hallway on each floor. Chimneys in the gable walls are common on nineteenth-century houses. I houses are often enlarged with rear extensions which give them an overall L or T shape in perimeter

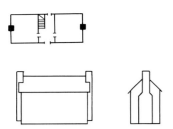

outline (see I Cottage, Figure B, above).

Kniffen 1936, 187; Kniffen 1965, 553; Glassie 1968a, 49; Pillsbury and Kardos c. 1970, 53; Newton 1971, 10; Glassie 1972, 44; Montell and Morse 1976, 32; Marshall 1981, 41; Patrick 1981, 63; Walker 1981, 74; McAlester and McAlester 1984, 80, 96.

Incised-Porch Bungalow

This gabled, 1- or 1½-story, double-pile structure features an incised or inset porch built into the structure (as opposed to being attached shed-style). Eaves of the low- to moderately-pitched roof are extended outward on all sides. Large dormers may be used both front and back to provide additional space in the half-story. Floor plans vary as do chimney placements. Generally, rooms connect one another without use of large hallways, and the front door opens directly into the living room. The main axis of the structure is parallel to the street. Such bungalows, as pro-

moted by commercial builders, were most popular just prior to World War I.

Finley and Scott 1940, 414; Lancaster 1958, 241; Mattson 1981, 75.

Incised-Porch Cottage (including the Creole Cottage)

This gabled (and sometimes hipped), 1- or 1½-story, double-pile cottage features an incised or inset porch built into the structure (as opposed to being attached shed-style). The porch is an integral part of the structure. Floor plans vary with two large front rooms, and either two or three smaller rooms variously arranged behind. Central or paired interior chimneys predominate in nineteenth-century "Creole Cottages" in the South. This general structure type also appeared in the nineteenth century Middle West, especially in areas of French and German settlement. The Incised-Porch Cottage may have inspired development of the Incised-Porch Bungalow in the twentieth century.

For nineteenth-century "Creole Cottages," see Kniffen 1936, 182; Glassie 1968a, 118; Newton 1971, 13; Jeane and Purcell 1978, 22; Fricker 1984,

218

137. For nineteenth-century Middle West types, see Van Ravenswaay 1977, 153.

Incised-Porch House

This structure is a 2- or 2½-story version of the incised-porch cottage. It has a gabled (and sometimes hipped) roof, but is distinguished by an incised or inset "gallerie" porch that is an integral part of the structure. Floor plans vary with two large front rooms and either two or three smaller rooms behind. Central chimneys or paired interior chimneys predominate in nineteenth-century houses.

Morrison 1952, 263; Walker 1981, 86.

L-Shaped Cottage

Like the upright and wing house this structure is L-shaped in perimeter outline. However, the floor plan is usually integrated under a single multiple-gable roof forming either a 1- or 1½-story dwelling. Floor plans vary as does chimney placement. The angle of the L frequently contains a shed-type porch with the front door usually in the "wing." This section is usually parallel to the street.

Finley and Scott 1940, 415; McAlester and McAlester 1984, 206.

L-Shaped House (Yankee House)

Probably a derivative of the upright and wing house, this L-shaped structure preserves a "temple and wing" effect. However, its integrated floor plan does not preserve the integrity of each house section as a separate unit as at least one room occupies space in both sections. Usually, this late nineteenth-

century form is capped by a multiple-gable roof. Floor plans vary as does chimney placement. The angle of the L frequently contains a shed-type porch. The front door is usually in the "wing" section (the section parallel to the street).

Finley and Scott 1940, 415; Marshall 1981, 35.

Minimal Ranch "House"

A one-story structure with low-pitched roof (usually gable), this dwelling is a scaled down version of the ranch "house." The garage, if existent, is most commonly a separate structure. This form, developed after World War II, is still popular with tradesmen who build on speculation.

Foley 1980, 220; Walker 1981, 237, 243, 244.

New England Classic Cottage (including the One-and-One-Half New England Cottage)

Like the Cape Cod cottage, this structure derived in the early nineteenth century from the central chimney hall and parlor cottage of New England. Two front rooms sit at either side of an entrance lobby from which a stairway ascends to two rooms in a half-story. Several smaller rooms are arranged across the first floor rear. Commonly, "lie-on-your-stomach" or "ankle" windows located below the eave of the gable roof (often in an entablature) light the upstairs rooms.

Hamlin 1944, 303; Lewis 1975, 10; Noble 1984, 105.

Octagon House

This structure, something of a curiosity of the mid to late nineteenth century, has an octagonal or near-octagonal perimeter outline, although extensions off the rear are common. Floor arrangement and chimney placement varies.

Fowler 1854, 1; Creese 1946, 89; Peat 1962, 92; Foley 1980, 159; Walker 1981, 140; McAlester and McAlester 1984, 235; Noble 1984, 139.

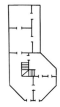

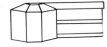

One-Half Cape Cod Cottage (House Cape Cod Cottage)

Here the full Cape Cod cottage of the early nineteenth century is reduced to one-half its size. This 1½-story gabled structure has one large room in front with two smaller rooms behind.

Connally 1960, 50; Walker 1981, 88.

One-Over-One House (Bandbox House or Stack House)

A set of one-room modules stacked to a height of two or three stories, this eighteenth- and nineteenth-century structure was usually capped by a gable roof.

Murtaugh 1957, 9; Marshall 1981, 41; Walker 1981, 74.

One-Over-One House With Rear Extension (City House)

One-over-one houses could be enlarged on a narrow urban lot by adding a one- or two-story rear extension. The extension was usually narrower than the front block and was normally aligned with one of the side walls. This form was most popular in the late eighteenth century.

Murtaugh 1957, 11.

One-Third Double-Pile Cottage

A 1- or 1½-story structure with gable roof, this cottage, common in the late eighteenth and early nineteenth centuries, is a reduced version of the two-thirds double-pile cottage. It is two rooms deep and one room wide. As in the gable-front shotgun cottage, there is no side hall.

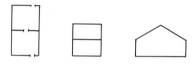

One-Third Double-Pile House (Two-Bay Town House)

A 2- or 2½-story structure with gable or hip roof, this house is two rooms deep. It is, in essence, the double-pile house reduced by two-thirds. Similar to the gable-front shotgun house, it does not contain a side hall, the staircase being located in the front room. Chimney placement varies. Common to the eighteenth and nineteenth centuries, this form has not enjoyed revived popularity in the twentieth century as has the two-thirds double-pile house.

Murtaugh 1957, 10; Glassie 1972, 38.

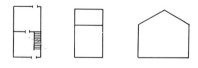

Pyramidal Cottage

This version of the square cottage (a structure two rooms wide and two rooms deep without central hallway) has a peaked-hip roof (sometimes truncated near the top). Stoves and associated chimneys are variously placed, although in structures with central heating a single chimney located at the peak of the roof is common. This form was most popular between 1890 and 1910.

Finley and Scott 1940, 417; Newton 1971, 17; Lewis 1975, 20; Bastian 1977, 126; Jeane and Purcell 1978, 21.

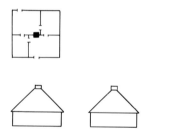

Raised Ranch House (Split Entry House)

This post–World War II two-story structure is organized around a central stairway located immediately inside the front door. Generally, the upper or main level is reached by a half-flight of stairs as one enters the front door. There the living room, diningroom, kitchen, and principal bedrooms are located. On the level below are additional bed-

rooms, utility space, and a garage. Floor plans vary.

Stith and Meyer 1974, 6.

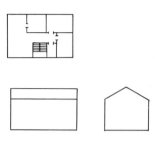

Ranch Bungalow

A one story double-pile structure with low pitched roof (usually a gable-front or hip roof) this post–World War II structure looks like a ranch "house" turned with the narrow end toward the street. Interior space, however, is organized in bungalow fashion with rooms arranged one behind the other. Incised corner porches are common. A garage is often attached to one side.

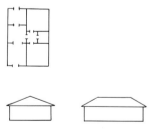

Ranch "House"

A 1- or 1½-story double-pile structure with low-pitched roof (either gable or hip), this form was popularized very rapidly after World War II by commercial builders. Interior floor plans vary. Garages may or may not be integrated into the structure.

Rickert 1967, 234; Stith and Meyer 1974, 3; Walker 1981, 235.

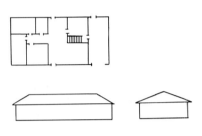

Saddlebag Cabin or Cottage

A widely used method of extending a 1- or 1½-story single-pen log cabin was to add another pen, its gable set up to the chimney end of the original structure. This method of enlargement produced a central-chimney dwelling two rooms wide and one room deep. The plan was widely replicated in the nineteenth century in frame construction. L and T extensions were common.

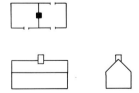

Morrison 1952, 168; Kniffen 1965, 562; Newton 1971, 7; Jeane and Purcell 1978, 18; Marshall 1981, 41; Walker 1981, 50; McAlester and McAlester 1984, 83, 95; Noble 1984, 116.

Saddlebag House (Saddlebag I House)

The saddlebag plan was also used in two-story houses in the nineteenth century.

Marshall 1981, 41.

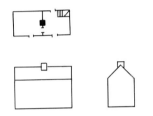

Salt Box House

An enlarged hall and parlor house of the late seventeenth and early eighteenth centuries associated primarily with New England. This structure, with lobby entrance fronting a central chimney, features a lean-to extension across the rear. The gable roof covering the extension assumes a "salt box" or "cat slide" profile in side view.

Kimball 1922, 33; Morrison 1952, 54; Williams and Williams 1957, 60; Glassie 1968a, 124; Pillsbury and Kardos c. 1970, 25; Cummings 1979, 24, 32–33, 70, 80, 86, 123–24, 138, 149; Foley 1980, 22; Rifkind 1980, 7; Walker 1981, 68, 257; McAlester and McAlester 1984, 78; Noble 1984, 25.

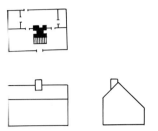

Shotgun Cottage

A single-story structure, one room wide and two or more rooms deep, this long linear cottage is usually capped by a gable-front roof. Hip roofs are also common as are shed-type front porches. Middle rooms frequently have a side exterior door. Chimney placement varies. This form was first introduced in the early nineteenth century.

Kniffen 1936, 186; Finley and Scott 1940, 417; Newton 1971, 15; Vlach 1976, 52; Rifkind 1980, 94; Noble 1984, 95.

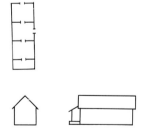

Shotgun House

One room wide and two or more rooms deep, this two-story version of the nineteenth-century shotgun cottage has either a gable-front or hip roof. Chimney and stairway placements vary. Shed-type front porches are typical as are exterior side doors that give access to a middle room.

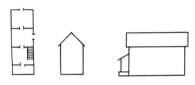

Southern Bungalow (Shotgun Bungalow)

With a front-gable or hip roof, this 1- or 1½-story, double-pile structure differs from incised-porch and cottage bungalows in that the main axis of the structure is perpendicular to the street. Eaves of the low-pitch roof are extended outward on all sides. Large side-dormers commonly provide additional space in the half-story. Floor plans vary. Generally, rooms connect one another without use of large hallways, the front door opening directly into the living room. The "Chicago bungalow," a common variation of the southern bungalow, has a hip roof extending over the front porch which is partially enclosed as a front room. As with other bungalows,

this form was most popular prior to World War I.

Kniffen 1936, 186; Finley and Scott 1940, 414; Newton 1971, 15.

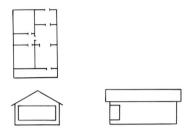

Split-Level Ranch "House"

This multi-level structure is comprised of a one-story section (which contains the living room, dining room, and kitchen) and a 1½- or 2-story section (commonly an L or T extension which contains the bedrooms with a garage below). The various levels, and, indeed, the two sections, are joined by a central staircase. A pair of gabled roofs covers the whole. Room arrangements vary. First introduced in the 1930s, this form did not become widespread until after 1950.

Rickert 1967, 238; Foley 1980, 221; Walker 1981, 262.

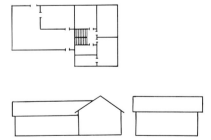

Square Cottage

This 1- or 1½-story, gable-roofed structure is two rooms wide and two rooms deep. It is very similar in appearance to the double-pile cottage; however, the absence of a central hallway produces a square or nearly square floor plan. Stoves and associated chimney columns are variously placed. This form was most popular between 1890 and 1910.

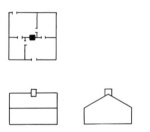

Three-Quarters Cape Cod Cottage (House-and-a-Half Cape Cod Cottage)

Like a Cape Cod cottage of the early nineteenth century but reduced one-fourth in size, this structure is two rooms deep and two rooms wide: the lobby entrance having been eliminated with one chimney column moved into a reduced front room.

Connally 1960, 51; Walker 1981, 88.

Two-Thirds Double-Pile Cottage

A 1- or 1½-story structure with gable roof, this cottage is two rooms deep and one room wide with a side hall containing a staircase to an upper half-story. This plan is essentially the double-pile cottage reduced one-third in size. A flat-hipped roof version usually has a rear extension. This structure was very popular in the late eighteenth and early nineteenth centuries. In New Jersey this type of dwelling, although often enlarged by a one-room deep lateral extension, is referred to as a Deep East Jersey.

For late eighteenth- and early nineteenth-century structures, see Glassie 1968a, 54. For Deep East Jersey, see Wacker 1971, 51, 53.

Two-Thirds Double-Pile House

A 2- or 2½-story structure with gable roof, this house is two rooms deep and one room wide with a side hall containing a staircase (a). In essence, this plan is the double-pile house reduced one-third in size. Such reduction accommodated the classical Georgian house to a narrow urban lot, although the plan also became popular in rural Pennsylvania, New Jersey, Maryland, and Virginia in the late eighteenth and early nineteenth centuries. Rural farmhouses were often enlarged through lateral extensions: appendages slightly set back from the line of the main house facade (b). Gable roofs predominated, but low hip roofs were common also. In twentieth-century derivatives, the side hall is reduced or eliminated with the front door sometimes opening into the living room (c).

Glassie 1968a, 54; Glassie 1972, 37; Lewis 1975, 6; Walker 1981, 75.

(a)

(b)   (c)

Two-Thirds Double-Pile House with Gambrel Roof

This two-thirds double-pile structure (two rooms with a side hall) has a gambrel roof. Twentieth-century revival houses only approximate nineteenth-century prototypes.

Two-Thirds Double-Pile House with Rear Extension (Town House or Three-Bay Town House)

A two-thirds double-pile house could be enlarged on a narrow urban lot by adding a one- or two-story rear extension. Extensions were usually narrower than the front block and carried back on one original side wall. This form was most popular in the late eighteenth and early nineteenth centuries.

Murtaugh 1957, 11; Rifkind 1980, 27, 81.

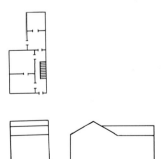

Two-Thirds I House (Half I House)

Two-thirds of an I house or one-half of an I house, depending upon the importance assigned the hallways, this 2- or 2½-story structure is one room deep with a hallway and a single room on each floor. Like I houses (see above), these structures were commonly enlarged with rear L or T extensions. The form was introduced in the eighteenth century, remaining popular throughout the nineteenth.

For two-thirds I house, see Glassie 1968a, 67; for one-half I house, see Montell and Morse 1976, 40.

Upright and Wing House (Temple Form House or Lazy T House)

Having evolved in New England and Upstate New York in the nineteenth century, this structure combines the New England classic cottage with the gable front double-pile house (or variations of the two) to form an L-shaped or T-shaped dwelling. The taller gable-front section was especially appropriate to Classical Revival styling and was responsible for the temple and wing label. Interior floor plans vary, although each section of the house usually stands as a unit with rooms totally contained within one part or the other. The roofs of both sections are totally separate in older dwellings of this sort: the gable of the "wing" usually joining the "upright" below the latter's eave line (a). In a later variety the roof of the "wing" intercepted that of the upright somewhere on its slope (b). The front door is usually in the "wing" section. Many houses were built in stages, the "upright" reflecting a latter stage of family prosperity.

Hamlin 1944, 306; Glassie 1968a, 132; Pillsbury and Kardos c. 1970, 29; Stith and Meyer 1974, 5; Lewis 1975, 13; Bastian 1977, 116; Walker 1981, 111, 127; McAlester and McAlester 1984, 93; Noble 1984, 109.

(a)

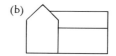
(b)

BIBLIOGRAPHY

Abramovitz, Moses. 1964. *Evidences of Long Swings in Aggregate Construction Since the Civil War.* New York: National Bureau of Economic Research.

An Account of the Celebration of the Fiftieth Anniversary of the Incorporation of the Town of Mattapoisett, Massachusetts, 1907. 1908. New Bedford, Mass.: n.p.

Alabama Historical Commission. 1975. *A Historic Site Survey of Blount, Chilton, Shelby, St. Clair, and Walker Counties.* Birmingham: Cather.

Alberts, William W. 1962. "Business Cycles, Residential Construction Cycles, and the Mortgage Market." *Journal of Political Economy* 70:263–81.

Alexander, Edward P. 1946–47. "Wisconsin, New York's Daughter State." *Wisconsin Magazine of History* 30:11–30.

Allen, Lewis F. 1860. *Rural Architecture: Being a Complete Description of Farm Houses, Cottages, and Out Buildings.* New York: Saxton.

Anderson, Sherwood. 1919. *Winesburg, Ohio.* New York: Huebsch.

Atwood, Daniel T. 1871. *Atwood's Country and Suburban Houses.* New York: Judd.

Backus, Samuel D. 1860. "Some Hints upon Farm Houses." In *Report of the Commissioner of Patents, 1859.* Washington, D.C.: U.S. Government Printing Office.

Bastian, Robert W. 1975. Architecture and Class Segregation in Late Nineteenth-Century Terre Haute, Indiana." *Geographical Review* 65:166–79.

———. 1977. "Indiana Folk Architecture: A Lower Midwestern Index." *Pioneer America* 19:115–36.

Baughman, A. J., and Robert J. Bartlett. 1911. *History of Morrow County, Ohio.* Chicago: Lewis.

Beadle, J. H. 1869. "History of Parke County." In *History of Vigo and Parke Counties,* ed. H.W. Beckwith. Chicago: Beckwith.

Bek, William G. 1907. *The German Settlement Society of Philadelphia and Its Colony, Hermann, Missouri.* Philadelphia: Americana Germanica Press.

Blumenson, J. J-G. 1977. *Identifying American Architecture: A Pictorial Guide to Styles and Terms, 1600–1945.* Nashville: American Association for State and Local History.

Bonner, Richard T., ed. 1909. *Memoirs of Lenawee County, Michigan.* Vol. 1. Madison, Wis.: Western Historical Association.

Brademan, Eugene M. 1939. "Early Kentucky: Its Virginia Heritage." *South Atlantic Quarterly* 38:449–61.

Braswell, O. Klute. 1889. *History of Carroll County, Arkansas.* Berryville, Ark.: author.

Brinkloe, William D. 1924. *The Small House: How to Plan and Build It.* New York.

Broemel, Greer E., and Ronald W. Cooper. 1981. *General Plan: Centerville, Tennessee.* Nashville, Tenn.: Tennessee Local Planning Office.

Brown, Robert. 1964. "The California Bungalow in Los Angeles: A Study in Origins and Classification." Master's thesis, University of California, Los Angeles.

Brunskill, R. W. 1971. *Illustrated Handbook of Vernacular Architecture.* London: Faber and Faber.

———. 1981. *Traditional Buildings of Britain: An Introduction to Vernacular Architecture.* London: Gollancz.

Bucher, Robert C. 1962. "The Continental Log House." *Pennsylvania Folklife* 12:14–19.

Bunnewith, Richard S., and Gene Pursley. 1976. *Mattapoisett: The Bicentennial.* Mattapoisett, Mass.: n.p.

Campbell, Burnham O. 1963. "Long Swings in Residential Construction: The Postwar Experience." *American Economic Review* 53:508–18.

Cartmell, T. K. 1963. *Shenandoah Valley Pioneers and Their Descendants.* Berryville, Va.: Chesapeake.

Chaddock, Robert E. 1908. "Ohio Before 1850: A Study of the Early Influence of Pennsylvania and Southern Populations in Ohio." *Columbia University Studies in History, Economics, and Public Law* 30:1–155.

Cleaveland, Henry W., William Backus, and Samuel D. Backus. 1856. *Village and Farm Cottages.* New York: Appleton.

Cohn, Jan. 1979. *The Palace or the Poorhouse: The American House as a Cultural Symbol.* East Lansing: Michigan State University Press.

Connally, Ernest A. 1960. "The Cape Cod House: An Introductory Study." *Journal, Society of Architectural Historians* 19:47–56.

Cooley, Solon. 1857. Letter to *The Genesee Farmer* 18:115.

Cooper, Patricia I. 1978. "A Quaker-Plan House in Georgia." *Pioneer America* 10:14–34.

Creese, Walter. 1946. "Fowler and the Domestic Octagon." *Art Bulletin* 28:89–102.

Crisler, Robert M. 1948. "Missouri's 'Little Dixie.'" *Missouri Historical Review* 42:130–39.

Croff, G. B. 1890. *Model Suburban Architecture, Embodying Designs for Dwellings of Moderate Cost.* New York: Roby and O'Neil.

Cummings, Abbott L. 1979. *The Framed Houses of Massachusetts Bay, 1625–1725.* Cambridge, Mass.: Harvard University Press.

Darnell, Margaretta J. 1972. "Innovations in American Prefabricated Housing, 1860–1890." *Journal, Society of Architectural Historians* 31:51–55.

[Davis, John W., and William E. Davis.] 1978. *Indiana Historic Sites and Structures Inventory: Interim Report—Parke County.* Indianapolis: Historic Landmarks Foundation of Indiana.

Dean, John P. 1946. *The Book of Houses.* New York: Crown.

Desprez, Annie. 1969. "Idealism and Reality in American Farm House Architecture: 1840–1880." Ph.D. diss., University of Kansas.

Dole, Philip. 1974. "Buildings and Gardens." In *Space, Style and Structure: Building in Northwest America, Volume One,* ed. Thomas Vaughn and Virginia G. Ferriday, 209–40. Portland: Oregon Historical Society.

Douglas, Ed P. 1974. *Architecture in Claiborne County, Mississippi: A Selective Guide.* Jackson, Miss.: Mississippi Department of Archives and History.

Downing, Andrew J. 1842. *Cottage Residences.* New York: Putnam.

———. 1850. *The Architecture of Country Houses, Including Designs for Cottages, Farm-Houses and Villas*. New York: Appleton.

Dunn, M. H. n.d. *Early Lincoln County History* ([Stanford] n.p.).

Durden, Marion L. 1983. *A History of Saint George Parish, Colony of Georgia, Jefferson County, State of Georgia*. Swainsboro, Ga.: Magnolia Press.

Egle, William M. 1883. *History of the Counties of Dauphin and Lebanon*. Philadelphia: Everts and Peck.

Egleston, Nathaniel H. 1884. *The Home and Its Surroundings*. New York: Appleton.

Embury, Aymar, II. 1913. *The Dutch Colonial House*. New York: McBride, Nast.

Faulkner, William. 1957. *The Town*. New York: Random House.

Ferguson, Jane E. M. 1975. "The Development of Domestic Architecture in Hickman County Tennessee: 1800–1910." Master's thesis, Vanderbilt University.

Field, M. 1857. *Rural Architecture*. New York: Miller.

Finley, Robert, and E. M. Scott. 1940. "A Great Lakes-to-Gulf Profile of Dispersed Dwelling Types." *Geographical Review* 30:412–19.

Foley, Mary M. 1980. *The American House*. New York: Harper.

Forman, Henry C. 1948. *The Architecture of the Old South: The Medieval Style*. Cambridge, Mass.: Harvard University Press.

Fowler, Orson S. 1854. *A Home for All*. New York: Fowler and Wells.

Frank, Lynn. 1979. "Houses and Structure Survey, Davie County, March and April, 1979." Manuscript, Davie County Public Library, Mocksville, N.C.

Fricker, Jonathan. 1984. "The Origins of the Creole Raised Plantation House." *Louisiana History* 25:137–53.

Fusch, Richard, and Larry R. Ford. 1983. "Architecture and the Geography of the American City." *Geographical Review* 73:324–40.

Galloway, Eloise. n.d. "History of Shelby County." Manuscript, Shelby County Library, Columbiana, Ala.

Garlinghouse Ranch and Suburban Homes. 1950. Topeka: Garlinghouse, L. F., Co.

Garnsey, George. 1885. "How to Build a House." *National Builder* 1:4.

Gasconade County History. 1979. Owensville, Mo.: Gasconade County Historical Society.

Gebhard, David, and Robert Winter. 1977. *A Guide To Architecture in Los Angeles and Southern California*. Santa Barbara, Calif.: Peregrine Smith.

Gerlach, Russel L. 1976. *Immigrants in the Ozarks: A Study in Ethnic Geography*. Columbia, Mo.: University of Missouri Press.

Glass, Joseph W. 1971. "The Pennsylvania Culture Region: A Geographical Interpretation of Barns and Farmhouses." Ph.D. diss., Pennsylvania State University.

Glassie, Henry. 1968a. *Pattern in the Material Folk Culture of the Eastern United States*. Philadelphia: University of Pennsylvania Press.

———. 1968b. "The Types of Southern Mountain Cabin." In *The Study of American Folklore*, ed. Jan H. Brunvard, 338–70. New York: Norton.

———. 1972. "Eighteenth-Century Cultural Process in Delaware Valley Folk Building." In *Winterthur Portfolio* 7:6–57.

———. 1975. *Folk Housing in Middle Virginia: A Structural Analysis of Historic Artifacts*. Knoxville: University of Tennessee Press.

———. 1984. "Vernacular Architecture and Society." *Material Culture* 16:5–24.

Glazner, J. Frank. 1938. *Geography of the Great Appalachian Valley of Alabama*. Jacksonville, Ala.: author.

Gottlieb, Manuel. 1976. *Long Swings in Urban Development*. New York: National Bureau of Economic Research.

Gowans, Alan. 1964. *Images of American Living: Four Centuries of Architecture and Furniture as Cultural Expression*. Philadelphia: Lippincott.

Gries, John, and James Ford, eds. 1932. *Publications of the President's Conference on Home Building and Home Ownership.* Washington, D.C.

Grills, Russell A. 1977. *Cazenovia, the Story of an Upland Community.* Cazenovia, N.Y.: Cazenovia Preservation Foundation.

Group, Harold E., ed. 1946. *House-of-the-Month Book of Small Houses.* Garden City, N.Y.: Garden City Publishing Co.

Grundy Center: A Centennial Portrait, 1977. 1977. Grundy Center, Iowa: Grundy Center Area Centennial.

Grundy Center Remembers: People, Places, Things. 1977. Grundy Center, Iowa: Grundy County Historical Society.

Hamlin, Talbot. 1944. *Greek Revival Architecture in America.* New York: Oxford University Press.

Handlin, David P. 1979. *The American Home.* Boston: Little, Brown.

Heimsath, Clovis. 1968. *Pioneer Texas Buildings: A Geometry Lesson.* Austin, Tex.: University of Texas Press.

Herman, Bernard C. 1978. "Continuity and Change in Traditional Architecture: The Continental Plan Farmhouse in Middle North Carolina." In *Carolina Dwelling,* ed. Doug Swaim, 160–71. Student Publication of the School of Design, vol. 26. Raleigh: North Carolina State University.

Hesse, Anna. 1981. *Centenarians of Brick, Wood, and Stone.* Hermann, Mo.: n.p.

Hickman County Sesquicentennial. 1957. Columbia, Tenn.: Columbia Printing.

History of Franklin, Jefferson, Washington, Crawford, and Gasconade Counties, Missouri. 1888. Chicago: Goodspeed.

History of Menard and Mason Counties, Illinois. 1879. Chicago: Baskin.

History of Morrow County and Ohio. 1880. Chicago: Baskin.

Hitchcock, Henry R. 1946. *American Architectural Books: A List of Books, Portfolios, and Pamphlets on Architecture and Related Subjects Published Before 1895.* Minneapolis: University of Minnesota Press.

Hogaboam, James S. 1876. *The Bean Creek Valley: Incidents of Its Early Settlement.* Hudson, Mich.: Scarritt.

Holbrook, Stuart. 1968. *The Yankee Exodus: An Account of Migration from New England.* Seattle: University of Washington Press.

Honorbilt Modern Homes. 1920. Chicago: Sears, Roebuck and Co.

Hubka, Thomas G. 1979. "Maine's Connected Farm Buildings." *Maine Historical Society Quarterly* 19:217–45.

Hugill, Peter J. 1977. "A Small Town Landscape as Sustained Gesture on the Part of a Dominant Social Group: Cazenovia, New York, 1794–1976." Ph.D. diss., Syracuse University.

———. 1980. "Houses in Cazenovia: The Effects of Time and Class." *Landscape* 24:10–15.

Isard, Walter. 1942a. "A Neglected Cycle: The Transport-Building Cycle." *Review of Economic Statistics* 24:149–58.

———. 1942b. "Transport Development and Building Cycles." *Quarterly Journal of Economics* 57:90–112.

[Jackson, J. B.] 1967. "To Pity the Plumage and Forget the Dying Bird." *Landscape* 17:1–4.

Jackson, J. B. 1972. "Metamorphosis." *Annals, Association of American Geographers* 72:155–58.

Jacques, D. H. 1868. *The House: A Manual of Rural Architecture.* New York: Woodward.

Jakle, John A. 1976. "The Testing of a House Typing System in Two Middle Western Counties: A Comparative Analysis of Rural Houses." Department of Geography, Occasional Publication Number 11. Urbana, Ill.: University of Illinois.

Jeane, D. Gregory, and Douglas C. Purcell. 1978. *The Architectural Legacy of the Lower Chattahoochee Valley in Alabama and Georgia.* University: University of Alabama Press.

Johnson, Paul C., ed. 1958. *Western Ranch Houses by Cliff May.* Menlo Park, Calif.: California Lane Books.

Jordan, Terry. 1978. *Texas Log Buildings: A Folk Architecture.* Austin: University of Texas Press.

Kelly, J. Frederick. 1924. *The Early Domestic Architecture of Connecticut.* New Haven: Yale University Press.

Kimball, Fiske. 1922. *Domestic Architecture of the American Colonies and of the Early Republic.* New York: Scribner's.

King, Anthony D. 1984. *The Bungalow: The Production of a Global Culture.* London: Routledge and Kegan.

King, David W., ed. 1868. *Homes for Home-Builders.* New York: Judd.

Kish, Leslie. 1967. *Survey Sampling.* New York: John Wiley.

Kniffen, Fred B. 1936. "Louisiana House-Types." *Annals, Association of American Geographers* 26:179–93.

———. 1965. "Folk Housing: Key to Diffusion." *Annals, Association of American Geographers* 55:549–77.

Lair, Jim, ed. 1983. *An Outlander's History of Carroll County, 1830–1983.* Berryville, Ark.: Carroll County Historical and Genealogical Society.

Lamme, Ary J., III, and Douglas B. McDonald. 1973. "Folk Housing Micro-Studies: A Central New York Example." *New York Folklore Quarterly* 24:111–20.

Lancaster, Clay. 1958. "The American Bungalow." *Art Bulletin* 40:239–353.

Lee, Lawrence. 1980. *The History of Brunswick County North Carolina.* Bolivia, N.C.: County of Brunswick.

Legner, Linda. 1979. *City House: A Guide to Renovating Older Chicago-Area Houses.* Chicago: Commission on Chicago Historical and Architectural Landmarks.

Lewis-Built Homes. 1918. Bay City, Mich.: Lewis Manufacturing Co.

Lewis, Peirce F. 1972. "Small Town in Pennsylvania." *Annals, Association of American Geographers* 62:323–51.

———. 1975. "Common Houses, Cultural Spoor." *Landscape* 19:1–22.

———. 1976. *New Orleans: The Making of an Urban Landscape.* Cambridge, Mass.: Ballinger.

———. 1979. "Axioms for Reading the Landscape: Some Guides to the American Scene." In *The Interpretation of Ordinary Landscapes: Geographical Essays,* ed. D. W. Meinig, 11–32. New York: Oxford University Press, 1979.

Lincoln County Bicentennial, 1775–1975. 1975. Stanford, Ky.: Interior Journal.

Lounsbury, Carl. 1979. *The Architecture of Southport.* Wilmington, N.C.: Southport Historical Society.

Lovett, Mrs. P. J. 1960. *History of Apalachicola.* Birmingham, Ala.: author.

Lynch, William O. 1943. "The Westward Flow of Southern Colonists Before 1861." *Journal of Southern History* 9:303–27.

McAlester, Virginia, and Lee McAlester. 1984. *A Field Guide to American Houses.* New York: Knopf.

McCall Corporation, 1945. *The American Woman's Home of Tomorrow.* New York.

Makinson, Randell L. 1977. *Greene and Greene: Architecture as a Fine Art.* Santa Barbara, Calif.: Peregrine Smith.

Marshall, Howard W. 1983. *Folk Architecture in Little Dixie: A Regional Culture in Missouri.* Columbia: University of Missouri Press.

Marshall, Willoughby. 1975. *Economic Development through Historic Preservation: Apalachicola Planning Study Phase One.* Cambridge, Mass.: author.

Mattapoisett and Old Rochester, Massachusetts. 1950. Mattapoisett, Mass.: Mattapoisett Improvement Society.

Mattson, Richard. 1981. "The Bungalow Spirit." *Journal of Cultural Geography* 1:75–92.

———. 1988. "The Gable Front House: An Historical Geography of a Common House Type." Ph.D. diss., University of Illinois, Urbana-Champaign.

May, Cliff. 1950. *Sunset Western Ranch Houses.* San Francisco: Lane.

Metz, Christian. 1980. "The Perceived and the Named." Trans. Steven Feld and Shari Robertson. *Studies in Visual Communication* 6:56–68.

Meyer, Douglas K. 1976. "Illinois Culture Regions at Mid-Nineteenth Century." *Bulletin, Illinois Geographical Society* 18:3–13.

Mitchell, Robert D. 1974. "Content and Context: Tidewater Characteristics in the Early Shenandoah Valley." *Maryland Historian* 5:79–92.

———. 1978. "The Formation of Early American Culture Regions: An Interpretation." In *European Settlement and Development in North America*, ed. James R. Gibson, 66–90. Toronto: University of Toronto Press.

Montell, William L., and Michael L. Morse. 1976. *Kentucky Folk Architecture.* Lexington: University of Kentucky Press.

Morrison, Hugh. 1952. *Early American Architecture.* New York: Oxford University Press.

Murtagh, Gilbert. 1924. *Small Houses.* New York: Doubleday.

Murtagh, William J. 1957. "The Philadelphia Row House." *Journal, Society of Architectural Historians* 16:8–13.

Nelson, Richard. 1874. *Suburban Homes for Business Men.* Cincinnati: author.

Newcomb, Rexford. 1928. *Mediterranean Domestic Architecture in the United States.* Cleveland: Jansen.

Newton, Milton B., Jr. 1971. "Louisiana House Types: A Field Guide." *Melanges*, no. 2.

———. 1975. "Cultural Preadaptation and the Upland South." *Geoscience and Man* 5:143–52.

Noble, Allen G. 1975. "Evolution and Classification of Nineteenth Century Housing in Ohio." *Journal of Geography* 74:285–302.

———. 1984. *Wood, Brick, and Stone: The North American Settlement Landscape Volume One: Houses.* Amherst: University of Massachusetts Press.

Omoto, Sadayoshi. 1964. "The Queen Anne Style and Architectural Criticism." *Journal, Society of Architectural Historians* 23:29–37.

Osborne, Charles F. 1888. *Notes on the Art of House Planning.* New York: Comstock.

Owens, Harvey P. 1966. "Apalachicola Before 1861." Ph.D. diss., Florida State University.

Owsley, F. L. 1945. "The Pattern of Migration and Settlement on the Southern Frontier." *Journal of Southern History* 11:147–76.

Palliser Brothers [Charles and George]. 1876. *Palliser's Model Homes for the People.* New York: Palliser Co.

Patrick, James. 1981. *Architecture in Tennessee 1768–1892.* Knoxville: University of Tennessee Press.

Peat, Wilbur. 1962. *Indiana Houses of the Nineteenth Century.* Indianapolis: Indiana Historical Society.

Pierson, William H., Jr. 1970. *American Buildings and Their Architects: The Colonial and Neo-Classical Styles.* Garden City, N.Y.: Doubleday.

Pillsbury, Richard. 1977. "Patterns in the Folk and Vernacular House Forms of the Pennsylvania Culture Region." *Pioneer America* 19:12–29.

Pillsbury, Richard, and Andrew Kardos. c. 1970. *A Field Guide to the Folk Architecture of the Northeast United States.* Geography Publications at Dartmouth, no. 8. Hanover, N.H.: [Department of Geography, Dartmouth College].

A Plan Book of Harris Homes. 1918. Chicago: Harris Brothers Co.

Plans of Modern Homes. 1913. Chicago: Chicago Millwork Supply Co.

Plews, Matilda J. 1974. *Some Interesting Menard County Homes.* Petersburg, Ill.: author.

Raitz, Karl B. 1980. *The Kentucky Bluegrass: A Regional Profile and Guide.* Department of Geography, Studies in Geography, no. 14. Chapel Hill: University of North Carolina.

Rapoport, Amos. 1969. *House Form and Culture.* Englewood Cliffs, N.J.: Prentice Hall.

Reed, Samuel B. 1878. *House-Plans for Everybody.* New York: Judd.

Reynolds, Helen. 1929. *Dutch Houses in the Hudson Valley Before 1776.* New York: Payson and Clarke.

Rhoads, William B. 1976. "The Colonial Revival and American Nationalism." *Journal, Society of Architectural Historians* 35:239–54.

Rickert, John E. 1967. "House Facades of the Northeast United States: A Tool of Geographic Analysis." *Annals, Association of American Geographers* 57:211–38.

Rifkind, Carol. 1980. *A Field Guide to American Architecture.* New York: New American Library.

Roos, Frank J., Jr. 1968. *Bibliography of Early American Architecture.* Urbana: University of Illinois Press.

Rosenberry, Lois K. M. 1909. *The Expansion of New England: The Spread of New England Settlement and Institutions to the Mississippi River, 1620–1840.* New York: Russell and Russell.

Sauer, Carl. 1941. "Foreword to Historical Geography." *Annals, Association of American Geographers* 31:1–24.

Saylor, Henry H. 1913. *Bungalows.* New York: McBride, Nast.

Schmidt, Mildred, and Joseph Schmidt. 1954. "German Influence on Hermann Houses." *American German Review* 20:13–17.

Sheldon, G. W. 1886. *Artistic Country Seats.* New York: Appleton.

Shortridge, James R. 1980. "Traditional Rural Houses along the Missouri-Kansas Border." *Journal of Cultural Geography* 1:105–37.

Sleeper, Catherine, and Harold R. Sleeper. 1948. *The House for You: To Build, Buy, or Rent.* New York: Wiley.

Sloan, Samuel. 1867. *Sloan's Homestead Architecture.* Philadelphia: Lippincott.

Smith, J. Frazer. 1941. *White Pillars: Early Life and Architecture of the Lower Mississippi Valley Country.* New York: Bramhall House.

Smith, James H. 1880. *History of Madison and Chenango Counties.* Syracuse: Mason.

Smith, Lil, ed. 1977. *Tales of Old Chilton.* Chilton, Wis.: Calumet.

Smith, Peter. 1975. *Houses of the Welsh Countryside, A Study in Historical Geography.* London: Her Majesty's Stationery Office, 1975.

Smith, William D., III. 1979. *Revitalization at Port Gibson.* Jackson: Mississippi Department of Archives and History.

Southern, Michael. 1978. "The I-House as a Carrier of Style in Three Counties of the Northeastern Piedmont." In *Carolina Dwelling,* ed. Doug Swaim, 70–83. Student Publication of the School of Design, vol. 26. Raleigh: North Carolina State University.

Spence, Jerome D., and David Spence. 1900. *A History of Hickman County, Tennessee.* Nashville: Gospel Advocate, 1900.

Sprague, Paul E. 1981. "The Origin of Balloon Framing." *Journal, Society of Architectural Historians* 40:311–19.

Steese, Edward. 1947. " 'Villas and Cottages' by Calvert Vaux." *Journal, Society of Architectural Historians* 6:1–12.

Stilgoe, John. 1982. *Common Landscape of America, 1580 to 1845.* New Haven, Conn.: Yale University Press.

Stith, D. J., and R. P. Meyer. 1974. *Styles and Designs in Wisconsin Housing: Pros and Cons of Popular House Plans.* Madison: University of Wisconsin Extension.

[Strouse, Issac, ed.] 1916. *Parke County Indiana Centennial Memorial.* Rockville, Ind.: n.p.

Stump, Roger. 1981. "The Dutch Colonial House and the Colonial Revival." *Journal of Cultural Geography* 1:44–55.

Swaim, Doug. 1978. "North Carolina Folk Housing." In *Carolina Dwelling,* ed. Doug Swaim, 28–45. Student Publication of the School of Design, vol. 26. Raleigh: North Carolina State University.

Todd, Sereno E. 1876. *Todd's Country Homes.* Philadelphia: McCurdy.

Town of Mattapoisett 100th Anniversary, 1857–1957, Souvenir Booklet. 1957. Mattapoisett, Mass.: n.p.

Upton, Dell. 1982. "Vernacular Domestic Architecture in Eighteenth-Century Virginia." *Winterthur Portfolio* 17 (2–3): 95–119.

Upton, Dell, and John Michael Vlach, eds. *Common Places: Readings in American Vernacular Architecture.* Athens: University of Georgia Press, 1986.

Van Ravenswaay, Charles. 1977. *The Arts and Architecture of German Settlement in Missouri.* Columbia: University of Missouri Press.

Vaux, Calvert. 1864. *Villas and Cottages.* New York: Harper.

Vlach, John M. 1976. "The Shotgun House: An African Architectural Legacy." *Pioneer America* 8:47–56, 57–70.

Wacker, Peter O. 1971. "New Jersey's Cultural Landscape Before 1880." *Proceedings, Second General Symposium of the New Jersey Historical Commission,* 35–62.

Walker, Lester. 1981. *American Shelter: An Illustrated Encyclopedia of the American Home.* Woodstock, N.Y.: Overlook Press.

Wall, James W. 1969. *History of Davie County in the Forks of Yadkin.* Mocksville, N.C.: Davie County Historical Publishing Association.

Wayland, John W. [1927] 1976. *A History of Shenandoah County, Virginia.* Strasburg, Va.: Shenandoah.

Wertenbaker, Thomas J. 1938. *The Founding of American Civilization: The Middle Colonies.* New York: Scribner's.

Whiffen, Marcus. 1969. *American Architecture Since 1780: A Guide to the Styles.* Cambridge, Mass.: MIT Press.

White, Alfred T. 1879. *Improved Dwellings for Laboring Classes.* New York: Putnam.

White, Charles E., Jr. 1921. *Successful Houses and How to Build Them.* New York: Macmillan.

———. 1923. *The Bungalow Book.* New York: Macmillan.

Williams, Henry L., and Ottalie K. Williams. 1957. *Old American Houses.* New York: Bonanza.

Wills, Barry. 1955. *Living on the Level: One-Story Homes.* Boston: Houghton Mifflin.

Wolf, Eric. 1982. *Europe and the People Without History.* Berkeley: University of California Press.

Wolfe, M. R. 1959–60. "Small Town. Puget Sound Region." *Landscape* 9:10–13.

Woodside, Robert E. 1979. *My Life and Town.* Millersburg, Pa.: author.

Woodward, G. E., and F. W. Woodward. 1866. *Woodward's Country Houses.* New York.

Woodward, George E. 1867. *Woodward's Cottages and Farmhouses.* New York.

———. 1873. *Woodward's Suburban and Country Houses.* New York.

Wright, Gwendolyn. 1980. *Moralism and the Model Home: Domestic Architecture and Cultural Conflict in Chicago 1873–1913.* Chicago: University of Chicago Press.

———. 1981. *Building the Dream: A Social History of Housing in America.* New York: Pantheon Books.

Wright, Richardson. 1916. *Low Cost Suburban Homes: A Book of Suggestions for the Man with the Moderate Purse.* New York: McBride.

Wyckoff, William. 1979. "On the Louisiana School of Cultural Geography and the Case of the Upland South." Department of Geography, Discussion Paper, no. 54. Syracuse: Syracuse University.

Yager, Verdie. 1983. *Reflections on the Bean: A History of the Hudson Area.* Hudson, Mich.: Hudson Public Library.

Zelinsky, Wilbur. 1973. *The Cultural Geography of the United States.* Englewood Cliffs, N.J.: Prentice Hall.

———. 1977. "The Pennsylvania Town: An Overdue Geographical Account." *Geographical Review* 67: 127–47.

INDEX